THIS THING CALLED LIFE

THIS THING CALLED LIFE

PRINCE'S ODYSSEY,
ON AND OFF
THE RECORD

NEAL KARLEN

ST. MARTIN'S PRESS
NEW YORK

For Michelle Kasimor Streitz
Baby, it's you . . .

First published in the United States by St. Martin's Press, an imprint of St. Martin's Publishing Group

THIS THING CALLED LIFE. Copyright © 2020 by Neal Karlen. All rights reserved. Printed in the United States of America. For information, address St. Martin's Publishing Group, 120 Broadway, New York, NY 10271.

www.stmartins.com

The Library of Congress Cataloging-in-Publication Data is available upon request.

ISBN 978-1-250-13524-7 (hardcover)
ISBN 978-1-250-13525-4 (ebook)

Our books may be purchased in bulk for promotional, educational, or business use. Please contact your local bookseller or the Macmillan Corporate and Premium Sales Department at 1-800-221-7945, extension 5442, or by email at MacmillanSpecialMarkets@macmillan.com.

First Edition: 2020

10 9 8 7 6 5 4 3 2 1

CONTENTS

It is strange to be known so universally and yet to be so lonely.

—Albert Einstein

PRELUDE

I pray to God Prince was dead by the time he hit the floor.

I pray Prince wasn't cognizant, even for a mite of a moment, that he was dying alone in a nondescript elevator, in a Wonder Bread suburb of the racially-fractured city that was one day too late in telling him his hometown—blacks, whites, the whole Crayola box of colors and ethnicities—loved Prince as much as he loved Minneapolis.

Because there's one thing I'm positive I know about Prince. After knowing him in forever-alternating cycles of greater, lesser, and sometimes not-at-all friendship over the final thirty-one years of his life, until our final peculiar phone conversation three weeks before he died: His greatest—and perhaps only—fear was dying alone.

Prince didn't care if the end came in a Chanhassen, Minnesota, elevator inside a building where he owned all the buttons, or in an opulent prime minister's suite in a Paris hotel, inevitably—and idiotically—redecorated for his arrival by a clueless management apparently determined to re-create for his pleasure Liberace's living room.

He just didn't want to die alone.

Yet he always accepted what was coming, and was trying to pre-
pare, he told me as far back as 1985.

Of course the questions must be asked whenever someone says
anything about what Prince actually said, or thought, or did: "How
do *you* know? Why would he tell *you*? Did you *see* that?"

Well, personally, on this and several other topics, in a wide array
of settings, yes, I witnessed this and saw that. Once upon a time, in
what feels like a previous lifetime, I wrote a gaggle of articles and interviews for *Rolling Stone* and then the *New York Times* with Prince
and about Prince—his thoughts, worlds, bands, and best friends of
the moment, what he wore on his head and the height of the heels
on his feet.

I still am not sure why he chose me to occupy one compartment
in his life—the most compartmentalized life I've ever seen, trapped
inside the loneliest soul I've ever met. Few of his real friends knew
who each other were, or even if they themselves were "real" friends.
He didn't like many people, and I still have no real idea why he
abided me.

And then, in the 1990s, I quit.

I didn't quit Prince, I just quit writing about him or hanging around
his world. I still don't know if I was brave or an idiot to walk away
from the only real scoop rock and roll had to offer in those days.

I was still young enough to believe it was worth trying to be a
"real" writer, writing real things, or at least running away to join
other circuses besides entertainment journalism, where life was the
proverbial high school with money—and the entire world reduced
to the simple binary equation of "*that's* cool" or "that's *not* cool."

If I didn't quit, I knew way back, I would never be taken seriously
as anything more than Prince's bobo, a slur in the baseball world
denoting a professional sycophant to a superstar player. In rock and
roll, I figured, the equivalent bobo might be, say, the only reporter
someone like Prince would give interviews to, or hang around with,
or divulge the inner meaning of his heels. ("I don't wear 'em cuz I'm
short," the five-foot-two musician told me in 1985. "I wear 'em cuz
the women like 'em.")

These are the first words I've written about Prince since back in the day. Until now I've kept a promise to myself that I wouldn't write about him anymore. In the years after the interviews, he asked me to write a couple of things with him, and I assented. The projects sounded so ridiculous I figured no one would believe they existed anyway.

In the nineties, I wrote the libretto to a rock opera called *The Dawn*, retitled for direct-to-video release in 1994 as *3 Chains o' Gold*. Prince had released the experimental set of narratively inter-connected videos on the marketplace as a present to Mayte, the first of his two ex-wives. For a story, he gave me a couple of details of what he wanted: a setting in the desert, and a princess being courted Valentino-style by an inscrutable, magical—ahem—prince.

He also gave me the indescribable experience of catching a true genius in the act of being a genius.

"Will you pay me?" I asked.

If he did, I knew, I'd be set free if I ever wanted to sell out. I knew I could never write another article about him again, at least not in the guise of an objective journalist. I would have to include so many caveats, full disclosures, and conflicts of interest as to render any scribbling about Prince worthless.

"No, I won't pay you," Prince said. "But you can say you wrote a rock opera with me."

Good point, little purple guy, I thought. And damn, looking back half a lifetime ago, that was the most profitable thing I've ever worked on, karmically speaking.

I also wrote a manifesto, composed as if I were writing a real third-person magazine profile, explaining why Prince was on the verge of changing his name to that goofy glyph—a fact then known only to him, his manager, and me. He told me the manifesto was for a time capsule to be buried on the grounds of Paisley Park with, among other things, his will. I have no idea if it ever was, though there is proof that such a time capsule exists.

I put my copy of the manifesto on a last-century floppy disk in a Minneapolis storage locker where I kept memories I didn't know where to put.

———

I always told Prince I knew he didn't honestly consider me a friend, but as one of the few people in Minneapolis who was probably awake, the way he always was, in the middle of the night, and was "Willing and Able," as my favorite song of his is titled, to talk about loneliness and death.

I even rubbed it in, in the opening of my third and last *Rolling Stone* story featuring Prince on the cover, published in 1990.

"The phone rings at 4:48 in the morning.

"'Hi, it's Prince,' says the wide-awake voice calling from a room several yards down the hallway of this London hotel. 'Did I wake you up?'"

No, you jerk, you never woke me. Well, actually you did a few times, but I was always happy to hear from you, even when you were so lonely and depressed you could barely speak. I told him I wanted to be a real writer, not the bobo formerly known as Neal. I wanted to be Nathanael West, and though he had no idea who Nathanael West was, he seemed to understand completely.

And we stayed in touch.

Sometimes we talked on the phone several times a year in the middle of the night for between several minutes and several hours. Sometimes I got letters, sometimes on purple stationery. Two of the eight times I published what I thought were "real" books, I received anonymous purple flowers. Over thirty-one years I'd guess we saw each other in preparation for published profiles on a couple of dozen occasions, saw each other socially thirty or thirty-five times, and talked on the phone a few hundred times in the middle of the night. About fifty unanswered (or unheard) calls from an "unknown" number registered on my phone during the hours when only Prince would call.

When he wrote, I'd always write him back care of Paisley Park. I have no idea if he ever got most of my letters, because I never had any idea what the hell was going on over there, even when I used to visit.

An hour before I quit on that story, I sent my editor a scan of an old letter he sent me that began, "Neal, Please treasure our friendship as I do"—yes, he drew an eye for an *I*—and ended "4 real. I love you."

I don't know why I sent the editor that letter; perhaps I wanted her to know I really knew him, we really were friends. Or maybe I just wanted to read it again and smarten up.

Still, like the rest of Minneapolis, I neglected to tell Prince I loved him back until it was too late.

He once told me he believed in heaven, and he thought if he made it there it would look exactly like earth. You can look it up: *Rolling Stone*, September 12, 1985.

If he was right . . . well . . . hey, Prince! Will you give me a call one last time? I forgot to tell you something.

I love you, too.

And so, that's what I wanted to actually tell Prince a week after he died, and for a little while beyond.

Leaving critical matters forever unmentioned, is, alas, a favorite track on the B-side of the civic album known as Minnesota Nice. On that reverse face of the local pleasant-at-all-costs ethos also lies a brutal passive-aggressiveness and meanness kept undercover.

And soon enough after he was gone, I was glad Prince wouldn't be calling ever again, even to hear my regretful un-saids. Dead, he was instantaneously embalmed in his own myths, deified and commodified. I was grateful there would be no Resurrection for a proper goodbye. If Prince reappeared again, I was sure, he would die a second time the moment he saw what was being done in his name, memory, and supposed honor.

Then, George Floyd was murdered. And I wished Prince could arise again, just to do battle with that Minnesota Nice flipside.

At its worst, that alternate face camouflages "racism with a smile," as one woman who immigrated to Minneapolis in 1998 from Somalia portrayed the duality of the local situation to the *New York Times* in June 2020.

It had only been days since a white Minneapolis cop put a knee to the throat of George Floyd, an African American, for almost nine minutes. The spot on the pavement is less than a mile away from where Prince went to high school, two miles from where I live.

And once again, after years being grateful he couldn't see what was going on, I pined for the presence of the actual Prince.

He often said he liked Minneapolis's brutally frostbitten winters, because it "keeps the bad people out." I wondered what he'd have to say, write, sing, and play now that Minneapolis had been exposed to the world as a place where the deadliest enemy had grown within.

Alive, Prince had become ever more politicized with the years. Near his end, in 2015, he'd released the song "Baltimore," centered on Freddie Gray, twenty-five and black, who less than a month before had died while in the custody of Charm City's police, sparking more than a week of protests and rioting. "Nobody got in nobody's way/So I guess you could say it was a good day/At least a little," Prince sang, "it was better than the day in Baltimore." True that, at least in Minneapolis, where Prince recorded his infectious gospel-like melody with a chorus of protest chants.

The day after the single hit Soundcloud, Prince played for almost three hours for a Baltimore "Rally 4 Peace." While performing "Purple Rain," Prince interrupted his own song to talk to the audience.

"The system is broken," he said. "Next time I come through Baltimore, I wanna stay in a hotel owned by one of you. I wanna leave the airport in a car service created and owned by one of you."

He didn't get specific about which "you" he meant in the crowd encompassing his usual spectrum of ages and colors. He didn't need to. Black, white, young, old, "woke," asleep—*you*.

Five years later, I stood at the spot where George Floyd had died days before. I wondered what if Prince had lived, what would the now almost sixty-two-year-old have told his own hometown, a dot on the map in Flyoverland, now at the center of the world?

I had no idea. But I knew it would be great, that *you* could probably dance to it—and it would probably be released in time for George Floyd's funeral.

I still miss the mamma jamma.

1

MEMOIRS OF AN AMNESIAC

Uptown—Set your mind free.
—"Uptown," 1980, by Prince

WINTER 2019

"*Another* book about Prince?" asked a friend of a friend in Sebastian Joe's, my local Uptown Minneapolis coffee shop, after I answered his query about what I was working on.

Yup. Another book about Prince.

Prince, the universally acclaimed genius deemed worthy of genuflecting toward even by other acknowledged global geniuses. Prince, the personification of hip to whom other intergalactic hipsters offered unashamed gush. Prince, the international cultural icon who defied and cross-bred genres from fashion to funk to apparent Three Stooges lunacy—and whose death made the Eiffel Tower, the cover of the *New Yorker*, the front-page above-the-fold headline picture of the *New York Times*, and all downtown Minneapolis glow purple.

Yes, I said, another book about. . . . him.

Prince at that point been gone for more than two years; a pretty compelling biography of his post-mortem life could probably already have been written about all that had happened *to* his name and *in* his name since his demise.

"Why"—my coffee shop interlocutor went on, honestly, genuinely curious—"do we need another book about Prince? I mean . . . sorry. But *why*?"

I *hmm*ed and took no offense.

"That," I told him, "is a very good question."

I glumly gathered my papers and notebooks, stowed my laptop in my backpack, and slowly, haphazardly ambled, with my head down, six blocks home to my apartment in Uptown, which Prince had made famous long ago with a joyful eponymous ode to that Minneapolis neighborhood.

I got to my apartment and turned on the lights. It was the middle of the afternoon, but I felt spooked into a morbid darkness. I then got in the shower to start the day over, felt the hot spray splatter my face, stared at the ceiling, and burst into tears.

"What," I shouted toward the ceiling, "do you want me to *say*?!"

I was talking to Prince: Seventy-eight days before a finished manuscript of this book was due, and I'd finally cracked.

Thank God I didn't hear an answer.

Instead of voices or a vision, the obvious response came to me in a memory on purple stationery inside a purple envelope on which Prince had written in a childlike scrawl, "NeAl." It was the first letter he'd ever written me, and I'd put it in a $3.99 Target frame after he'd died. It had hung for two years above my desk, easy to see but hiding—the way Prince used to do himself—in plain sight.

After my first interview and story about Prince came out in *Rolling Stone*, he'd written me a note, which—unlike the third-grader's handwriting of my name on the envelope—was filled with the florid ink flourishes of the charmingly affected penmanship he'd been practicing since junior high.

"Thanx 4 telling the truth!" he'd written. "Love God, Prince."

It was the first thank-you note I'd ever received from anyone I'd written about. It was the only note I've ever received thanking me for telling the truth. I never expected one: It's kinda sorta the gig.

And there was my answer.

"Thanx 4 telling the truth!"

That I can do.

This is a work of nonfiction.

That's a grandiose claim to be sure, considering I am purportedly presenting a historically sound and journalistically accurate account and accounting of Prince, who ranks among the most seemingly unknown and unknowable people of our time: Prince, this . . . Genius. Clown. God. Demon. Riddle. Joke. Teller of immutable truths. Purveyor of temporal lies. And everything in between.

I also want to make clear this is not a work of "*creative* nonfiction," a genre of writing I have taught here and there in assorted MFA and journalism programs. I lack the moxie to claim that what follows is creative. If this book is remembered at all, I'd much rather it be for its accuracy than its creativity.

This book is also not Mezz Mezzrow–style nonfiction. It pains me to slur the name of Milton "Mezz" Mezzrow, author of the 1947 classic jazz memoir, *Really the Blues*, a wonderful tale of an astonishing jazz figure. So swell a read are Mezz's memoirs that in 2016, New York Review Books reissued *Really the Blues*, complete with toney introduction by *New York Times* music critic Ben Ratliff.

"Most memoirists enter a complicated relationship with the truth," Ratliff wrote, "especially when they are not household names, and when the key events they describe are not a matter of public record. . . . (The most dubious assertions here—[include] that Mezzrow had a role in the invention of the term 'jam session,' and that he was directly responsible for the popularity of [Louis] Armstrong in Harlem. . . .) But the reader probably expects some rearrangement of the verifiable truth."

It doesn't especially blacken the brilliance of *Really the Blues* when one quickly just *senses* that Mezz is blowing a fair gale of bullshit. After all, he *was* Mezz Mezzrow.

Finally, I'm also not writing a clip job of my own previous scribblings on Prince, which I guess would be easy enough to do—but how sad! A clip job is a book or story with stories or anecdotes wholly lifted from other publications. When I quote from *Rolling Stone* I say so—among other things it means the quote was fact-checked. Once upon a time *Rolling Stone* had the best fact-checking department in the business.

But that's another story.

And frankly, I'm not good enough a writer to want to swipe my own stuff from thirty years ago, when I was even worse.

For real.

That's how we roll in Minneapolis. We begin by apologizing.

Perhaps I sound as if I protest too much. But when it comes to Prince, and the truth, and the connection between the two, I don't think it is *possible* to protest too much. The contradictions elucidated by too many credible sources are just too mighty.

To many trustworthy sources, he was simply unable to tap into anything emotional. Over the years, Alan Leeds served Prince in virtually every critical executive role imaginable, not to mention duties as one of his few trusted confidants. In 2017's *When Doves Cry*, a curious biopic/documentary, Leeds movingly, humanely described Prince's inability to simply discuss feelings without sounding obnoxious.

"I remember when Kim Basinger had been his significant other for a while, living in Minneapolis and holding an office at Paisley Park," he remembered. "And that relationship, for whatever reason, ended abruptly."

"And he came into my office and just sat on my desk," Leeds continued, "and I said, 'Hey man, you okay?'"

According to Leeds, Prince veritably spat out the words with overmacho venom: "How do you *think* I'd be?" and walked out. He wasn't, Leeds said, "okay with compassion. [What I said] was intended as 'Do you want a hug?' You know, a brotherly, 'You okay, dude?' And the only thing I could get back was a very snide 'How do you *think* I'd be?'"

Alternatively, there is the take of André Cymone, the loudest echo from his past, who reached a rapprochement with Prince in the last year of his life: "If you were close, Prince wanted to talk," he said—but Alan Leeds, whom he'd blown off, *had* been close.

"It was good for me, because I never did find too many people I could relate to on a lot of different levels," André continued. "And [Prince] was one of the few people throughout my life I could relate to. He was one of the few people throughout my life that I could connect with."

He could talk from the heart, discuss life and death in the middle of the night, but he could also vent from the spleen, spewing bilious comments to those who only meant to express concern about his well-being.

He had myriad levels of relationships over the years, so contradictory that it seems impossible that all those facets could be held in one personality. I don't think it hurt that I wasn't on his payroll, kept my distance, and never wanted anything except to do what needed to be done so I'd never have to write about him again, or talk about a "friendship" I was never sure I had in the first place.

And yet here I am, writing a book, contradicting myself.

Yet in many ways, contradictions were the very essence of Prince. Yes, he was astonishingly unknowing, yet also shockingly wise. He was cruel, and he was kind.

And I know what I know.

Taking stock of the eruption of paper in my living room, I paused, looking at the three faded and cracked pieces of luggage long ready for the glue factory. They had looked so shiny and bound for glory, sitting there in the Columbus Avenue store window on Manhattan's Upper West Side, when I lived only a block away—and a planet away from Minneapolis.

Now the baggage was tattered with age, over- and misuse, its once-efficient packing compartments overflowing with thousands of sheets of paper. There were transcripts of several formal, days-long questionings of Prince for a half-dozen interviews sometimes bound for publication, sometimes not.

Reporter's notebooks spilled out of the battered suitcases, organized, sorted, and re-sorted so many times over the last two years that I had no idea if there was an order there or not. Perhaps Prince's story was all there in my living room, somewhere; perhaps it wasn't; perhaps there was no Prince story or tidy narrative to explain what had been?

Poking out from other baggage were other interview transcripts, printed on a 1986 dot-matrix printer, stained with the coffee I'd been drinking when I first looked over the interviews I'd recorded back when with . . . who can remember? I looked at the pages.

Ah, yes, threescore pages of interviews with the Revolution's Lisa Coleman and Wendy Melvoin, for a *Rolling Stone* cover story in 1986—thirty-three years before. Under those were the quotes I'd scribbled down on index cards during my last conversation with Prince, three and a half weeks before he died on April 21, 2016.

The baggage held hundreds and hundreds of those index cards, each with a date, a note, a quote, a half-thought, or full paragraph scribbled on it, many of them barely decipherable, taken down while on the phone in the middle of the night. Many, I knew, made no sense at all, even when I could make out the words.

There were great wads of toilet paper spilling out of one of the suitcases. Over a quarter-century before, I'd taken secret notes on the tissue, hiding from Prince and pretending I had to pee in the cavernous hotel bathrooms of whatever grand hotel suite in Paris or converted castle in Switzerland he was staying in as he conquered Europe on his 1990 *Nude* tour. I'd been tagging along for weeks, conducting an interview for *Rolling Stone*.

Except—Prince told me five seconds before our interview began—I couldn't record or take notes of our conversations. I knew he was fucking with me, but it wasn't funny.

This isn't funny.

That tour was the last time I'd publish a word he said until he died thirty-one years later.

Under the toilet paper in the baggage were more notes, these scribbled days, months, or years after the fact. Here was the time, memorialized on a four-by-six-inch index card, when Prince brought to my attention the curious coincidence that we'd met as preteens.

That would have been the late 1960s. We'd both been on the fringes of groups that hung out in the Dairy Queen parking lot on Plymouth Avenue, the main boulevard of Minneapolis's mostly black Northside, one door down from my immigrant grandparents' Oliver Avenue shack. (My behind-my-back nickname was "Casper," Prince told me in his laugh/sneer, I had noted on one card.)

Paper, quotes, notes taken in real time—a treasure trove of the being and nothingness, the in-betweenness, the contradictions, of Prince's life.

And then there were the tapes of Prince and me talking, dating back to 1985. I hadn't listened to them since transcribing the first cassette some thirty years before.

I tried to listen for almost a year after he died. But I couldn't stand hearing the ghosts—not just his, but mine as well. I felt haunted, hearing the past me, my everything-will-work-out-fine optimism. And why not? Especially on those first tapes. I was just twenty-six, Prince was twenty-seven, and both of us were in love for what we were sure was the first and last time.

Then there was a floppy disk with a rock opera we'd collaborated on, which he liked, produced, and which got the worst reviews of anything he ever did, a fact I am perversely proud of. Underneath that were typewritten, never-used liner notes for a greatest-hits collection.

He'd hated my liner notes, my midcareer summation of his career, and the collection came out, annotated by the wise Alan Leeds, a highly reliable narrator who has served as everything from James Brown's road manager to president of Paisley Park Records.

And then, spilling out of a large shoulder bag that was hip at roughly the same time as Don Johnson jackets, were the notes that held our private conversations—conducted for nobody, neither on nor off the record—talks that went on until the last weeks of his life.

What had come from those discussions were the hundreds upon hundreds of manuscript pages on which I'd been typing, fourteen hours a day, for most of the past two years: every memory, story, quote, inflection of his, reflection of mine, plus everything I'd ever been told about Prince by someone I trusted.

What a fucking mess, I thought.

The papers literally flowing out of the sad-sack luggage reminded me of a molten lava of facts and acts and quotes and articles signifying . . . a great artist who almost escaped history.

Except I wouldn't let him, and I won't let him. We always exacted playful if spiteful revenge upon each other for wrongdoings, and this was no exception. The only not-terrible thing about knowing Prince, in the end, was simply knowing Prince.

That part was fun.

Having shitty, personal, untrue things written about you in your hometown paper since you were twenty-six *wasn't* so fun, I knew from personal experience, stemming directly from being granted direct journalistic access to Prince. So I will have my revenge on the purple guy for subjecting me to slurs simply for him giving me the honor of quoting him directly. Prince will not be allowed to run away from history, as he'd planned.

And besides, it's what he really wanted, I think.

"Thanx 4 telling the truth!" I remembered again.

I took a nap.

Revived, I dared myself to look at the streams and reams of paper taken down in informal interviews Prince and I had done for no reason at all, taped or contemporaneously noted, in the last thirty-one years of his life. There were printouts of jungles of verbiage from others, too; reflections from those he loved and who had once loved him back.

True, a certain number of those folks had evolved from loving Prince to wishing they could kill him. Ironically, it wasn't until 1999 was over that Prince actively began learning empathy, becoming aware that others exist for reasons beyond using or being used. Until then, he usually thought any bad karma directed at him came simply from others' thwarted professional ambitions.

It wasn't his fault. Just be glad you weren't on his payroll or in one of his bands. As longtime Prince saxophonist Eric Leeds explained: "In order to do production rehearsals we would start to perform the show and literally every 30 seconds or every minute he would say, 'STOP,' and then would say 'Okay, continue.' We'd pick up the song where we left off, we might get a minute into it, and he'd say 'STOP.' And that would go on, eight or ten hours a day, day after day."

Prince never really got it back then, though I think he tried. "I can make people famous for fifteen minutes, but I can't make them famous forever, and they never forgive me," he said to me in 1998, feeling especially lonely, a feeling he said never went completely away, the way the noise in his head, simultaneously holding his next six creative ideas, never abated—the curse of brilliance.

"My head feels like a pinball machine," he said. "It's when I think too much and can't sleep from just having so many things on my mind. You know, stuff like I could do this, I could do that. I could work with this band. When am I gonna do this show or that show? There're so many things. There're women. Do I have to eat? I wish I didn't have to eat."

But *other* people's feelings?

He generally didn't care for or consider them until the calendar page on 1999 literally turned. In 1999 Prince filed trademark infringements in New York state against the Uptown and two other fanzines, and nine fan sites. Ron Herbert, who had worked from Atlanta promoting albums for Prince, said straightforwardly: "I would be advising Prince not to sue [his own fans]. There just has to be more to the story than what you and I know."

The ultimate contradiction: He'd turned on his fans, the one demographic Prince always seemed determined to take along for the joyride to wherever he was going.

2

LAST CALL

"Hi, it's Prince," said the unmistakable voice on the other end of the line.

But I was mistaken.

Someone who sounded a hell of a lot like Prince—alive for another three and a half weeks—was on the other end, no doubt. Yet it *wasn't* quite him: A smidgen of something I couldn't put a name to was missing from the person and voice I'd come to know over the last thirty-one years.

Someone who sounded astonishingly like Prince was on the other end of the line. But something was undefinably, ineffably off, *missing*, in the timbre of that voice. This fellow sounded like an excellent simulation of the musician, like the Prince impersonator I once saw in a Las Vegas celebrity lookalike "Legends" show. The voice on the phone was nearly a pitch-perfect soundalike, a Prince robocall, talking the way you start talking back to before you realize there's nobody there.

Nearly.

I've got nerves that jangle easily, and now, for no specific reason, they were jangling hard. Knock it off, I chastised, reminding myself I hadn't talked to him in ten months, and during all that time hadn't had to deduce instantly, the way I usually did, which of the hues in Prince's profoundly compartmentalized box of emotions he was feeling at that moment. He sounded uncharacteristically flat, as if he was a smushed drawing utensil that needed a spin through a pencil sharpener.

Nah, I was crazy, I thought. I always thought there was trouble when there was none; my major in life had long been worrying over nothing. Paranoia runs deep.

I mumbled nothingisms, not following our usual script for greeting each other.

"It's Prince," he repeated, sounding annoyed.

"Prince *who*?" I finally asked back, returning his "It's Prince" in the telephone shtick we'd been replaying with each other for more than a generation.

"*The* Prince," he responded in 2016, his annoyance alchemizing more toward the tone of animated bonhomie I'd grown accustomed to when he was in a good mood.

Our telephone shtick had begun in 1985, when Prince, bringing his impatience up to its usual Formula One speed, had called my folks' house in Minneapolis to find out if my plane had landed yet from New York for our first might-be-if-he-liked-me interview, for an if-he-did-he'd-talk *Rolling Stone* cover story. When he announced himself to my mother the first time, demanding to know if I'd arrived yet, she said, unimpressed: "Prince *who*?"

"*The* Prince," he'd responded.

When I got home to Minneapolis a few hours later, she told me "*the* Prince" had called, a moniker she used, without a hint of disingenuousness, for the rest of her life: "Say hello to *the* Prince!"

Back then, he hadn't spoken to the press in three years, had vowed never to speak publicly again, and in the meantime, had become via *Purple Rain* the biggest rock star on the planet. I didn't know that this interview wasn't a lock, but rather an audition. I'd falsely figured I'd already landed the story of him finally talking on the recommendation of Wendy Melvoin and Lisa Coleman of his band The Revolution. I'd interviewed Wendy and Lisa several weeks before for their own *Rolling Stone* cover.

Check that, I learned a generation later. Ultimately the critical "Why don't you talk to him?" came from Susannah Melvoin, Wendy's identical twin sister and lead singer with "Saint" Paul Peterson of the Prince-tutored band the Family—and Prince's girlfriend for years. According to most of Prince's folklorists, Susannah was also his fiancée, which is actually truth, not fable. She was also a woman who took no shit, and his last opportunity to be with a woman who could keep him tethered to planet Earth.

Among the songs Prince is known or believed to have written about or for Susannah are "Nothing Compares 2 U," "The Beautiful Ones," "Forever in My Life," "If I Were Your Girlfriend," and the almost mythical "Wally," a lost love ballad to Susannah that Prince had had erased after recording what engineer Susan Rogers had said was an indescribably brilliant song.

The original deal had been that Prince, still living under his vow never to speak to the press again, would let Wendy and Lisa speak for him—and that he'd pose with them for *Rolling Stone*'s cover. By recommending to Susannah Melvoin (and perhaps positing the idea with Prince himself) that the Little Big Man talk to me, Wendy and Lisa did the unthinkably generous: They gave up their own cover story.

True, they would make it the following year. But they didn't know that, and once you give up the cover of any major magazine, it's always doubtful that the wheel will come around again. People in rock and roll just don't give up being on the cover of *Rolling Stone*.

But Lisa and Wendy did. They talked to Susannah, who talked to Prince, and in 1985, after watching me putz around his assorted bands' rehearsal space and test-driving me for conversation and karma while playing Ping-Pong and showing me around the place for a couple days, he agreed to give talking on the record one last try.

"Um, how are you?" I asked Prince over the phone in 2016, thirty-one years later. We'd been on for about a minute, but I remained so lost in my reverie of fretting about why he was calling me during daylight hours that I hadn't homed in specifically on what he'd been talking about.

"I'm tired," I heard him say numbly, after a long pause. "I feel like sleeping all the time."

I hadn't paid much attention to Prince's career, to be honest, in the last decade. And he didn't seem to mind that I no longer seemed to know which of his new albums he was talking about, where he'd been on his last tour, or that I never, ever came to Paisley Park for one of his three-in-the-morning, announced-at-the-last-second shows that famously finished near dawn with him serving pancakes to the gathered and devoted.

I sat down on my bed, as Prince related why he'd called: He'd just heard something he'd thought I'd find funny on a Netflix rerun of the sitcom *The Office*, his favorite television show of the moment.

"He always loved his sitcoms," André Cymone (né André Simon Anderson) said in 2018. Cymone, Prince's high school best friend and musical coconspirator, had his family take Prince under their roof in the mid-1970s. To my mind, André had been brutally betrayed by the purple guy, and was still, I believed, the last actual friend—in most traditional senses of the word—that Prince ever had.

"There is a lot about Prince that people don't understand," Cymone said when we first talked after Prince died. "He was extremely into Americana. *Happy Days*, he watched *Happy Days* religiously," André went on, beginning to enumerate Prince's favorite television shows. "*The Jeffersons*. And he watched *Welcome Back Kotter* religiously. And I'm not kidding—*Barnaby Jones*, he just loved *Barnaby Jones*."

Ah, that ancient show from the seventies, featuring the even more ancient Buddy Ebsen as the old-coot private eye; Ebsen had played Jed Clampett on *The Beverly Hillbillies*—another sitcom Prince loved (he watched the *Hillbillies* in reruns; he thought Elly May Clampett, Jed's blonde daughter, was hot).

"You know," said Cymone. "I used to get on his case for watching that stuff. I'd say, 'You're never going to make it wasting all your time watching those television shows.' And he would laugh and say, 'But you *gotta* hear what they're saying!'"

"Watching those shows was his *thing*, literally," Cymone said. "A lot of people don't know that, but obviously when you live with someone, you know their habits. And watching those shows was one of his *main* habits."

Prince had so many habits one wouldn't think possible, contradictions that simply didn't make sense. Just as one suspected he was barely a resident of reality, he'd come out with a perfect impression of Fonzie saying "Eyyyy, Mr. C!" to Tom Bosley on *Happy Days*.

Just as one would be given reason to suspect that Prince suffered from savant syndrome and was cognitively impaired, he would come out with a line from "Big Blonde," arguably Dorothy Parker's best short story. Or somebody might be of the correct opinion that Prince had just read the front page of that day's *New York Times*—and he would then say something so ignorant about the illuminati running the universe that the best one could do was simply shake one's head.

Everything, it seemed to me, depended on who and where he was that day, what he felt and needed that hour, and what one might provide that second. I was not his shrink, his rabbi, or his confessor. And I most certainly wasn't a Prince Whisperer. I knew what I knew; I had an idea of the extent of what I didn't know, and I had no idea of what I had no idea about.

Even though I was introduced as "Prince's friend" so many times in the old days that for my own sanity I had to drop as conspicuously as possible out of his life, I never said once while he was alive that we were in fact friends.

And so, the last time Prince and I ever talked—fittingly on the phone—was so he could relate a scene he'd just seen on *The Office*, a sitcom about life in a workaday Scranton, Pennsylvania, paperselling company that ran for almost a decade on network television, and was, for years, one of Netflix's most popular warhorses.

In the particular episode Prince was calling about, it seemed, Creed Bratton, the ancient lunatic of the cast, had used my forever all-time-favorite Prince jive pronoun from back in the day when we were both young and thought everything would work out all right for both of us in this thing called life. He'd used the jive pronoun so often, and I'd always laughed so hard when he did that it became my off-and-on nickname in the private patois we developed from the first moment we began talking: "mamma jamma."

I always suspected he had a similar secret language with every-body he had any kind of relationship with: It's an easy way to co-opt somebody's unquestioning loyalty, and Prince was a master of exerting personal power. He knew how to drive colleagues like slaves, but he also knew when and how to make them feel special with a nickname, or even private language.

John F. Kennedy understood. No one co-opted Ben Bradlee, the former marine and tough future executive editor of the *Washington Post*, who had the courage to oversee and run with the Watergate story that destroyed Richard Nixon. Except Kennedy, who nicknamed and alone called Bradlee "Benjy" while he was president, and Ben was the Washington bureau chief of *Newsweek*. For the rest of his life JFK had one of the least corruptible icons of journalism safely in his pocket.

Prince had read Niccolò Machiavelli's *The Prince*, the classic sixteenth-century meditation on deviously getting and keeping power. And no matter which spirituality he actually officially followed at the moment, he forever religiously practiced Machiavelli's dictum that "It is better to be feared than loved, if you cannot be both."

And so, if Prince was expert at making peers feel like shit—which he did automatically if he was paying you a salary—he was also adept at making you feel special. For me, that meant in the old days his use of "mamma jamma"—the word Prince had used obsessively when we first met to try unsuccessfully to break his habit of saying "motherfucker."

"Mamma jamma"—the jive, Ebonics, or African American English vernacular pronoun was the word he chose when still in the first blush of his "Purple Rain" above-the-law rock star fame. At the time, he thought it might be a good commercial idea to clean up his language, if not necessarily his lyrics.

"Mamma jamma." He'd known since the day we met that the mellifluous sound of his long-retired use of the jive term was my all-time favorite expression in his profoundly catholic vocabulary. Unfortunately nostalgia was not a place Prince visited too often anymore, and now, in the spring of 2016, the fact that I hadn't heard him say "mamma jamma" in several years seemed another indication to me that *something* was wrong.

Ach, I told myself again, everything's fine. I looked at the clock: One in the afternoon. Well, *that* was wrong. Or, as we say in Minneapolis, *different.*

After all, I was his middle-of-the-night-angst guy, I thought. And though I could and would talk to him about sitcoms or the Minnesota Vikings, romance, raising a family, or suicide, it was usually between three and six in the morning.

I was *not* his middle-of-the-afternoon talk-trash-about-television-and-sports guy. For decades he'd called in the dead of night, politely inquiring after saying hello, "Did I wake you up?"—as if he might have caught me in the middle of a brief nap or doing the crossword.

I assumed for some reason his middle-of-the-day guys were perhaps his BNs, Prince-talk (at least with me) for "Big Negroes," an abbreviation he'd borrowed from *Homicide,* one of his favorite television shows, created by David Simon, who later invented *The Wire,* his favorite show of all time.

"BN, BG," the quite-brilliant cops-and-robbers show delineated, was Baltimore police shorthand for the only details most white mugging victims tended to remember when quizzed for descriptions of African American assailants: "Big Negro, Big Gun."

In our private language "BN" came to mean Prince's hired muscle. He privately called his bodyguards or other pumped-up members of his entourage "my BNs," and he seemed tickled when I presumptuously adopted the term to refer to the men who kept the little fellow safe by radiating menace at thirty feet.

So if he wasn't calling his BNs right now, where were his morning women—why wasn't he calling or talking to one of them right now, in the light of day? When Prince's parents were alive, he'd bring his special lady friend—or friends—of the moment to both of his folks' houses to say hello at daybreak. Why wasn't he talking to *those* people in *those* compartments at *this* time of day?

———

Calling anybody at any time of day or night wasn't just another Machiavellian tool of power and intimidation for Prince. Fellow Twin City native F. Scott Fitzgerald wrote in *The Crack-Up*, his chilling 1940 account of his own unraveling, of the "real dark night of the soul [when] it is always three o'clock in the morning, day after day." For Prince three o'clock in the morning wasn't meant for existential shivers. It was a normal working hour, day after day, night after night.

He was proud that his lifelong vampire's schedule was prime time not for self-torture or mental disintegration, but to continue his day labors that resulted in the release, during his lifetime, of thirty-nine studio albums and four soundtracks that sold one hundred million units, and won a gazillion Grammys, one Academy Award, and, perhaps most astonishingly, the veritable ownership of his own color (by which, of course, I mean purple, not black).

When did he sleep? Late morning, early afternoon, a few hours at most, those who seemed to know seemed to say. Yet it had always been an open question, as far back as junior high school. "Anyone who was around back then knew what was happening," he told me. "I was working. When they were sleeping, I was *jamming*. When they woke up, I had another groove. I'm as insane that way now as I was back then."

In 1985, the first time we'd talked on the record, Prince even acted out, in self-mockery, his own death, saying he'd mostly likely die during the witching hours of exhaustion *extremis*. Stretching out on a recording console, limbs awkwardly splayed like a body ready to be chalked by the coroner, he crossed his eyes and stuck his arm out.

That's all this was, these heebie-jeebies I was feeling, I tried in vain to reassure myself less than a month before he died. On this, our final exchange of words, maybe Prince was verbalizing one facet of his multifacets, maybe it was a cartoon version of . . . something *real* he was trying to express, he did that, too. Something that I unconsciously buried, at least for the duration of that call, intimations that what I was hearing was perhaps the death rattle of a rock star on the verge of a drug-induced overdose, which still haunts me.

I felt better after he complied with my request to do one of his best impressions, one of many. I asked him for his impersonation of

Stanley Hudson, the curmudgeonly middle-aged African American, a former Black Panther who grudgingly put up with the subtle and not-so-subtle foibles and unknowing racism of his fellow paper sellers in *The Office*. So he did several spot-on Stanley impressions for my benefit, including my favorite, his furious, shouting Stanley, the one he said reminded him most of his father.

Prince threw in one of his magnificent, animated Don King imitations, and I felt better. He finally said keep in touch, and my last thought as we hung up was that I wished I'd asked him to do Fonzie from *Happy Days*!

I loved his Fonzie.

"Next time," I thought. "Eyyyy."

There never would be a next time. And the out-of-time oddness of that last call nagged at me periodically for days. But lots of things bother me off and on for days, always had. For whatever reasons he liked me, it wasn't for my preternatural calmness. As potatoes went with Prince, this was pretty small, I reassured myself.

And yet, others across the city had felt weirdness emanating, too. Prince had uncharacteristically gotten back in touch with several people from his past over the last year of his life, and he'd mentioned in our last conversation how he'd been reaching out, though I didn't even wonder if he was trying to signal an end or a beginning. I'm nostalgic for times I wasn't even alive for; I get nostalgic for other people's nostalgia.

Yet suddenly, events became even more worrisome. A week after I talked to Prince, his plane made an emergency landing in Moline, Illinois, after a concert in Atlanta: Secretly, he was to be revived from an opioid overdose that was covered up as a touch of the flu. He was down to 112 pounds from the 130 he'd weighed several years earlier.

But even when news broke of the weirdness in Moline, no one from his old days could get to him. André, his old best friend and among those old pals he'd gotten back in touch with in the last year, tried texting Prince a dozen times, falsely telling him he was homeless, needed a place to stay, asking if he could hang out at Paisley

Park for a few days until he got on his feet. (André was fine, as were his wife, children, house, and career.)

And then there was Alan Leeds, who over the years had served Prince in every role from production manager during the filming of *Purple Rain* to road manager on his most grandiose world tours to president of Paisley Park Records to confidante above all others. Disturbed by the reports of the Moline incident, he called Paisley Park and wasn't able to get through either to Prince—or the truth.

"I called someone I knew, and they assured me he was okay," Leeds remembered. "But even though I knew them, they sounded like a press release. I could tell something was wrong."

What could Alan, among the best business and personal allies Prince ever had, *do*?

And so, Prince died.

He'd shown me where, in 1985, when Paisley Park was just another unnamed, featureless field in the middle of nowhere, adjacent to the Twin Cities. It was the Drivepastland of Flyoverland, and for reasons my know-nothing twenty-six-year-old self never understood, my Spidey sense spooked me the second he showed me the field and told me of his dream of what he would soon build there.

Soon enough Paisley Park was indeed built, a 65,000-square-foot, $10 million creative production center and temperature-controlled storage facility encompassing a capacious layout of studios, soundstages, and practice spaces. Paisley Park also provided a Superman-worthy Fortress of Solitude for its creator. Staring at the empty field where he would die in another century, he defined the concept of "Paisley Park," presciently, spookily, as a "place in your heart where you can go to be alone."

I don't believe in visions, but it was a hell of a coincidence what popped into my mind all those years before when he showed me that field. I flashed suddenly on Orson Welles in *Citizen Kane*, dying unloved, tended to by a barely caring nurse in "Xanadu," Kane's equivalent to Paisley Park, his stately pleasure dome built to shut out the world forever knocking for *him*. In the end, I guess, Prince got what he wanted: Like Charles Foster Kane in the film, he was left alone to

die, without even his version of "Rosebud," Kane's remembrance of
a more innocent time.

If "the Big Sleep" was the slang moniker Raymond Chandler
used for death, then Prince's yearning to be by himself was "the Big
Alone." For the musician the need to be by himself proved a road
map straight to Chandler's destination.

Kirk Johnson, then fifty-one, was one of the few inside the Prince
bubble when he died, and virtually his only contemporary. Aware
to whatever extent one wishes to believe he was aware of what was
going on with his boss, Johnson at least gets credit for taking action
when his boss was so obviously ailing.

Johnson is the one who demanded the plane make an emergency
landing on the way back to Minneapolis from Prince's show after
he'd overdosed on board in front of singer and protégé Judith Hill,
who later told investigators that among Prince's final words before
nodding off were "I'm tired. I think God is calling me home."

Johnson carried Prince off of his private plane during the emergency stop, and watched as paramedics at the Moline airport gave
Prince naloxone, the come-back-to-life antidote for opioid over-
doses. The first hit didn't work; they shot him up again, and Prince
opened his eyes.

"Are you all right?" paramedics asked Prince. He didn't answer.

"He's fine," Johnson said, on behalf of his boss.

Later Prince scolded Johnson for having him revived.

Johnson didn't give up. He'd helped procure the services of a local doctor to try to manage Prince's addiction, while a Los Angeles
drug rehab the rock star had been referred to by a San Francisco–
based business associate made preparations to send a representative
to Paisley Park and Prince, stat.

But not stat enough. Of all the horrific details to emerge from the
morning of April 21, 2016, the most sickening and revelatory was
the transcript of the 911 call made to the Carver County police from
Paisley Park by Andrew Kornfeld, the premed son of Dr. Howard
Kornfeld, the putative drug-rehab genius from Mill Valley, California. The father would get to Minneapolis just as soon as he could; in

the meantime his son, who was still fulfilling his requirements to get into medical school, would have to do.

Though the world-famous Hazelden drug and alcohol rehabilitation center—and its on-site emergency room—was only a gallon of gas away, Andrew Kornfeld had taken the red-eye all the way from the Coast. Illegally armed with naloxone and Dr. Daddy's blessing, Andrew was ready to sit in for the moment while his father took care of business in California and prepared to set his watch two hours ahead, to Central Daylight Savings Time—Prince time.

Dispatcher: 911, where is your emergency?

Andrew Kornfeld: Hi there, um, what's the address here? Yea, we need an ambulance right now.

D: OK.

Kornfeld: We have someone who is unconscious.

D: OK, what's the address?

Kornfeld: Um, we're at Prince's house.

D: OK, does anybody know the address? Is there any mail around that you could look at?

Kornfeld: Yeah, yeah, OK, hold on.

D: OK, your cellphone's not going to tell me where you're at, so I need you to find me an address.

Kornfeld: Yea, we have, um, yea, we have, um, so, yea, um, the person is dead here.

D: OK, get me the address please.

Kornfeld: OK, OK, I'm working on it.

D: Concentrate on that.

Kornfeld: And the people are just distraught.

D: I understand they are distraught, but—

Kornfeld: I'm working on it, I'm working on it.

D: OK, do we know how the person died?

Kornfeld: I don't know, I don't know.

D: OK.

Kornfeld: Um, so we're, we're in Minneapolis, Minnesota, and we are at the home of Prince.

D: You're in Minneapolis?

Kornfeld: Yea, Minneapolis, Minnesota.

D: You're sure you are in Minneapolis?

Kornfeld: That's correct.

D: OK, have you found an address yet?

Kornfeld: Yea, um, I'm so sorry, I'm so sorry I need, I need the address here?

Unidentified Female: 7801.

Unidentified Male: 7801.

D: 7801 what?

Kornfeld: Paisley Park, we are at Paisley Park.

D: You're at Paisley Park, OK, that's in Chanhassen. Are you with the person who's—?

Kornfeld: Yes, it's Prince.

D: OK.

Kornfeld: The person.

I had heard Prince called many, many things during his lifetime, on a spectrum from Mozart reborn to Satan revisited. But rarely, at least in the decades I knew him, had he been called this: just a person.

3

THE POWER OF THE JUST-DEAD

Silence invaded the suburbs,
The current of his feeling failed; he became his
admirers.

. . . .

The words of a dead man
Are modified in the guts of the living.

—W. H. Auden, "In Memory of W. B. Yeats"
(1940)

Every society honors its live conformists
and its dead troublemakers.

—Mignon McLaughlin, *The Neurotic's Notebook*
(1960)

APRIL 21, 2016

So, this guy I knew died before dawn on April 21, 2016, best guessti-mate somewhere around four. Timing was a drag. "The Dawn" was always a big deal to him, at the end of "Purple Rain," the last line after the credits was "May You Live to See the Dawn."

The apocalypse and resurrection and all that: He lived for seeing the Dawn. He was denied, heckuva thing, as they say in Minneapolis.

And so Paisley Park announced Prince's death, and it was still morning when the Associated Press sent word around the world. In my world it was a Wednesday at one o'clock in the afternoon when I found out: Jesus, the phone had been vibrating a lot that morning. Unknowing, I ignored it.

So it wasn't until the afternoon that a close friend, comedian Elizabeth Ess, somehow broke through my cone of silence by banging on my front door to give me the news. My knees buckled, and for the first time in decades I remembered an old editor of mine in New York when I was a cub reporter writing obituaries for a newsmagazine. I was always first to be brought the wire copy on the newly deceased, and I marveled to him of the "Oh, wows!" and frequent disbelief that greeted my mentions to other staffers of who'd died, even if they weren't that "big."

"It's the power of the just-dead," my editor said. "Never underestimate their power. The power of the just-dead will never let you down."

I remember asking Elizabeth if Prince had been alone when he died. The words sounded strange coming out of my mouth. I didn't say "How did he die?" but "Did he die alone?"

Yeah, she said, inside an elevator.

"Do they know if it was instant?"

Elizabeth didn't know.

And then Elizabeth was gone, and I remember praying, *actually praying*, closing my eyes as tightly as I could, gripping my mitts until they turned white, praying that he was dead before he hit the floor.

The last thing I remember is my ninety-two-year-old father calling.

"Suicide?" he asked.

No, I said to my father. "It was probably the flu."

Maybe, I wondered, aware of one of Prince's occasional and random obsessions over the decades, could he have either done it himself—or allowed himself to get got by circumstances he might have guessed were already in place? I didn't and don't want to know.

Prince had been talking to me about killing himself as early as 1985, soon after he'd called an early halt to the triumphant *Purple Rain* tour that followed the boffo smash of the film. "Sometimes I'd be onstage and [feel] a little tired and run down, like maybe I wasn't going to make it," he said back then, so softly you could hear a heart break.

"I would hurt myself," he continued, "like I'd hit my arm with my guitar, or slide down the pole the wrong way and twist an ankle or something. . . . I was afraid that I could kill myself out there, and nobody would notice."

I remembered how after he'd first talked about killing himself back then, I'd tried to make him laugh by sending him a copy of Dorothy Parker's famous "Resumé." I mailed *The Portable Dorothy Parker* to Paisley Park, bookmarked at the mordant poem that went one by one over the usual ways of committing suicide, then ruling them each out as painful, unpredictable, or aesthetically unpleasing.

In fact, he'd memorized "Resumé," back in those days when he still gratefully accepted reading suggestions from me (and suggestions of many kinds from various people). I sent him *The Portable Dorothy Parker* after he'd broached the topic on the phone the previous night.

In the poem, Parker enumerates how guns are against the law, the rope used to hang yourself could break; and gassing yourself would give off a terrible stink. She concluded: "You might as well live."

I know he got that envelope addressed to Paisley Park, because the book also includes Parker's best short story, "Big Blonde." Conventional wisdom has it that he had no idea who the author was when he wrote "The Ballad of Dorothy Parker," which appeared on the 1987 classic double album *Sign o' the Times*, but . . . well, read the short story, listen to the song, you decide.

Prince was not a sentimentalist, and anyone who knew his . . . well, um . . . *tart* sense of humor can probably guess what he would have said if he'd witnessed his own remarkable bounce into the pantheon of all-time genius, which began at 10:08 a.m., April 21, 2016, when the Associated Press reported via Twitter: "BREAKING: Publicist: Pop music superstar Prince has died at his home in suburban Minneapolis."

Over the next several days, sales of Prince's albums spiked 44,000 percent above what his records had sold shortly premortem. No, that's not a typo—44,000 percent. *Billboard* magazine counted four of the top ten albums of the week as Prince product, with *The Very Best of Prince* clocking in at number one; *Purple Rain* snared the second spot.

"*Good career move*," Prince would have said, snickering, echoing the apocryphal tale of this or that record executive or rock star, observing the effect of Elvis Presley's death, tumbling off the toilet in 1977, and the King's ensuing great good fortune as he rebounded from laughing stock to legend as his catalog zoomed up the charts as if it were 1957.

Indeed. In the end Prince sold more albums than any other artist in the United States in 2016, outselling even Drake and Adele. More than two million of his records were sold in the months after he died; he sold a total of 5.4 million digital songs that year. No one else sold more than a million digital and physical albums.

In his first days as the just-dead, the *New Yorker*'s postscript article read: "Prince and the Mystique of Genius." *People* magazine's cover read "Prince: The Private World & Shocking Death of a Musical Genius." *Newsweek* put out a "special commemorative edition" titled *Prince: The Life and Death of a Musical Genius,* while Condé Nast put out their own distinct edition, *The Genius of Prince.*

Q, the British magazine that bills itself "The World's Greatest Music Magazine," headlined its issue "Prince: Portrait of a Genius," while India's edition of *Rolling Stone* blared "Prince: Rock Star, Funk Lord, Genius."

Apparently he'd been some sort of genius.

But who *was* he?

Antoine de Saint-Exupéry, author of *The Little Prince*, is widely credited with saying, "Tell me who admires and loves you, and I will tell you who you are."

If that is true, tell me then who, exactly, this man Prince was, loved, on one hand, by President Barack Obama, who tweeted upon learning of Prince's death: "'A strong spirit transcends rules,' Prince once said—and nobody's spirit was stronger, bolder or more creative." And yet, in perhaps the only case where the two men agreed on anything, Prince was also admired by Donald Trump, who tweeted on the same sad news the day the musician died: "I met Prince on numerous occasions. He was an amazing talent and wonderful guy. He will be greatly missed!"

That twist of universal adoration, where *everyone*—the entire world, it seemed—admired and loved Prince, only made him seem more unknowable than ever to those of us who remembered the cumulative decades when he seemed to exist in the popular imagination more as a cultural freak than a creative phenomenon.

U.S. Representative Adriano Espaillat (D-NY) remembered that his grandmother had a slight twist on de Saint-Exupéry's who-admires-and-loves-you equation. She "used to say, '*Digame con quién caminas, y te diré quién eres*,'" Espaillat explained. "'Tell me who you walk with, and I'll tell you who you are.'"

But just as everyone wanted to walk alongside, Prince didn't walk too close with anyone. Not for too long, anyhow, with any particular person: Knowing Prince too soon was a sure one-way ticket to exile in the Palooka-ville of Prince ex-friends.

Prince's death certificate may have listed an overdose of fentanyl as the cause, but the fact was that he died of multiple causes, including a loss of spirit that resulted in what might most dramatically be called a passive form of suicide, as tragic as it is blameless.

First, he died in part because he'd never really recovered from losing two children by his first wife, Mayte—one to miscarriage, and one to a congenital defect at ten days. "No one is living for me, and I'm not living for anyone," he once observed, while we both kvetched miserably in equal parts self-pity and self-loathing over the phone in the middle of the night how, somehow, neither of us had the families we'd planned—and had no one to blame but ourselves.

I'd only heard that loss of spirit, determination, and hope once before—and just as it had been over the phone talking about families, it had sounded a little bit like death. The situation didn't seem to call for melodramatics, but it was the last time I could look at Paisley Park even semi-benignly. It was 1991; the Special Olympics were taking place in Minneapolis; Prince had played for the opening ceremonies and thrown open his doors for a party afterward.

I never liked Paisley Park. Even when it was new and shiny a generation before, a mirage in a cultural desert, known only when I was growing up as home to the Chanhassen Dinner Theatre, where Minneapolitans (that's what we're called) could attend what is today the world's largest professional dining and drama venue.

Among the gathered was Bobby Shriver, whose mother, Eunice Kennedy Shriver, was one of the driving forces behind the elevation of the Special Olympics to most-favored-charity status. I was standing behind a group of fancy, fancy people blocking the elevators—my escape from the party, where I didn't know a soul, and this scene, which was most assuredly not mine.

Shriver later accurately recalled what I'd witnessed for the benefit of *GQ* writer Chris Heath, author of an excellent oral history of Prince for the magazine that ran at the end of 2016. When Prince came out of the elevator that night, I happened to be a few feet from a smirking Warren Beatty.

Prince approached, and Beatty said: "I love your music." Prince replied: "I love your movies." Warren said: "Here we are! At your house! It's great!"

Suddenly Prince deflated as if a ventilator had sucked all the air out of his body. And Prince said: "Yeah. Yeah, it is. But I'm still short." He sounded like a dead man talking, or—in Jewish mysticism, a *golem*—a physical body with no spiritual soul. I had no idea why Beatty's compliment, uttered at a party, should so take the wind out of Prince's spirit. He walked away, and Shriver said: "That's *sad*. He meant it." Beatty looked around, unknowing, unmoved. I was invisible, Prince was gone, and Beatty slithered a few feet toward a friend.

I didn't come back to Paisley Park for a long time after that.

What had also done him in, I was convinced, were the combined effects of those lost children's lives, and the fact that his hips hurt so much from decades of jumping off speakers in four-inch-high heels that he could barely dance in—an unsurprising occupational hazard aggravated by the attendant accidents endemic to intricate stage shows.

All that, and add that in his final months, a growing numbness in his arms from repetitive strain made it clear his days as a pianist and guitar player were numbered. And how could his arms *not* ache? According to Alex Hahn and Laura Tiebert, coauthors of *The Rise of Prince*, he'd spent more time playing and practicing the guitar and piano than anyone in the history of recorded music.

"Oscar Wilde said we kill what we love," George Plimpton says in the Academy Award–winning documentary *When We Were Kings*, the story of how the aging, fading Muhammad Ali—with cunning, grit, and the "rope-a-dope" strategy—won another heavyweight title in 1974, from the then-invincible George Foreman.

"But with Ali, I think it might have been the opposite," Plimpton goes on, alluding to the astonishing amount of punishment the Greatest had taken during his career. "What he loved killed *him*."

It isn't much of a stretch to say that what Prince loved—dancing, playing guitar, and piano, the dream of being a father—had also killed him. Boxing led Ali to glory, and boxing led him to brain-injured silence. Prince, his body and soul racked with pain, was similarly killed by the one thing he always adored and never was unfaithful to—his own music.

"He was just all worn down," said Patricia Kasimor, ninety-four, the mother of Michelle Kasimor Streitz, who designed the canes and jewelry Prince used to such great dramatic effect on the *Sign o' the Times* and *Lovesexy* tours.

He was just all worn down.

Three years before his death, Prince and I had promised what we'd do for each other, depending on which of us died first. The agreement was, if I went before him—I was sure that's what would happen, I was positive he'd be like B.B. King and be playing at ninety-three—he was going to perform for an hour unannounced after lunch at my high school, St. Louis Park High. I knew he'd play three hours, and the kids wouldn't have to go back to class.

My task, if by some fluke he went first? "Write just one thing for the hometown paper?" he asked.

I hadn't written about him for decades, but I promised, figuring this was one bet I couldn't win.

When I found out I had won the wager, survived Prince, and either had to keep my part of the bargain or be a lying sack of shit, I did nothing. I'd been so sure I'd never have to pay up that I'd made the agreement. Now I was paralyzed.

There is a scene in an episode of *The Office* where Kevin, the gambling-addict accountant, tells the camera that if "anybody offers you ten-thousand-to-one odds on anything, take it. If John Mellencamp ever wins an Oscar, I'll be a very wealthy man."

Well, if somebody had offered me fifty-thousand-to-one odds that I would either (*1*) outlive Prince, or (*2*) become so emotionally and cognitively paralyzed by the death of any pop star, even one I knew, I would have taken the bet and gambled every cent I have.

In the weeks before he died, Prince had appeared at a couple of Paisley Park parties. He noodled out "Chopsticks," the first song he ever learned, and reminisced about his late father, John Nelson, and how he'd harshly criticized Prince and his childhood piano playing for their wretchedness.

One can find meaning wherever one wants; he'd also been playing "Motherless Child" on the tour: as was to be expected when a father physically abuses a son, the son blames the mother for not protecting him.

Mattie Shaw, a singer-turned-public-school-social-worker who'd married John Nelson, sung in his band, borne him children, and taken her beatings, too, was so proud of her son that she didn't seem to care when he told reporters she was "the wild side of me," and bullshat other journalists with fables about how Mattie was a hard-core pornography addict whose stash had provided Prince's first guidebook to gynecology and perversion. "Oh, that boy!" Mattie, always proud and dignified, defended him the few times I met her, usually with a chuckle.

I had to take care when checking facts with Mattie: She'd agree with whatever Prince said was the truth. I quizzed her twice at length. Because I couldn't put a notion in her head or else she'd agree with whatever I said to be polite and agreeable, I had to wait almost a dozen years for her to volunteer, without prompting, that Prince had indeed adopted purple as his favorite color in honor of his favorite children's book, *Harold and the Purple Crayon*.

The famous 1953 story by Crockett Johnson tells the tale of young Harold, who, armed with a purple crayon, could draw himself in and out of his own reality. He could draw a window and climb out of his house. Sail a boat. Tuck himself into his cozy safe bed for a quiet night unpunctuated by parental screaming.

Baloney, I thought, when Prince told me the story; it was the kind of piffle he'd peddled to credulous reporters his entire life.

But I couldn't ask Mattie: "Was Prince's favorite book growing up *Harold and the Purple Crayon*?" Having already blown a couple of chances to accurately fact-check other points with her, I knew she'd reply: "What did my son say?"

Then she'd laugh, and add: "Well, however he remembers it, that's the truth. What did my son say? I know my son told you something."

In the 1990s, accompanying Prince on his morning rounds to both his parents' houses—a routine he followed for years—I sat down with Mattie, in a conversation I wrote down in her bathroom. I'd asked her if Prince had liked to play pretend as a child.

"Oh yes, Prince loved 'pretend,'" Mattie said. "And his favorite book was *Harold and the Purple Crayon*. You remember that book? It was his favorite book ever since John took him to work one day at Honeywell and told Prince what he really did for a living at Honeywell—the child must have been six or seven, it was one of those 'take your kids to work days' they used to have. Did Prince tell you about that?"

Yes, he had, and I'd thought the story was also too perfect to be true. I was overjoyed that years before I'd stopped writing about Prince and didn't feel any compunction to cash in with a perfect Prince story such as this one, even if unverified. (Unverified had never been a hindrance to anybody if they wanted to get a Prince story published somewhere.)

Then Mattie Shaw Nelson told me the tale of John Nelson telling

young Prince Rogers Nelson what he actually did for a living as
the first full-time African American employee at Honeywell. He
was officially a "plastics molder" at the company famous for its
thermostats—and during the Vietnam War, for its production of napalm and the timing devices that set off cluster bombs, meant to be
used against Vietnamese civilians.

And now I could publish it.

Mattie died in 2002, and Prince was friendly at the funeral with
Hayward Baker, the man she'd married soon after divorcing John
Nelson in 1968. By the time Prince was in his twenties, he was admitting that Baker had been a beneficent stepfather who had been
kind to him. But he clung to his story that he'd learned the piano
after Hayward had locked him into the parlor as punishment for six
months, and there was nothing else for the prepubescent Prince to
do but practice.

Prince had indeed been locked in the parlor for six months, learning the piano. What he neglected to mention to early reporters was
that it was he, not Hayward, who'd locked himself in.

By 2016 Prince had already found his version of freedom a dozen
years before he died. At the least, it was enough freedom to keep
him rich, artistically satisfied, and the critics crowing that his genius
hadn't left him entangled and entombed in the La Brea Tar Pits of his
own brain. And all those years when he seemed cuckoo, what with
the often sketchy music, minuscule sales, or his name reduced to a
glyph? By 2004, it seemed he had simply been lying in wait to get
over once again with the public—his way.

"Baby, I'm a Star, Again," ran the headline in the *Wall Street Journal* that year, when he'd morphed out of the joke he'd become in
the music business with the release of his *Musicology* album, which
climbed rapidly to number four on the pop charts, marking his first
hit record in several years. And he was, indeed, doing it his way: The
soundtrack to *Purple Rain* had made Prince $19.5 million over the
previous twenty years, selling twenty-five million copies, reported
Ronin Ro in his 2016 biography, *Prince: Inside the Music and the
Masks*.

Meantime, *Musicology*'s sales for just 2004 of 1.4 million units had already brought Prince a previously unthinkable $9.1 million. According to the *San Francisco Chronicle*, "Having once revolutionized rock'n' roll, Prince can now say he defied the rock establishment and survived."

Yet survived for what? The artistic and financial freedom he'd risked everything for didn't necessarily bring happiness. As the French philosopher Jean Baudrillard wrote: "It's always the same: once you're liberated, you are forced to ask who you are."

Or, now that he was dead, who had he been?

4

KILL 'EM AND LEAVE 2.0

While Prince was alive, dead, and alive in death, forests have been felled with reportage and criticism on his life after death. Oh, and then there's his music. There have been well-written and -researched biographies and memoirs, and a quite fascinating autobiography/ scrapbook; bookstore shelves sag with oral histories and tomes of revenge and fond remembrances; deconstructions of Prince's discography, not to mention comic and coloring books for adults. There have been so-called pathographies positing theories about every one of Prince's warts, faux pas, and social miscues, real or imagined; and hagiographies all but concluding, like the old joke (originally told about Elvis Presley), that God had two sons, Jesus and Prince— Prince was just the fucked-up one.

Ben Greenman wrote in his worthy book, *Dig If You Will the Picture,* published on the first anniversary of Prince's death, that his was not just an "investigation" and "celebration" but "a frustration as well." He meant the frustration of trying to capture the experience of Prince's music in words, never mind the difficulty of piecing together the details of his life. Prince was a teenager when he took up residence with a friend's family, but the what happened and why of his upbringing had largely escaped getting pinned down. His death brought more stories about his life as an adult, the tales so odd and contradictory that the job of discerning fact from fiction seemed impossible.

Indeed, the dirty little secret of people who actually knew Prince is that they really don't know that much. They would breathe a sigh of relief and usually admit the same when you told them: "You know, I never thought I knew more than 15 percent of him."

Many of the most reliable narrators of the Prince saga had not spoken to him in decades. Many knew him very intensely for short periods of time a long, long time ago.

In many of these worthy efforts of parsing who exactly Prince was, virtually everything, it seemed, was covered. Harder, smarter, and groovier writers than I all took their swings, yet there seemed always to be at least one variable missing.

The guy, Prince.

The *guys*, Prince.

AKA, at various times as: A Prince Roger Nelson.

Prince Rogers Nelson.

Skipper Nelson.

Roger Nelson.

Rogers Nelson.

Prince Nelson.

His Royal Badness, per Minneapolis writer Martin Keller.

Roger Nelson.

Rogers Nelson.

An unpronounceable glyph.

The Artist Formerly Known as Prince.

The Artist—per Jay Leno's monologue—Who Formerly Sold Albums.

Brother Nelson, per the Jehovah's Witnesses.

And finally, just Prince again.

And then there were the personae he was so expert at inhabiting or transforming into actual people, actually living *inside* them, not just impersonating them. The excellent simulations of real people he'd been perfecting since he'd been named after a disreputable dog. To save himself, he'd mastered the innards of people and archetypes.

The pimp. The lover. The gangster. The magnificent doe-eyed innocent. The terrifying tyrant. The dawg. The joker. The gentleman. The actual magician who could materialize and vaporize, seemingly, directly, before someone's eyes. The loyal-until-death friend. The man who would sell out his oldest pal for a fistful of coin, and never speak to them again.

Then there was the man of the ghetto street, like John Shaft, who knew the secret equation wasn't play or get played—but to make the other guy play *himself*. The fighter who only fought dirty because that's what he had to do.

The proud black man unafraid to change his already-perfect name to nothing at all in 1993, even though he knew the ridicule that would come, as it had to his all-time hero Cassius Clay when he became Muhammad Ali in 1966; the book-smart man of issues; the seemingly, willfully misinformed zealot who thought the answer lay in the apocalypse. The Earth child waiting for God and the Dawn.

The genius, like Mozart. The genius, like James Brown.

And of course, the just plain batshit crazy man playing the role of Prince.

The just plain guy, or as Andrew Kornfeld identified him to the 911 dispatcher on Prince's death, "the person almost never seen."

Who was he?

Prince didn't find it too difficult to keep his truths secret, rendering his fictions as history. First, nobody got the whole picture of his life, and most of those who got close—usually by virtue of their proximity to his work or mentoring—didn't stay too close too long. One could be reasonably sure that if Prince called you his best friend this Tuesday, by next Thursday he'd never speak to you again—ever. Second, once you were gone—you were *gone*. "I was always an expert at turning my back, never to be seen again," he admitted at age twenty-seven.

It's hard not to laugh, hearing the familiarity with which so many now speak of Prince—most of whom in fact hadn't talked to him since far into the last century—as though they were just yakking the week he died.

I think of William Hurt's character scoffing at notions of closeness among the college chums gathered in *The Big Chill*. Hurt picks a fight with a long-unseen friend, a war of words which Kevin Kline's character tries to break up: "We've known each other too long for—"

The curmudgeonly Hurt interrupts: "Wrong. A *long* time ago we knew each other for a *short* period of time."

And so it went with Prince. In a general epoch I shall label "a *long* time ago," a great number of people knew Prince for a *short* period of time.

Added to this dearth of reliable witnesses is the sheer tonnage of bullshit Prince himself tossed into the already hopelessly muddied waters of his truthful history. Egregious mistakes litter Prince's biography and bibliography, many of them planted by Prince himself.

In 1985, the year after *Purple Rain*, Prince was unapologetic about spreading so many falsehoods about his background early in his career. "I used to tease journalists early on," he told me, "because I wanted them to concentrate on what music was coming out of my system that particular day, and not on the fact that I came from a broken family."

By 2004, he finally deemed his mission of misinformation a success. Never mind that that was also the year he was inducted into the Rock and Roll Hall of Fame, gave what can be called without hyperbole a historic performance at that year's ceremonies, led all artists that year in revenues generated by touring, or once again had a top-selling album.

Rather, Prince said, his biggest accomplishment of that year was that his true "story," though not his work, had disappeared from history. "Everything has been said [so] that nobody will ever know what really was," Prince said happily. "Now all anybody will have to focus on that they know is true is my music."

James McBride, in writing the brilliant *Kill 'Em and Leave: Searching for James Brown and the American Soul*, spoke to Buddy Dallas, who worked closely with Brown for almost a quarter-century as his personal attorney. "You did not get to know James Brown because he did not want to be known," said Dallas. "In twenty-four years of working with him I have never known a person who worked harder at keeping people from knowing who he was."

I'm still not sure exactly how much I knew who Prince was. A lot. At least more than I thought while he was alive. It was no secret that when his father died near the turn of the century, Prince had his own old purple house, where he had let John Nelson live out his days, immediately knocked down—destroyed, erased, like he did almost everything and anybody he no longer needed or wanted to deal with.

And yet—the incongruities. I also learned from Prince's father's hospice nurse that the son, for months, had been a daily middle-of-the-night visitor to his dying dad. I learned that three years after Prince himself died. How does one reconcile those two facts? A doting, caring son, who—once visiting hours are permanently over—becomes a destructive agent who needs not only to forget the unwanted, unhappy parts of his history but to *obliterate* them?

Prince, thank God, is dead and unable to see, we can hope, what has happened to his $300 million estate, the relatives picking over his bones, the lawyers still mooching off the rewards of his creativity, putative friends vying to execute his putative will of personality, if not an actual will. If he were to come back to life—and saw the consequences of what I have more than reasonable belief was his last practical joke—hiding his will—he'd die again.

He told me in 1993 that he had a will and it would be buried on the grounds of Paisley Park; I typed up the seven-page document to accompany it. But alas, Prince suffered the occupational hazard of many geniuses of thinking he was a genius at all things, be it directing films—or plotting practical jokes to make avaricious relatives scramble a bit for his money. Or maybe he was just fucking around and hid the directions to his will too well. Or maybe there is indeed no will at all.

But geniuses have off days and off projects. He was hilarious when he wanted to be, but when his jokes, like his films, didn't work—the way *Under the Cherry Moon* or *Graffiti Bridge* didn't work as cinema—they very *much* didn't work.

I think when developers start digging up the hundreds of acres of Paisley Park that have already been sold off, Prince's will will be found. Whether there will be any money left in the estate by then is anybody's guess, but I'll bet the five thousand dollars he actually paid me to interview him and type up the story of the end of Prince that he made . . . arrangements. I won't be in it, the bastard, but Jesus Murphy, I think he was telling me the truth when he said he'd made a will. If there was one thing I could do it was usually tell when Prince was lying—and that man was telling the truth. He made a will the central plot point of *Graffiti Bridge*!

Call it PrinceLit: the number of actually quite worthy books and articles about this guy that have been published in the years since he died, or republished postmortem from the back catalog of Prince life stories and artistic dissections that have appeared regularly since his 1984 *Purple Rain* breakthrough. Despite the wealth of scholarship and informed enthusiasm, at his most knowable Prince is a Cubist painting where people can, if they have the time to kill, argue about the corners, contours, colors, or negative space of his being, ad infinitum.

Or is it really just about his music? His music! What are we to make of his music?

The first sentence of the *Los Angeles Times*, March 16, 2004, account of that year's Rock and Roll Hall of Fame induction ceremony and grandiose showbiz hoo-ha at New York's Waldorf-Astoria Hotel made mention of one of the newly enshrined as "the dynamic funk enigma that is Prince."

Very apt. Very righteous. Very right on.

Just one question: What *is* a "dynamic funk enigma"?

Perhaps it's actually close enough to describing what Prince actually *was*. How else to designate a musician who, with equal facility, shredded guitars, tinkled ivories, conquered a symphony's-worth of other instruments; cut rugs with his feet and hearts with his lost love ballads; sang on a spectrum of registers ranging from Muddy Waters to Eartha Kitt—all the while making one swallow one's sandwich with lyrics about incest, songs titled "Jack U Off," and sounds heretofore unheard from Bangkok to Bakersfield?

And yet, didn't he indeed have the industry medals to prove his place in the eternal rock-and-roll pantheon? One hundred million records sold and induction into the Rock and Roll Hall of Fame in his first year of eligibility in a career that encompassed, well, *everything*?

The best modern description I've read of Prince came in *Pitchfork*'s 2019 ranking of all 221 members of the Rock and Roll Hall of Fame. Prince made the top half dozen, immediately following James Brown:

> Prince has to come after Brown, but it should be noticed that he could do virtually everything Brown did—and also wrote cosmic songs, and also played guitar just about as well as anyone on this list, and also sang like both an angel and devil, and also was a venturesome and sure-footed rock, pop, and soul producer and songwriter. Prince kidnapped rock's pretensions to perversion, skinned them and fashioned them into a frock coat he pulled out on special occasions or just because.

In any case, hadn't the *Village Voice*'s Robert Christgau written all the criticism really *needed* to "get" Prince anyway, in his review of his 1980 release, *Dirty Mind*? Christgau's line has become an old saw:

"Mick Jagger," Christgau had written, "should fold up his penis and go home."

Indeed. What else need be said? True, his music was, at times: punk, funk, new wave, no wave, rap, sap, romantic, pedantic, heart-breaking words, brain-breaking curves, loathable, lovable, shocking, mocking, one-man symphonies, solo cacophonies, fragile and brilliant, unbreakably resilient, white-boy power-rock ringing, anybody-in-the-shower-singing, unheard-of, can't-hear-enough-of, genius or fool with equal ease and seeming comfort, dancing with the sizzle of frying, more boring than watching paint drying, hater, hated, jack of forever fades, master of seemingly every single one of his industry's trades.

Prince.

And how does one quantify nerve, sheer gall, which often enough is enough to "get over" in the music business, never mind if one is talented or not? And I say this sans snark or sniffiness, but rather with embarrassment for my apparent rock snobbery, engaging in the de rigueur pastime of quoting from the late Lester Bangs for a definition of the meaning of rock and roll:

"Anybody can do it," wrote Bangs:

> Learn three chords on a guitar and you've got it. Don't worry whether you can "sing" or not. Can Neil Young "sing"? Lou Reed, Bob Dylan? For performing rock and roll, or punk rock, or call it any damn thing you please, there's only one thing you need: NERVE. Rock and roll is an attitude, and if you've got the attitude you can do it, no matter what anybody says.

And if you've got the attitude and nerve of Prince, along with virtuosic abilities that placed him alone on this planet in terms of sheer musical talent? Someone with the unmitigated shamelessness to record songs for a major label before he was old enough to drink, with titles invoking sleeping with one's sister and the wonders of oral sex?

Well, as we say in Minneapolis to denote passive-aggressive disapproval, *That's interesting.*

And so, here was a man-child able to play every instrument needed in any band better than anybody he could possibly get. And nerve?

Here, at twenty-two, was a musician willing to open for the Rolling Stones in 1980 in lingerie in front of a bedrugged and boozed-up crowd of one hundred thousand made up mostly of angry *muy macho* white boys waiting in the Los Angeles Coliseum's sweltering heat for the main act?

Suddenly said masses are confronted by a Lilliputian African American Martian wearing nothing but leg warmers, a trench coat, and a leather thong. Full whiskey bottles flew back toward the stage; Prince flew back to Minneapolis, blowing off a second show scheduled for two days later.

He came back to Los Angeles to play when he couldn't answer sympathetic promoter Bill Graham's question of "What are you going to do instead of a music career if you don't come back?" (After Prince had walked away from the first concert, Graham, in one of his famous quaking rages, had berated the gathered one hundred thousand for not recognizing Prince's genius.)

Prince.

And how does one adequately, or even idiotically, begin to dissect the musical ties that bind his fans, critics, and the scholars, and critique a musician who on his first album, *For You*, recorded when he was a teenager, featured Prince adeptly playing twenty different instruments, not counting, as the liner notes say, "all vocals"? Among the instruments he is credited with playing on that record are electric guitar, acoustic guitar, bass, bass synth, singing bass, Fuzz bass, electric piano, acoustic piano, mini-Moog, poly-Moog, Arp string ensemble, Arp Pro Soloist, Oberheim four-voice, clavinet, drums, syndrums, water drums, slapsticks, bongos, congas, finger cymbals, wind chimes, orchestral bells, woodblocks, brush trap, tree bell, hand claps, and finger snaps.

How in Minneapolis does a teenage African American male even learn the clavinet? For that matter, what *is* a clavinet?*

---

* A clavinet is a stringed, electronically amplified instrument based on the Renaissance clavichord and utilized mainly in funk, reggae, and soul. For more than you'd probably want to know see Dave Hunter's 2013 book *365 Guitars Amps, & Effects You Must Play.*

Even more disheartening, how does a critic approach the widely thought irrelevant Prince of the 1990s, rendered a Luddite by the plate-tectonic shift in the music business to hip-hop, where a superstar need not know how to play even one instrument, sing on or off key, or possess anything much beyond samples of other artists' work, and words that rhyme with whatever street definitions of the second are available to any weekend gangsta on the Urban Dictionary (urbandictionary.com)?

Well, you can try to approach Prince's music differently. Instead of relying on the standards of standard rock crit, explaining ye olde who, what, why, when, where, and how of an album, and instead trying to understand how a panoply of songs—taken in no particular order, some not even necessarily by Prince—washes over his myriad lives, real or imagined, past, present, or future, with themes ranging from the orgiastic to the apocalyptic, and personae infinitum ranging from the feminine mystique of his alter ego "Camille" to his alter alter ego, the invisible producer "Jamie Starr"?

To me he was the mere but reassuringly human man behind the curtain in *The Wizard of Oz*, pulling the levers to make impossible visions—but so painfully human one felt embarrassed for him when the curtain was pulled back to reveal the reveal. When people asked what Prince was like, I always said: "He was the loneliest person I ever knew."

It is an easy line, but it was true, and it gave the quasi-insidery whisper of intimacy people pine for when looking for the skinny on the celebrated. It wasn't exactly breaking news, but most people, it seemed, hadn't heard that—or anything, really—and quasi-insidery was as far as I would go. He was a friend, even if I dared not admit it.

Like the Wizard's shadow, I saw Prince in places where he *wasn't*. Take John Leland's most excellent 2004 book, *Hip: The History*, a smart, funny, and humane book covering the historical woof and weave of who was hip, what it meant, and why it might matter.

Prince seemed visible between lines of the book, if not in the actual text or back matter. For anybody else it would seem an insult to be left out, an egregious snub: After all, "The proper way to read the book," Leland wrote, "is from the back, checking to see if your name is in the index."

For Prince, not appearing seems his due: He is above a mere alphabetical indexing of the putatively hip. In 1965 it would have seemed almost unseemly for "Dylan, Bob," to be included in such a list, just as it seemed kind of sad that Dylan had fallen so far from his perch above everyone that twenty years later he joined, even for charity, the mass gathering of mere celebrities—and legends—in the recording of "We Are the World."

(Prince infamously didn't show up, and though he made mountainous amends in time, effort, and creativity, his absence and in-the-moment behavior remain a blot on his biography. To him it wasn't a case of charity withheld, but of his arm being twisted by Quincy Jones and Michael Jackson—and though it would have been easy to slide right into that studio that night, he took the early Dylan-esque, if questionable, way out.)

"Hip comes of the haphazard American collision of peoples and ideas," wrote Leland, "thrown together in unplanned social experiment: blacks, whites, immigrants, intellectuals, hoodlums, scoundrels, sexpots, and rakes. It feeds off antennae as well as roots. Born in the dance between black and white, hip thrives on juxtaposition and pastiche. It connects the disparate and contradictory."

Using these criteria, isn't Prince the very definition of hip? The "disparate and contradictory"? You don't need a weatherman to know where the Minneapolis sound blew in from. It came from Memphis, Motown, Nashville, Philadelphia, Los Angeles, Laurel Canyon, and even, occasionally, Minneapolis, where fifteen years before "Jack U Off" was released, the epochal "Surfin' Bird" was recorded.

Prince could both pay homage to and trounce Los Angeles power pop bands praying at the altar of sex, drugs, and rock and roll, and New York nihilist noise groups, praying while playing dirges onstage, about humanity's eve of destruction. He had alchemized the Memphis sound, with the Nashville sound, with the Motown sound, with the Stax-Volt sound, with the sound of one hand clapping,

Like Duke Ellington, Prince had the elegance to wait, albeit impatiently, for his time to come around again after he swung and missed at relevance during the birth and adolescence of hip-hop. Still, like Duke Snider, the late majestic slugger of the late Brooklyn Dodgers, Prince had the power and longevity to hit the towering home run when it was needed, be it 1984 with *Purple Rain* or 2007 and his halftime performance at the Super Bowl.

And despite the aforementioned forests felled over the decades in aid of explaining his music and his musicianship, few seemed to realize that whatever point one thought Prince was making—he probably wasn't. Prince didn't want to go anywhere with a "sound," he wanted to go everywhere with tones he described as a gift he'd been granted and an albatross he'd been cursed with, all found amid the noise of genius that filled his head every second he was awake.

"Wouldn't it be cool to line up your records at the end of your life and each of them flies you to another city?" he asked in the first flush of *Purple Rain* international fame. "That," he said, "would be *cool*," sounding like a black Beavis in the mid-1980s.

Perhaps one considers Prince a musical god, like Mingus or Ellington, or even regards him with the awe with which he judged his own father's musical brilliance (half the time, that is, when he didn't consider John Nelson to be Satan).

Or perhaps one thinks Prince nothing much at all—though his rise and fall, then rise and fall, do at the very least provide a time-lapse X-ray of the star-making machinery that has evolved over the last forty years—from *Here today, gone tomorrow,* to something like *Here today, gone before lunch.*

One might not even need to be able to stand Prince to be fascinated by his life—and many couldn't stomach him. His ability to inspire loathing was almost part of his majesty: "It's quite interesting because you never seem to get a middle ground with this guy," said Eric Clapton, a fan. "There's no one I've ever met that can just say, 'Well, he's okay.' You either hate him or love him."

Indeed, to be authentically enthralled, saddened, or sickened at the concomitant grandeur and tragedy of his life, I don't think you need to tap your toe to his music, admire or even abide the way he comported himself in public, or be curious how, in the days after his death, he achieved one of the greatest, most grandiose, split-second mass comebacks in rock and roll history.

Still, *who* was he?

Well, there were the assorted Princes I knew. But why trust me? It would take me a lot more than a prelude and three chapters to trust anyone claiming to know anything about anything about Prince. Instead, let me tell you about where I felt aspects of his spirit.

I heard echoes of Prince in those artists who legitimately wanted to be lost to history, who simply didn't want to be known. Souls as diverse as Emily Dickinson and James Brown actively tried to get lost. Dickinson, an artist at both poetry and covering her own tracks, never dated a poem and named only a handful. She followed her own lyrical advice: "Tell all the truth but tell it slant—/ Success in Circuit lies." She was a master of circuitry, and I think Prince intuited her sense that "The Riddle we can guess /We speedily despise."

And James Brown? In *Kill 'Em and Leave: Searching for James Brown and the American Soul,* James McBride writes a paragraph in which "Prince" could be substituted for "Brown" and nothing would need to be corrected. "Brown was always foggy about his past," McBride says:

> When asked by reporters he weaved and bobbed. He told a biographer this, he told a reporter that. What difference did it make? . . . There's lots of versions of the story: a white version, a black version, a historical version, a record company version. There's even an official version in his [auto]biography.

And with Prince, if one was able to pierce the patina of bullshit that seemed to coat just about everything he said about himself, the contradictions in his character were so vast as to make him almost impossible to decipher as an individual. He offered up multiple versions of who he was. Each correct, each wrong.

Personal incongruities, of course, are not the domain just of the artist. Bill Moyers, decades before he reigned as the éminence grise of civic-minded journalism, served as one of President Lyndon Johnson's top aides. "Lyndon Johnson was 13 of the most interesting people I ever met," Moyers once observed.

> He could be magnanimous one day and petty the next. Women loved to dance with Lyndon Johnson, he was the best dancer in the White House since George Washington. But he could also at times be uncouth and clumsy and stubborn. And he could do the virtuous thing, and he could do the vile thing, and all in the course of a 24-hour period. Very difficult to work for. Ourselves magnified, right? We're all capable, as [Walt] Whitman said, of great contradictions. Lyndon Johnson was capable of great contradictions. I didn't like him, but I loved him.

Similarly, Prince was the most interesting, well, multitude of people I ever met. And I *did* like him. But how many other *hims* were there? I was determined to find out, verifiably.

I'm still not sure. But more than you'd think, or than I thought. He was, in the bebop jive he so loved to play at—as if it were a hobby, or Esperanto—one complicated cat.

The task of capturing this man is not simply describing the dozen or so people I could deduce and describe, plus all the others I could put together from others' descriptions. For how do you describe someone who is so seemingly knowable by all, yet unknowable by any—simultaneously?

He created his own Rashomon effect—telling five different people five different versions of the same occurrence. When he was elected to the Rock and Roll Hall of Fame in 2004, he said in his speech that one should always have a mentor and a friend not on one's payroll. He told me after the concert where he gave his most famous guitar solo that he'd meant me. I'm positive he'd told several different people the exact same thing.

His egotism was so infamous it seemed even gravity could barely bring his profound sense of self to earth. And yet how different and more egregious was Prince's narcissism from that of almost any given mass superstar at any given moment? (Okay, there was what happened in Los Angeles that 1985 night when "We Are the World" was recorded and Prince didn't show up. No excuses, just explanation—he was quite young, at the height of his international fame, and also could always behave, for such a smart guy, like an extraordinary nitwit.)

Still, in less memorable circumstances, how was Prince's general expression of his stardom so different than the leather-lunged Ethel Merman? Merman, who in 1955, accurately perceived the reality of her own existence with, "When I do a show, the whole show revolves around me, and if I don't show up, they can just forget it."

But he wanted to be known, I'm convinced. He just didn't want to be there as people went about the business of figuring out what he himself could never figure out: himself. Me, I kept my distance, never asked for anything—and wondered if this guy was my friend in a world where I take nothing more seriously than friendship—nothing. Now I know, but once again it's too late.

And so Prince was whatever he was, except when he wasn't. Just as he was a devout Jehovah's Witness—except when he wasn't, which was often. Or the way he was a devoted vegan—except when he ordered rib tips at Rudolph's Barbecue, located a few blocks away from my apartment. In virtually all forms, Prince was what he was—except when he wasn't. Which was often.

At Paisley Park, Prince's "swear jar" ethos was strictly enforced, and woe to the musician who said "damn." Those on *that* scene never saw the boss even descend to the level of profanity of "Aw, heck." But if he felt like a Rudolph's brisket sandwich for dinner instead of kale and picked me up a few hundred yards from the joint, during the course of the meal he would say "motherfucker" more often than ever.

———

So Prince lived a life where nobody—nobody!—knew more than 15 percent of what was going on in his life and brain. Still, that 15 percent could encompass a lot of surprises. And the problem, I repeated to friends over and over, dozens of times over the years, "is how do you write something that, if you read it, you'd yell: 'Bullshit!'"

That said, I need not look beyond my own mirror to find a culprit to call out for spreading, albeit unwittingly, misinformation, disinformation, and bullshit about Prince that has been reprinted and reprinted and come to be thought of as fact. Over the decades, his mother, Mattie Shaw, the singer in his father's quasi-professional jazz combo, has repeatedly been said to have had a voice spookily reminiscent of Billie Holiday's. Truth be told, I first compared the two, saying she had a "hint of Billie Holiday in her pipes," because (1) I had no idea what her voice sounded like, and (2) Billie Holiday was my favorite singer.

It was a "factoid" as the word was originally meant by Norman Mailer, who coined the term in his otherwise portentous and forgettable biography of Marilyn Monroe. A factoid was almost like a fact, Mailer explained his neologism. Except a factoid was accepted as true not because it was true, but simply because it had appeared in print.

I made an egregious error in the very first *sentence* I ever wrote about Prince. At *Rolling Stone*, I began my first Prince interview/story by talking about Prince's father, who (I'd already decided) had ruined his son and in the process forced the creation of a star.

It took me thirty-four more years to find out if I was right.

"John Nelson turns 69 today," that story began, "and all the semi-retired piano man wants for his birthday is to shoot some pool with his firstborn son."

Wrong.

Prince wasn't John Nelson's firstborn son. Prince was his firstborn son by his second wife, young Mattie, seventeen years his junior for whom he'd left his first wife, Vivian, who once looked exactly like Mattie. His actual firstborn son was John Roger Jr.

I had just turned twenty-six when we met for the story. Prince had just turned twenty-seven, and as Joseph Heller titled his second novel, *Something Happened*.

Well, they put "PRINCE TALKS: The Silence Is Broken" on the cover of the *Rolling Stone*, and thus began the ruination of my life.

Just kidding.

Just sometimes.

Fucking Prince.

This is a story about genius. My editor friend Alison, in Chicago, who doesn't even like Prince, tried to talk me out of writing this book with an email that only made me want to do it more.

"It is hard to write about genius when you, yourself, are not a genius," she said (honest woman). "Prince may not have known he was a savant, he may have thought he was just a strange man. Yet everything he said was a surprise to anyone who was listening. Or he might not talk at all, maybe never say a word again; and any words you hear might be the last words ever spoken by this . . . being."

Alison continued:

> He saw things you just never saw. All he can do is explain from where he is, which could be underwater, or in a secret cave, or on a mountain in Nepal, somewhere you will never be. I understand why the world loved him and actually let him be "him," which is actually in itself rare. Prince himself was actually a work of art; and I am sure he had no more idea than we do about why him, and no one else.

This is also a story about Mozart, who also liked purple and shooting pool, and whom Prince ridiculed for spending his youth as a piano prodigy known "as the most kissed child in Europe."

"No kisses for me, man," Prince said. "I was the most *kicked* child on [Minneapolis's] Northside."

"Also, the most talented," I said, not sucking up, but merely stating the obvious. (And anyway, Prince suffered brown-nosing suckups as little as he did his backing musician fuck-ups.)

"True that, I feel you," Prince said, speaking in 2008 of his talent vis-à-vis the rest of Minneapolis's Northside, never mind the rest of the world. "But a lot of good that did for me. I know most of them hate me. That's okay."

This is also a story about hearing music where before there was none. I am reminded of the way the late, great Jack Newfield, the *Village Voice* political sleuth, who moonlighted as a boxing expert, described the transcendent 1940s–60s welter- and middleweight boxer Sugar Ray Robinson.

Robinson was not just a quick-footed palooka, said Newfield, but an artist who "created a new place for the imagination of a fighter to go, the way Louis Armstrong or Frank Sinatra or Marlon Brando did in their art forms."

As it went for the original Sugar Ray, so it went for Prince, who "created a new place," a new space, almost a new race, for artists and those who appreciated them to bask in. While he wasn't doing that, I'd estimate he spent about 15 percent of his time equally divided between talking about the majesty of Jehovah, or the Minnesota Vikings, or perhaps, that day, why nothing he did seem to satisfy his father—or, of *course*, "You want to play Ping-Pong?"

And it is a story of shame. In the beginning I used to say Prince talked to me because we were joined at the shame bone. True, that. Who cares about my shame, but a case could be made that he died of it just as surely as from an accidental—ahem—overdose of black-market opioids purchased over the dark web. Those were merely the means—not the motive—for his death.

It's about ghosts. Not just of the dead, but of the living. It's why I couldn't bear to listen to the voices of Prince and me in conversation back when I was twenty-five and he was twenty-six.

It is about finding in the ashes what was lost in the fire.

It's about knowing who your friends are, and the people who love you, and telling them that you love them.

It's about living by a code, as agreed upon by the lascivious cop "Bunk" and the breathtakingly larcenous Omar in *The Wire*, in the pantheon of Prince's favorite television show ever.

It's about showing you can have a lonely or unhappy life—but still lead a wonderful life.

And this is also about a gravel-voiced Miles Davis, decades later, commanding a broken-down Sugar Ray Robinson, lying supine and bereft in his dressing room after being mauled in a match: "Pack it in, Ray."

And Prince saying, "Fuck Miles Davis. I mean I respect the man's talent, I'll give him my music, but I won't stand in the same room as him"

Davis was in fact the son of a dentist, a prominent and prosperous one servicing the African American community of East St. Louis with such success that he could send young Miles to Juilliard. In Prince's mind this marked Davis as soft and black bourgeois, and he'd most assuredly just call him a "motherfucker," and again, never mind the swear box Prince made visitors to Paisley Park pay into for using profanity.

Like Miles Davis, he loathed Spike Lee at the very beginning of the filmmaker's career, not because he didn't admire his films— but because of his access to college-kid bonbons like the NYU film school.

Then of course Prince forgave Spike for daring to be born solidly middle class because of a few lines of dialogue in *Do the Right Thing*. John Turturro, playing the unashamedly racist Pino being challenged by Lee himself, playing "Mookie," to admit that his favorite musician was Prince, the unabashedly uppity black man.

"But Prince ain't no nigger," Pino explains.

That's right, Prince said, saying there was only one worse word he could be called as a kid to provoke him—a master of the sucker punch—to violence. Back when he was universally known as "Skipper"—he'd fight if he was called "nigger," but friends thought he might kill if anyone dared call him "Prince."

This is a story of time capsules and rock operas.

And magic. Because in Minnesota, as the Prince song says, sometimes it snows in April.

5

DADDY DEAREST I: THE BAD SON

"You know 'The Crusher'?" I asked Prince, as he slowly tooled down Plymouth Avenue, the Northside's main drag. I'd invoked the demented novelty song about our local gravel-lunged pro-wrestling hero, recorded by the Minneapolis band the Novas in *1964*. Somehow "The Crusher" had reached all the way to number eighty-eight on the national pop chart.

"Know it? Prince said. "I probably still own it!"

And so, trolling down Plymouth in June 1985, I sang a duet with Prince, both of us singing in the Crusher's voice, which sounded less like a man trying to communicate than someone trying to gargle sandpaper.

We sang repeat choruses about applying the hammerlock hold to our enemies, which the lyrics referred to as "turkey necks."

Oh my. For the only time I knew Prince, I was singing with Prince. We went on:

The next chorus we sang together was of the beauty of gouging the eyes out of one's opponent.

To this day, I am unduly proud of having sung "The Crusher"

with Prince, rolling down Plymouth Avenue. Forget if there's a will or not, I say when people ask me if there is a will or not, and if so, if I am remembered.

"Oh, I've never thought I'd ever see any money," I say, on the occasions when they ask. "But no matter what happens the rest of my life, when I die I can say Prince drove me down Minneapolis's Plymouth Avenue, together singing at the top of our lungs "The Crusher.""

They can put that on my grave. It is more than enough. I've been blessed.

Prince was the best of sons; Prince was the worst of sons.

And his father? John Nelson, who gave himself the stage name "the Fabulous Prince Rogers"?

The name was neither mere showbiz handle nor piano-man persona. Rather, the Fabulous Prince Rogers was the uninhabited soul Nelson always presumed he would shortly inhabit, personify, and *be*, he told me in 1993.

"It was the kind of name my talent *deserved*," he said.

I waited for him to laugh at his own joke. It wasn't a joke.

My opinion of John Nelson? My impressions, which I wrongly thought I'd made sufficiently evident in print, providing narration to his noxious aura from the second I met him? As Mike Tyson, former heavyweight boxing champion of the world and convicted rapist, said of Don King, his former manager who'd once kicked a man to death on the streets of Cleveland: "He's a wretched, slimy, reptilian motherfucker."

With all due respect.

And I thought that before I discovered that John Nelson, the Fabulous Prince Rogers, claimed for twenty-five years to have written "Purple Rain."

"You say it was a name your talent deserved?" I asked.

"I suppose," he began anew, "that's what I supposed that the ladies would soon enough yell down the street after me," John Nelson said. "'It's the Fabulous Prince Rogers!'"

He sounded neither wistful nor sad, just bitter and unjustly wronged, speaking of what should have been. Years later he made clear that should have been a lot more than a hand-me-down purple house from his famous son. I'd called Prince's father from Los Angeles, where I was meeting with Prince, having just garnered his permission to call his father back in Minnesota with a get-'er-done hosanna.

As I dialed the digits, Prince, meantime, was shooting pool a few feet away from where I sat, prompting me with waves of his cue that on second thought, *Hang up*. I needn't talk to his father, I should continue my questioning in this informal/formal interview with him. I hunched my shoulders in the international sign of "Too late whaddya going to do?"

"*Just . . . Hang . . . Up!*" Prince commanded me, but I couldn't. John Nelson was an old man, and he was already answering my first question, somehow before I'd had time to ask it.

"I was ahead of my time," Nelson—then seventy-seven—groused. "Too far ahead for my own good."

"Your son was ahead of his time, too," I offered, benignly.

"Nah, I made sure that boy come along *right* on time," John Nelson said, stopped, considered, then resumed talking in a tone that might be termed "smoothly formal," accompanied by the pulpit cadence of a Southern Baptist minister:

"Prince says I gave him my name out of spite, as a *curse*, for him being born and taking away my career, while he got the life that was to be mine," Nelson continued. "He's wrong. That name 'Prince Rogers'—that was a blessing, a blessing from God. I gave that blessing to Prince, so he achieved what I myself was never given the chance to achieve."

"Uh-huh," Prince said with a nasty chortle when I got off the phone, peppering me for the answers his father had given to my questions. "He said he gave me my name as 'a blessing from God'?" Prince said. "He didn't tell you he took the name 'Prince' off a dog he once knew—a dog he didn't even *like*?"

No, he'd left that part out.

Is that why, when his father died, Prince had the house he'd regifted him bulldozed?

"He made enough of a living off me while he was alive," Prince said to me at the time. "I'm not carrying him through the afterlife too, having people driving by *my* old house saying"—Prince then adopted an exaggerated falsetto—"'That's where Prince's daddy lived, he's the one give Prince all his talent.'"

Prince paused. "I kept his name alive while he was alive, gave him songwriting credits when he couldn't write *shit*." He paused again. "I ain't keeping his name alive when he's dead."

"'Honor thy father'?" I plaintively asked, testing the putative recent Jehovah's Witness convert.

"Oh, I *honored* the no-talent sidewinder," Prince said, using one of his most pejorative epithets. "I just couldn't s*tand* him."

All I'd needed from Prince's father when I was calling was some paternal description for an extremely cuckoo-sounding project of Prince's that he'd hired me to write a narrative of. I should have waited to call the old man when I got back to the hotel, when I didn't have Prince trying to listen to every word he said over my shoulder.

"I have to go, Mr. Nelson," I'd said in signing off. "We're working on this, well, time capsule, and—"

"What do you mean 'time capsule'?" his father spouted. "He's gonna bury a *time capsule*? Where? At Paisley Park? Is there a will? He *says* there is a will, or there *is* a will? Are you his lawyer? Can you find out? Am I in it?"

John Nelson was a wretched, slimy, reptilian motherfucker, indeed.

And Prince totally agreed.

Except, between a third and half the time, when Prince refused to second the motion that his father was a wretched reptile. At those times his father, Prince thought, was more than a great talent unto himself. Prince also thought he himself *was* his father. "Me and my father, we're one and the same," he said in 1985. "My father's a little sick, just like I am."

"Papa," the fifth cut on Prince's 1994 subtly titled album *Come*, is less a song than a plaintive screech for help by an abused four-year-old. With lyrics like—and worse than—"Smack, Smack" and "... baby starts to cry / Please don't lock me up again, without a reason why," the song is redolent of a family court deposition, not a tune on an album titled *Come*.

And yet, the song generally is not taken at face value in the Prince or critical community, or considered *prima facie* evidence that John Nelson smacked his wife Mattie and son Prince around. (I have absolutely no idea if he struck Tyka, Prince's younger sister.)

Prince told me several times, without a detectable agenda for why he'd lie, that he and his mother had indeed been knocked about by Papa John, much as portrayed in the purportedly fictional part of Prince's *Purple Rain*. Then again, in *Purple Rain*, Prince's father shoots himself in the head—now *that* didn't happen.

But the physical abuse suffered by his family at the hands of John Nelson? That happened. I guess that's why they called it a semiautobiographical piece of work.

"True, that," Prince said. "But you can't say that, that he hit me" going off the record the only time during the dozen hours of interviews that encompassed my first *Rolling Stone* story on him. He was ashamed, he later told me, in dribs and drabs, that he hadn't bounced back up from the periodic beat-downs and fought back.

Even if he was only seven—he'd already rightly deduced that for himself it was be bullied or learn to fight dirty, with sucker punches and a mad dash to safety. That he didn't even try to get away from John Nelson's beatings, let alone land a few punches of his own into the old man, where he knew it would work, made him, he said, feel weak.

A master of not giving due credit, Prince was also wise about knowing when to give credit when no credit was earned.

"That [bad] stuff about my past and my father hitting everybody was part of [director-writer] Al Magnoli's story," I quoted him back when. "We used parts of my past and present to make the story pop more, but it was a story. My dad wouldn't have nothing to do with guns. He never swore, still doesn't, and never drinks."

And beats the shit out of his family? I left the answer to that question aside, left the question itself besides, quite blatantly and transparently, I thought.

I thought I was pointing a big neon sign reading "child abuse," but I was very wrong. And anyway, Magnoli gladly took full credit for coming up with the idea of Prince's father smacking Prince, aka "the Kid," in the movie. Magnoli even wove a myth about the filial violence that made John Nelson popping his son a critical element of Magnoli's very participation in *Purple Rain*.

According to Magnoli's telling, most prominently to *Rolling Stone*'s David Browne in an article published a week after Prince died, upon meeting the star, the utterly untested-as-a-professional director demanded that there be a scene where the Kid gets smacked by the father. To hear Magnoli tell it, he saw it in a magic vision—kismet.

From Magnoli's first look, he said, "Suddenly I saw the violence, the dysfunctional relationship with his mother, his father as a musician writing music and hiding it in a box." The would-be director and musician then went for a wild-ass drive, Magnoli recounted, Prince driving, finally slamming on the breaks and demanding: "'Do you know me?' I said no. 'Oh, you know my music?' I said. 'Just *1999*.' And he said, 'Then how is it that you essentially tell me *my* story without knowing me?'"

"I said, 'I don't know, but if you're willing to commit to this story we have an opportunity to make a great picture.' He said, 'Is that important for you, my father hitting me?' I said, 'Yes.' He said he was willing to commit."

The words Magnoli has Prince speaking bear no relation to any vocabulary, syntax, or sentence construction I ever heard Prince use in thirty-one years. Despite Magnoli's attempt to make himself sound like a twenty-five-year-old Orson Welles choreographing every twitch in *Citizen Kane*, the truth in *Purple Rain* was more of a downer for Magnoli.

From every direction he was being hazed or ignored. Alan Leeds, who served essentially as production manager for the film, spoke to Alan Light on the thirtieth anniversary of *Purple Rain* for Light's masterful book on the film and its effect on its intended audience: "You also had drama with Magnoli, who didn't have the complete faith of the crew, because he was not an experienced director. . . . All you need is one underling who's frustrated, who thinks he should be a director, and all of a sudden he's stirring shit up."

More critically, Magnoli's personal artistic visions, that he said began with Prince being pummeled by his old man, weren't helped by Prince's ongoing script revision.

"Prince took everything away from Magnoli, he was writing the script himself," said vocalist Susannah Melvoin. "He would be like, 'Nah, that's not what I had in mind. There are no rules here—this is my movie, so I can do it myself.'

"He would read something and say: 'It's not popping enough, it doesn't say what I'm saying,'" Melvoin continued, "and next thing [Prince is] sitting on the floor rewriting it. He'd give it to Steve [Fargnoli, Prince's manager] to take to the office, and the next day it's changed. It was always his way, or the highway and you just facilitated it."

And when they were finished, they had a script resembling the one that was more or less the one seen up there on the screen, in vignettes pretty much as Prince had described happening in his household down here. Though down here he fingered his father for the beating, Prince blamed his blameless mother, telling scurrilous lies about the woman who would provide the biggest support system he had in his entire life.

Yet he would badmouth her for years, telling his forever hairstylist Kim Berry she was a drug addict who stole from his piggy bank; telling other reporters not that Mattie Baker held a master's degree from the University of Minnesota and was a valued social worker for two decades in the Minneapolis schools. Rather, he'd weave fables that found their way into biographies, about his mother leaving a fictional cache of hard-core pornography around the house for a prepubescent Prince to find. (This particular fiction gets the biggest guffaws from those who knew how "proper" Mattie always was.)

Mattie, his mother, whose advice he relied on like no other human being's until the day she died in 2002. Who took him on dentist and doctor appointments, bringing the teenager to work with her sometimes, all through high school, because the father couldn't be bothered?

Of course, he blamed her for the beatings they both took from John Nelson. As renowned psychotherapist and researcher Phyllis Chesler put it in *Tablet* magazine, a "victim bears up under the weight of it, absorbs the blow, and tries to move on . . . but never forgives the mother who did not protect."

"A single person is missing for you"—wrote French philosopher Philippe Ariès to the point of this aversion in *Western Attitudes toward Death*—"and the whole world is empty."

Try as righteously as she might, Mattie was not that single person for Prince. It was the father who gave the son his own stage name, which, I repeat, he'd taken from a dog he didn't like.

I could never deduce whether there was always a real reason Prince flipped between particidal-minded disgust toward his father and Wally-to-Ward Cleaver obeisance. It seemed he did it, as was always the case with Prince, for no particular reason at all.

Prince was the best of sons; Prince was the worst of sons.

Either way, it was heartbreaking to watch.

I knew the first entire day I spent with Prince, which included a half-day spent with Prince's father, that John Nelson had long since killed off his son.

"That's what time it is," Prince said, our second day in each other's company. He slowed his whalebone-white 1966 convertible Thunderbird to a crawl, threading his way through North Minneapolis, his native stomping grounds, and mine on weekends with my grandparents when I was a kid.

"My father named *himself* the '*Fabulous* Prince Rogers,'" Prince said with a cackle. "Now, if you're James Brown, it's all right to name yourself the Godfather of Soul, because he's James Brown, you feel me?" Prince asked. "It ain't braggy if you can do it."

———

There it was, the Minneapolis "Braggy"!

"Satchel Paige said that," I chimed in faux-helpfully.

"Who made you a Negro, who taught you how to tell time?" he asked dismissively. "These are my streets," he said.

I looked out the passenger window at all the familiar sights. Every weekend I'd go to my grandparents' house, only a few alphabetized blocks from Prince's home while we were both growing up. He lived at 915 Logan Avenue North; then came Morgan and Newton Avenues; my grandparents lived at 1252 Oliver Avenue North. I remembered my father's peasant parents, who never learned English in fifty years in America.

Prince drove like a proper Minnesotan, a good citizen, cruising under the speed limit, hands at the ten and two positions, stopping completely at four-way stops, indicating his turns with his blinkers, even when no pedestrians or automobiles were in sight.

The old neighborhood was brimming with life—jump-roping girls, men stuffing impossible shots into hoops. Prince kept trilling memories, real and/or imagined and/or bullshit, as we drove toward his old man's house.

On Oliver and Plymouth, I said: "That's where my grandparents lived. Right there."

"When?" asked Prince.

"You were there," I said. "A few blocks up on Plymouth."

"What them old Jews, your grandparents, doing staying here North?" he asked.

After walking across Europe and somehow ending in *farkakte* Minneapolis, I explained, they decided they'd walked far enough, and refused to move from the Northside, even when the summer riots of the 1960s burned down the neighborhood they'd shared in poverty and relative peace for half a century with their African American and Slavic brethren. My grandparents' synagogue was still in necessary walking distance.

I started drifting off, sleepy from Prince's and my long first day together yesterday. I was still thinking of my grandmother, and of the only thing I understood that she did or said in the twelve years I was alive before she died.

Professional wrestling, aka "rasslin'."

Every Friday night we'd sit and watch, live, *All-Star Wrestling*, the professional matches on independent television station 11, broadcast live from the Calhoun Beach Manor adjacent to Lake Calhoun, smack in the middle of Minneapolis. (The lake was named for mid-nineteenth century statesman John C. Calhoun from South Carolina, most remembered for his virulent defense of slavery. Oy, Minneapolis!)

Pro wrestling was the international language, it turned out, the bridge between the old-world bubbies and the American boychiks. I don't know what my grandmother was saying, but I'd never seen her rage like she did whenever she saw the evil Japanese "bad guy," Kinji Shibuya. She screamed when Shibuya threw salt in the eyes of his opponents. She'd yell something that sounded like a gargle at the referee—"Look, ref, not that way, the other way! Shibuya is hitting his opponent, the poor yutz, with a foreign object!" she'd shriek in Yiddish.

In the eyes of the ruling elite, her lower-class shtetl-tinged passions and predilections were all part of the minor blot that constituted Minnesota's tiny population not with roots that took them back to Scandinavia, Germany, or at least the "right side" of Europe—the undeniably *Western* side of Europe—the undeniably non-Italian, non-Slav, non-Jewish *white* side of Europe. When those other people immigrated to Minneapolis from the wrong side—or from the Deep South—they were largely sequestered on these Northside streets.

Most of the whites fled with the riots, except, it seemed, my grandparents. As for African Americans?

Five months after Prince signed his first contract with Warner Records in 1977, Calvin Griffith, owner of the Minnesota Twins baseball team, gave less than a stemwinder to the Lions Club of Waseca, Minnesota, a town of 9,200 located some forty miles south of Minneapolis. Griffith had been enjoying fellowship with the gathered Lions before his speech. Blotto, he concluded the conclave by taking questions.

One interlocutor innocuously asked Griffith why he'd decided to move his Washington Senators to Minnesota in 1961. The most recent census had put the white population of the state at 99 percent.

"It was when I found out you only had 15,000 blacks here," Griffith said, unaware that amidst the Waseca Lions sat young Nick Coleman of the *Minneapolis Tribune* scribbling quotes. "Black people don't go to ball games," Griffith continued, "but they'll fill up a rasslin' ring and put up such a chant it'll scare you to death. It's unbelievable. We came here because you've got good, hardworking, white people here."

It was a thoroughly unsurprising remark. Though Minneapolis's chamber-of-commerce-on-steroids-like publicity machine has painted the town as a bastion of progressive liberal harmony, it is by far the most racist, segregated city I've ever lived in. (And I wrote that last sentence *years* before George Floyd was killed and it became fashionable to slag Minneapolis's racial duality.)

But I was also irritated by Griffith's remark for the disrespect it showed wrestling, not least of which was that both I and my immigrant grandmother loved watching rasslin'.

Indeed, I never saw her as angry as she got once a week at that cheater, Kinji Shibuya on *All Star Wrestling*.

Blocks away on Logan, young Prince Rogers Nelson was watching wrestling too, live from the Calhoun Beach Manor.

"Moolah," I said, back in the present, my head bobbing back in exhaustion—Prince had picked me up at home at my parents' house at seven thirty that morning. "The Fabulous Moolah."

"What?" Prince said, at first sounding delighted. "Did you say 'the Fabulous Moolah'? How do you know the Fabulous Moolah? The women's champ! She didn't even wrestle here."

"Right," I said, still groggy from Saturday-night sleep deprivation, hoping Prince didn't notice that I might have fallen asleep for a second, talking up a cyclone, trying to distract him: "We had midget wrestlers. Remember the Indian midget, Billy Red Cloud?" I said.

"Him and Little Beaver, the Indian midget tag-team champions," he shot back knowingly.

"But we didn't have any women wrestlers, no Fabulous Moolah. How do *you* know the Fabulous Moolah? You must have got the magazines," I said.

Prince looked at me as he drove and said, bemused: "Shit, I thought I was the only one who got the wrestling magazines. I was the only mamma jamma at John Hay Elementary who knew who Bruno Sammartino was, or 'The Sheik.'"

"Los Angeles territory," I said. "The champ babyface and the champ heel," I retorted, using the professional-wrestling jargon for, respectively, a "good" guy and a "bad" guy. Sometimes the babyfaces, or faces, turned into heels, I noted, still hoping to divert attention from my profound exhaustion. "Remember when good-guy Cowboy Jack Lanza turned into bad-guy Blackjack Lanza overnight?"

Yeah, Prince affirmed, he remembered, delighted to have some-one with whom he could talk intricate pro-wrestling details from the early 1970s: He'd been playing "kayfabe" with his own life for vir-tually his whole life—"kayfabe" being wrestling's inviolable code of never-let-the-rubes-unsuspend-their-disbelief-that-all-this-theatrical-hoo-ha-was-fake.

But Prince was more astonished at catching me falling asleep before him, even momentarily. Prince always knew when my mind drifted from *his* thoughts, on those occasions when he chose to be fully engaged, even for just a sentence.

"Mamma jamma, you listening to me?" he demanded.

"'Course I'm listening," I said, a terrible liar. "Bruno Sammartino. And we're off the record now anyway."

"You said that, not me."

"I got what I needed. I got much more than I needed." I paused. "And I was betrayed. They're getting much more than they deserve."

"Yes, they are," Prince said. "They wanted to give you up, get their *music* editor to be you," he said, laughing, one of the most fa-mously disloyal humans on earth having stuck up for me before my own bosses in ways unheard of.

"Everyone dying to hear me talk, and you falling asleep on me," Prince said, and laughed aloud, half–Jerry Lewis, chump; half–Muhammad Ali, champ.

"I was resting my eyes," I said. I don't mind late nights, but just because he wants to go cruising around town again at 7:30 a.m. the next day didn't mean I had to *indulge* him.

"Yes, it does," Prince had said before dropping me off at my parents' home the night before, when he told me the itinerary for the next morning. "What else you got to do?"

True, that. So maybe I did fall asleep while the world's biggest rock star was talking.

"Man, you gotta wake up!" Prince had commanded. "You know how many lives God gives you?" he went on.

"No," I said. "None before noon?"

"Too many," Prince said, starting up the car again. "Let's go see Satan," he said. "Let's go look in on the Fabulous Prince Rogers."

And besides, I didn't miss anything, my tape recorder is running, I thought.

Except that I also thought: I didn't realize at the moment that I was so pooped I was talking out loud.

"I *see* that your tape recorder is running, Prince said. "Don't let anybody have any of those tapes."

"I won't," I promised. "Where were we?"

"My father," Prince said. "See, my father didn't have the talent to be the Fabulous Prince Rogers," Prince continued, literally spitting out the words, "and had to get his black ass a job and properly feed his new baby and wife. Now that would be my mother who helped ruin his life, this nobody, this John Nelson, now Mr. Nine-to-Five Negro, not Mr. Pretend Duke Ellington, not the Fabulous Prince Rogers. The Fabulous Prince Rogers killed himself the first breath I took, when he had to quit saying music was his life, not his *hobby*."

Prince said "*hobby*" the way most people say "*Nazi*."

With malice. "Extreme prejudice," I think it's called in spy novels.

"Nobody gets those tapes," he doubled back on topic. "Promise me."

"I promise, I promise."

Something had happened between Prince and his father sometime between his dropping me off late the previous night and picking me up early that morning.

They'd fought.

In what for most people would constitute half a night's sleep, Prince had changed his opinion of his father 180 degrees. Yesterday, his father's birthday, Prince had been the lapdog son trying to please or at least appease the unforgiving father. He'd alchemized from a little boy adoring a hero to a man loathing his archenemy.

Yesterday, picking up his father, Prince had lost that ineffable luminescence that glows off a newly minted international superstar within a second of coming within sight of his father waiting for him outside his house. Now I suddenly felt nothing but menace vibrating off Prince.

John Nelson saw it, too, the second we pulled into his driveway. John's physiognomy went from a mellow dapper dan to a blues-racked John Lee Hooker. Even though I already despised John as a bully and batterer of his own beloved, one couldn't help but feel heartbroken by the expression on his face.

I think the *New Yorker*'s Amanda Petrusich got it just right while critiquing a 2018 documentary about playwright Arthur Miller, made by his daughter, Rebecca. Miller's plays, wrote Petrusich, "often feature older, failing men, who baffle and horrify their children. This has to be one of the most excruciating things a person can endure: your own child looking at you with disappointment. It's devastating."

It was.

"Why, if it isn't the Fabulous Prince Rogers," Prince said, with a tone, as it were, of disgusted disrespect.

"Good morning," his father said quietly, chastened by whatever had happened.

We stayed outside the house.

"You know, you just couldn't make a living in this town playing jazz back when," John Nelson said to me, sounding apologetic. "I hadn't mentioned that yesterday."

He went on to explain, sounding shamed, as if Prince had ordered him to explain it to me, how it was an ugly but necessary bit of domestic alchemy that he had to make me understand, that made it possible for the persona of the Fabulous Prince Rogers, always cool, to coexist with John Nelson, company man, with a banal handle and a 1958 family man's responsibilities, including, worst of all, having a dull-as-dishwater, full-time day job.

In reality John had had to become a part-time jazzman well before he'd had Prince, his first child with his *second* family. Both a cad and a dawg, John had abandoned his first legal mate and brood for the attention and affection of his soon-enough-wife Mattie Shaw, Prince's mother, a singer seventeen years John's junior.

But he never dropped the pretense that he was a profoundly gifted, full-time jazzman. Once they were together, Mattie had taken over vocals for the Prince Rogers Trio. She quit the Prince Rogers Trio when she got married, soon bore Prince, and soon enough began hectoring her husband to give up the trio—she wouldn't dare say he didn't have the chops, but she did mention that they now had a family.

"Not my fault he didn't have it," Prince said, of his father.

"'It'?" I asked, idiotically.

"*It*, man," Prince said, a little irritated. "T-a-l-e-n-t. Talent. When you got down to it, she told me secretly a few times, my father was a 'legend in his own mind.'"

I reached for a metaphor of megalomania. Prince and I had been watching old boxing matches on VHS, mostly Muhammad Ali, back at the purple house.

The first day I ever spent with Prince (mere days before) I'd seen John Nelson's original sin—perpetrated against Prince, and his mother and sister, Tyka—explained, the crime replayed in miniature, passively rationalized, and/or aggressively denied by that same cast of victims.

Before that night's end I'd witnessed the aforementioned mamma jamma reenact with Prince their entire doomed past. I'd seen the collateral damage and emotional defenses erected forever by the mere reality of what Prince Rogers Nelson's birth had done to John Nelson's career.

By morning, Prince had described what had been lost in the flames of that domestic forest fire he'd unwittingly set by having the temerity to be born. And what he found—or, more accurately, invented—out of his own ashes.

The first thing Prince remembered was his father's apocalyptic rage, so different from his neighborhood persona as the coolest, smoothest, best-dressed cat in the surrounding blocks. When he drank—no matter what the public relations machinery churned out in later years—John Nelson *drank*.

John Nelson heaped physical abuse on his wife and child whenever he felt they impinged on his personal space by, in Prince's case, trying to sneak a few scales on John's off-limits piano; or, increasingly with Mattie, whenever she breathed her husband's air or asked him a question.

Prince, I'm positive, was telling the truth. Problem is when trying to discern the truth from the blarney, Prince could make himself believe the fibs he told, at least for the length of time it took to tell them. And being able to actually believe your own fables, for just the necessary moments to send off convincing honest vibes that don't show deception, I saw with Prince, can be a powerful tool indeed.

Soon enough, though, within a year of releasing *Purple Rain*, Prince didn't have to lie much anyway, except for his own amusement. Just about everything said about him was untrue.

When Prince was seven, in 1966, John Nelson moved out of the house; he and Mattie were divorced three years later. John often refused to pay child support, so Mattie took three jobs, and also began taking classes at the University of Minnesota toward a degree in social work.

Footage from *A Current Affair* provides perhaps the best recorded proof that exists of just what an asshole John Nelson was. Sitting at a piano for one piece of the segment, John's wrists wander up and down the keyboard in a cacophony of nothingness, then slide into "Purple Rain," purporting to show the direct influence he'd had on the song, which he "demonstrated" that he essentially wrote.

This could not be true. My great-uncle Augie Ratner owned Augie's, the eponymous déclassé strip joint on the seamier side of downtown Minneapolis's Hennepin Avenue. Augie, proprietor of the dive from its opening in 1944 to 1964, was one of John Nelson's most frequent employers during the years Prince Rogers labored under the delusion that he was a historic jazz figure who'd so far just lacked the requisite break.

Though John Nelson hinted on *A Current Affair* that he noodled around on his revolutionary compositions while accompanying downtown strippers during their acts, it just wasn't so. That just wasn't done. Downtown joints like Augie's, Curly's, and Brady's—the kind of places that employed broke, broken-down, and even artistically thriving local jazzmen to play behind what *Billboard* called "peelers"—that is, club strippers—were most definitely not encouraged to try out their own material, even if they believed they combined the very best of Thelonious Monk and Duke Ellington in their numbers. On downtown Minneapolis's Hennepin Avenue, black musicians weren't even allowed to mingle with the white customers.

They were there to play bump-and-grind music, unbilled. That was it.

John Nelson very much minded that the duties and costs of raising a child and supporting a wife meant punching a clock, as it were, for Honeywell, the Minneapolis-based company whose thermostats seemingly kept the entire *world* just warm or cool enough to be comfortable.

Honeywell was a *happy* company, whose products made people *happy*.

Except, that is, during the Vietnam War. Then Honeywell, and the plastic molders in their employ—John Nelson among them—made other things, too, besides widgets of comfort. During the war Honeywell was also one of the largest purveyors of the most critical components of weapons of mass destruction of the U.S. military, and the object of one of the most sustained and vehement organized war protests of the era, known officially as the "Honeywell Project."

There were still the remnants of fear in Prince's voice when he described his father telling him drunkenly what exactly he had made during wartime at Honeywell: napalm and the euphemistically named "antipersonnel" devices, weapons meant to maim, burn, and vaporize the Viet Cong, any Vietnamese civilians mixed into their ranks or villages, and the villages themselves.

Cluster bombs. Land mines. Missile guidance systems.

And napalm. He made napalm.

"I make hell, boy, I make it rain orange hell."

It was after watching an episode of *The Office* that Prince revealed that the simple narrative handed down was that Honeywell was "an industrial supplier," as one comprehensive Prince biography put it.

So Honeywell made napalm, the chemical jelly that burned most of Vietnam and untold millions of citizenry. It burned, and the more you tried to rub it out, the deeper it ran. It literally was hellfire.

"My father made that 'neigh-palm,'" Prince said, stretching the word out. One day in sixth grade, he said, "it was take-your-child-to-work day" at Honeywell. "They showed us this film that showed napalm being dropped from a jet into a jungle. I don't know if it was Vietnam, I just remember how it looked so beautiful. Just all this blue sky, and the planes dropping these things that ignited orange on the ground against all this brilliant green. But they didn't tell us what it really was, and what it really did.

"My father told us what he did when he got home: 'It made hell. You just saw hell. You see all that green that napalm fall on? That was life. That orange was hell.'"

Later we watched *Apocalypse Now*, the famous scene where Robert Duvall says, "I love the smell of napalm in the morning," and he goes surfing amid the action. "It smells like—victory."

Fans have been trying to work out the meaning of "purple rain" for decades now. Some believe it's about the end of the world, an apocalyptic theme that was never far from his mind:

"When there's blood in the sky," he said, "red and blue equals purple. Purple rain pertains to the end of the world and being with the one you love and letting your faith in God guide you through the purple rain."

Purple, detailed Ronin Ro in *Prince: Inside the Music and Masks*, was becoming a motif in the fifth album Prince had been working on, the album that would make the man synonymous with the color. "Prince used the word [purple] now to describe a bloody conflict that waged in blue skies between angels and demons," Ro wrote, "which would cause red and blue to mix. He tried the word in a title for a droning dance number called 'Purple Music.'"

The blue skies over Vietnam were where the American planes flew, and the red fire of hell was what they rained down on the people below. Prince couldn't let the color go. After trying out some new songs for his Los Angeles management team for his upcoming *1999* double album, Ro wrote: "Back home, Prince returned to his new trademark, purple skies, and fear of nuclear war. He programmed another dance beat and recorded a Sly-like multiplayer vocal about a dream, a nuclear 'judgment day' in which the sky was 'all purple,' with 'people runnin' everywhere.'"

John Nelson didn't care about that; he was making a fine wage, though most of it seemed to go into his wardrobe and other women: Neighbors grew used to young Prince knocking on their doors and asking for food.

Nor did John Nelson seem to care that he was thought to be Honeywell's first full-time African American employee. Rather, his nightmares were that men whose work he respected, and whom he believed would respect his own compositions and piano playing, would never hear his art. Men who made a living from their instruments and souls, most nights until four in the morning. John Nelson was as good as they were; why couldn't he sleep until three in the afternoon? And wear parakeet-colored jackets?

(Thelonious Monk is indeed wearing a parakeet-colored jacket in Art Kane's historic black and white 1958 picture for *Esquire* of fifty-seven jazz kings and queens lined up and down the stoop of a Harlem brownstone. All the greats were there—and John Nelson minded mightily that he wasn't. A few years later, he angrily refused when I asked him to take a peek at the photo and point out whom he had met.)

Indeed, well into his seventies, John Nelson looked, dressed, and personified—at least outwardly—the stereotype of an authentic, get-down, old-school jive hepcat, who fancied himself a Duke Ellington/Thelonious Monk–level talent that the gods had unfairly denied a break, and whose son, he felt, had none of his chops, inspiration, or soul.

To paraphrase ancient homespun humorist Sam Levenson, talent is genetic; John Nelson got his from his son. "It wasn't my fault he didn't have *it*," Prince said, interrupting his own narration to disrespect his father midway through his tour of the old neighborhood, pointing out names of old streets, and this old friend watering that fresh lawn, and the church he attended growing up and the black tar sprouting bent basketball hoops, where his (and my mother's) elementary school, John Hay, once stood.

"Why," he asked, "is it *my* fault that his biggest accomplishment, besides thieving credits from me for songs he didn't write, was to be the only *Negro* at Honeywell, ya feel me?"

Well, yes, I thought. And no. Prince had given his father those credits; there was no thievery.

Wasn't John Nelson the same man who, in only the previous seventy-two hours, Prince had humiliated himself in front of a heart-breaking attempt to receive what seemed *conditional* conditional love from his father? Whose ass Prince kissed for approval, in front of the dozens of people His Royal Badness employed, all of whom stood watching him genuflect as if to the pope—people who gener-ally wondered what day Prince would kick *their* asses?

Eli Grba, a vowel-challenged New York Yankee, used to say there was "an aura around the aura" of Mickey Mantle, his All-American-boy teammate and slugger for the ages. Prince similarly seemed to have an aura *surrounding* the natural aura that can envelop interna-tional superstars of a certain magnitude. But around John Nelson, the aura as well as the aura it surrounded disappeared.

Around John Nelson, I wondered, where was Prince, the wunder-kind with the guitar that literally ejaculated during the 1980 *Dirty Mind* tour? Prince, with the 1984 single "When Doves Cry," a song that not even Bruce Springsteen's biggest hit up to that time, "Dancing in the Dark," could dislodge from its number-one ranking on the *Bill-board* charts for five weeks. Prince, who could play any instrument better than anyone in any band you might mention, would battle any band that dared challenge him, to the death if need be, to prove that not only was he better than you, he *owned* you; would slash your band, steal your girlfriend, eat your heart, and piss on your grave?

Where was *that* Prince?

Prince was non-nonplussed by my queries, and I was stunned by the polarizing effect his father had on Prince's being. I couldn't ask, let alone get a word in, while he continued his recitation of the mediocrity that plagued his father. And then, he suddenly lightened, brightened, and offered a laugh, an ominous chuckle—malevolent, if not borderline homicidal.

"You know," he said. "The music business should give me a Grammy for just being born and stopping that man's career in music. Addition by subtraction, feel me? Lord knows he made me suffer for it."

Prince grew quiet, mindfully navigating his astonishingly groovy, mint, vintage convertible through his neighborhood as a student driver during his first lesson. "I was just the excuse, the one to blame," he said soberly. "Ain't *my* fault he didn't have the talent to feed his wife and baby."

"He said he named you Prince so you could achieve everything he didn't have a chance to," I reminded him.

"Motherfucker!" Prince almost spat.

"Anyone called me 'Prince' growing up—well, they didn't," he continued the next day, with his father sitting mostly wordlessly in the back seat of the card. "I punched hard and fast and dirty because I had to. Nobody calls me a dog's name."

At home and on the streets, Prince bore the prep-school sobriquet "Skipper," the nickname his mother had given him at birth. (Mattie called John "Prince." Prince said it was to taunt her husband for his failure at fabulousness, fame, or establishing an existence, even as much as an alter ego to salve his permanently and gravely wounded sense of self.)

The younger Nelson would remain mostly "Skipper" until his superhero origin story unfolded when he was a young teen and he emerged from a phone booth as "Prince": a man-child from another planet, a Munchkin giant, a being granted—and tormented by— powers no one had ever seen before.

Prince then offered a short symposium on how he delivered a sucker punch if anyone dared call him by his given name. "You just punch—a second faster," he said, pulling a jab to my stomach, "before they realize you're going to punch at all."

Then he laughed, hard. He had two great laughs, one from the gut, the other more a sideways snicker, both profoundly, reassuringly, the laughs of an authentic human being.

"Yeah," Prince said, then sighed. "So, you wanna know what that mamma jamma did? He sinned so bad he's had to live hell on earth." Pause. "He got me."

Out of nowhere, then, he asked me what my first memory was.

"Jack Ruby shooting Lee Harvey Oswald live on TV," I said. "I was four." I waited a second. "What's yours?" I asked.

"I'm one," he said. "I've just had my first birthday. My mother puts me on her lap in front of my father's piano. She puts my fingers on the keys and we play 'Chopsticks.' My father comes in, hits my knuckles with a yardstick, and slaps my mother with an open hand."

Well, I knew what I was going to write.

"I know what I'm going to write," I told him.

"Well, you gotta hear this other story first."

"Okay."

"But you can't write it."

"Okay." And it made me so sad I didn't write the first one either.

"It's about Vietnam. You know anything about Vietnam?"

"Yeah," I said, "I know about Vietnam."

"You know who said, 'No Viet Cong never called me nigger'?"

"Muhammad Ali. The man you had me watch knock out Sonny Liston yesterday."

"He was Cassius Clay back then," Prince instructed me.

I know. I know.

"Ain't that a pretty name? And he changed it to a name every white person and almost every black person hated, not just the name, but the man who dared take it."

"I know," I said. "Brave man."

"You know who his inspiration was?"

I did. But I didn't know what his point was.

I wouldn't know, yet.

"You know yesterday I said my father was a little sick, just like I am?

"Sick," Prince said, "was him buying this car. He told my mother he needed it, it was a musician's car, the leader of a band's car. He bought it in 1965, a white convertible Thunderbird. I was seven."

"We was all hungry, except he had his clothes and he bought this car new. He was right, this is a star's car, so what was he doing buying it all those years after music was just his hobby, his butterfly collection?"

"No need to be mean, boy. You had an allowance," John Nelson finally said.

Prince had been speaking to me as if his father weren't thirty-six inches away in the back seat.

"The really sick thing, and I mean go-to-the-mental-hospital-sick, is that the mamma jamma never drove it!" Prince said. "He was so afraid of it getting dented that it's twenty years old and has"—he checked the odometer—"22,000 miles on it."

"How'd you get it?" I asked.

"I gave him a purple BMW for his birthday last year," Prince replied. I still don't know if it was a trade or a gift from his father.

Prince made John Nelson's mint old car famous, putting it in the video to the hit song "Alphabet Street" as a major supporting character, while John Nelson hid the BMW.

The palpable tension in the car was making my stomach ache.

Prince's father said nothing, letting his son answer for him.

"Yesterday was the second time I've seen the mamma jamma take it out of the garage since I gave it to him," Prince said.

6

DADDY DEAREST II: THE GOOD SON

We have the same hands. We have the same dreams. We write the same lyrics, sometimes. Accidentally, though. I'll write something and then I'll look up and he'll have the same thing already written. . . . Our personalities are a lot alike, but his music is like nothing I've ever heard before. It's more complex. A lot of beautiful melodies are hidden beneath the complexity. That's why it takes me [so long] to pull all that out. That's why we work so well together.

—Prince on his father, *Ebony*, 1995

On April 21, 2017, the first anniversary of Prince's death, I finally girded my loins, and actually did what I was beginning to fear I'd never be able to do. I read a handful of the thousands upon thousands of words I'd published about Prince, or quoted in his name, a lifetime before.

I hadn't read a syllable of any of these articles since I'd written them.

Still, I took consolation that even in my twenty-five-year-old idiocy, my opening sentence had at least attempted to convey what I'd been able to deduce after a few days spent around John Nelson, and what I still believe is the crux of the story.

———

In prose so nuanced nobody could possibly have understood, I'd tried to foreshadow that Prince's was a tale of how John Nelson—whose malignant narcissism had revealed itself to such an extent during those days, at some not-very-subterranean level—truly thought that the story was about him, not his son, and that the headline on the front cover should read: "John Nelson Talks: The Silence Is Broken."

Well, I couldn't do that. But I would surely make him the key supporting player.

And Prince? He got the second sentence, in which he reveals just what a good son is, dutifully doing whatever his father desires for his birthday, and then fervently complimenting him on his skills and his style.

"He's real handy with a cue," was Prince's first quote in that first story, spoken in true admiration of John Nelson's acumen at pool, as he drove us to his father's house in the North Minneapolis ghetto.

And his father's acumen, in general?

"He's so cool," Prince said. "The man knows what time it is."

Prince was a very good son that day, as he was most days. Or maybe half the days. Or, at times, never.

Prince seemed almost to make a willful point of projecting onto others—often father figures—his well-earned, never-quenched rage against the abusive John Nelson. Or he internalized the fire and ire his father had directed against *him* as a child and teenager—and alternately infantilized, criticized, betrayed, or demoralized his friends, patrons, underlings, protégés, collaborators, and minions.

The crime had been capital, even Prince would sometimes mumble in wrath: He felt his very being had been effectively snuffed out by the man who didn't give him his name, but his stage name.

Looking back, perhaps I shouldn't have begun with Prince talking about his father being cool and, even at sixty-nine, knowing what time it was.

Maybe I should have begun with his very first response to my very first question when he'd finally agreed to go on the record with me.

So why, after all this time, do you finally want to talk? I asked, when he was at last settled and ready to be quoted.

"I don't want people to think I live in a prison," he said.

Strange; I'd never read anywhere that people thought he was imprisoned in himself, his life, his art, his house. Prince? In prison?

Well, one needn't be Columbo, or anything more than a twenty-five-year-old reporter who knew fuck-all about anything, to know what this meant.

Prince was in prison.

Even though "Prince is imprisoned," was my first, second, and third thought as soon as I heard him say it, I didn't really *hear* it. I couldn't have. I got it, but I missed it. I knew it, but it somehow didn't dawn on me to say it.

So, by the end of the third paragraph of my first story on Prince, I placed him not in a psychological Alcatraz, a fact I might have caught at some point all those days if I'd paid more attention to who and what was swirling around Prince at that curious, discombobulating moment in his young life, and less attention to his attempts to rationalize, compartmentalize, and explain away everything that had happened because he was the Fabulous Prince Rogers's son.

Such bullshit.

Prince's love of Minneapolis, like his love for his father, was not the love of someone who wanted to stay where he knew he was loved. "I feel homesick, even when I'm home," he said at least a half dozen times while I knew him, uttering a phrase I thought was wholly his own, but which I later heard Sarah Silverman use.

And staying in Minneapolis? He didn't want to—he said so in his first interview given to his high school newspaper in 1976. "I'm from Minneapolis," he said. "Unfortunately."

So what I should have written was: "Cruising peacefully through his old neighborhood, where he learned to live by the law of the streets in lieu of getting bullied, Prince is proof in a paisley jumpsuit that sometimes it's not just criminals who return to the scene of their crimes. Victims, too, often return to the scene of the crimes done to them."

In certain ways, their manners had become like father, like son. "He was always smooth, still is," Prince said that day. "He's got girl-friends, still, lots of them. Young ones, too."

It would be a family curse. Each of John Nelson's three wives looked virtually the same when he married her: light-skinned, much younger than him, genteel. He traded them in as if they were leased, and in the last couple of decades of his life, there was a similar sameness to the women Prince hung around with that mirrored his father.

Still, he was a good son enough of the time. In Minnesota, that counts for a lot.

He'd come to forgive his father for the terrors he'd inflicted on his family when Prince was a child. Said Prince, "Once I made it, got my first record contract, got my name on a piece of paper and a little money in my pocket, I was able to forgive. Once I was eating every day, I became a much nicer person."

But it took many more years for the son to understand what a jazzman father needed to survive. Prince figured it out when he moved into his purple house.

"I can be upstairs at the piano, and [his chef] Rande Laiderman can come in," he said.

> Her footsteps will be in a different time, and it's real weird when you hear something that's a totally different rhythm than what you're playing. A lot of times that's mistaken for conceit or not having a heart. But it's not. And my dad's the same way, and that's why it was so hard for him to live with anybody. I didn't realize that until recently. When he was working or thinking, he had a private pulse going constantly inside him. I don't know; your bloodstream beats differently.

Prince pulled his car into an alley behind a street of neat frame houses, stopped behind a wooden one-car garage, and rolled down the window. Relaxing against a tree was a man who indeed looked just like the perfectly, dapperly aged Cab Calloway in *The Blues Brothers*. Dressed in a crisp white suit, collar and tie, a trim and smiling John Nelson adjusted his best cufflinks and waved.

"Happy birthday," said the son. "Thanks," said the father,

laughing. Nelson said he wasn't even allowing himself a piece of cake on his birthday. "No, not this year," he said with a shake of his head. Pointing at his son, Nelson continued: "I'm trying to take off ten pounds I put on while visiting him in Los Angeles. He eats like I want to eat, but he exercises, which I certainly don't."

Father then asked the son if maybe he should drive himself to the pool game, so he wouldn't have to be hauled all the way back afterward. Prince said okay, and Nelson chuckled and said to the stranger: "Hey, let me show you what I got for my birthday two years ago."

He went over to the garage and gave a tug on the door handle. Squeezed inside was a customized deep-purple BMW. On the rear seat lay a copy of Prince's latest LP, *Around the World in a Day*. While the old man gingerly backed his car out, Prince smiled.

"Wait!" called Prince, remembering something. He grabbed a tape off the Thunderbird's seat and yelled to his father, "I got something for you to listen to. Lisa [Coleman] and Wendy [Melvoin] have been working on these in L.A."

Prince threw the tape, which the two female members of his band had mixed, and his father caught it with one hand. Nelson nodded okay and pulled his car behind his son's in the alley. Closely tailing Prince through North Minneapolis, he waved and smiled whenever we looked back.

Prince looked in his rearview mirror at the car tailing him. "He don't look sixty-nine, do he? He's so cool." Prince drove alongside two black kids walking their bikes. "Hey, Prince," said one casually. "Hey," said the driver with a nod. "How you doing?"

Nearing the turnoff that led from Minneapolis to suburban Eden Prairie, Prince flipped in another tape and peeked in the rearview mirror. John Nelson was still right behind. "It's real hard for my father to show emotion," said Prince, heading onto the highway.

He never says, "I love you," and whenever we try to hug or something, we bang our heads together like in some Charlie Chaplin movie. But a while ago, he was telling me how I always had to be careful. My father told me, "If anything happens to you, I'm gone." All I thought at first was that it was a real nice thing to say. But then I thought about it for a while and realized something. That was my father's way of saying "I love you."

A few minutes later, Prince and his father pulled in front of the Warehouse, a concrete barn in an Eden Prairie industrial park. Inside, the Family, a rock-funk band fronted by Susannah Melvoin and "Saint" Paul Peterson that Prince had begun working with, was pounding out new songs and dance routines. The group was as tight as ace drummer Jellybean Johnson's pants. At the end of one hot number, Family members fell on their backs, twitching like fried eggs.

Prince and his father entered to hellos from the still-gyrating band. Prince went over to a pool table by the soundboard, racked the balls, and shimmied to the beat of the Family's next song. Taking everything in, John Nelson gave a professional nod to the band, his son's rack job, and his own just-chalked cue. He hitched his shoulders, took aim, and broke with the dexterity and skill of Minnesota Fats. A few minutes later, the band was still playing, and the father was still shooting. Prince, son to this father and father to this band, was smiling.

I hate destroying any of Prince's sacred origin myths, especially the ones pertaining to back when he was a kid being teased as "the Great Gazoo," the diminutive alien in the Flintstones with the outsize head as big as his childhood Afro. The poor bastard, legally pretagged his father's stage name, his reality tempered for the worse from the womb on his father's art and artifice, not the needs of a neonate.

He'd been playing with reporters when he said, early in his career, that he learned his life's destiny, quest, and destination when he was just five years old and first saw the Fabulous Prince Rogers playing piano on a stage that his description made sound like a wonderment. In some iterations of the saga, which evolved over the decades, Prince said he accompanied his mother, Mattie, to the downtown Minneapolis club where his father was headlining, and Prince was supposed to stay outside.

In another version, he was simply in the alley behind the club, alone. In both versions Prince slithered inside, unseen—which in real life he called "playing sneaky sneaks"—to see a scene taken straight from the pages of Harlem's fabled Cotton Club, where black jazz artists played for rich white slummers, their Generation Lost, acting out their lostness through Fitzgerald flappers.

As the tale of kid Prince's first night out unfolded, he was as bedazzled at the first sight of showbiz as Dorothy was when she first spied Oz.

And in the middle of it all was John Nelson, putting on a bravura performance, went the Pecos Prince tall tale, and his father was truly, artfully, in Prince's actual words, "*tinkling* those ivories." Prince saw glory in the glamour and sheen surrounding his father—the strippers slinking around him, the high-class-whorehouse orange lights of the joint casting the proper glow on the scene.

Well, erase that one from Prince's "true" column. John Nelson had no problem telling people how he was forced to play out his lackluster career as a part-time piano player for strippers. On YouTube, one can find John and his daughter by his first wife—Prince's half-sister, Sharon—yakking it up in an instructive, if hideous, 1996 segment of *A Current Affair*, a tabloid entertainment news show of the kind that eventually begat the likes of TMZ. John and Sharon give, say the teases, a tell-all, tight-as-blood look at the unknowable Prince.

They had less than nothing to offer in the tabloid TV gossip department. And though John *did* note that his compositions were ahead of their time, he neglected to say that for the last several years of his music career, he had a full-time nine-to-five job, and was stealing another night away from his family whenever he wanted to play the piano man.

In 1964, when Prince was five, his father took him, Prince said, to see at the Minneapolis Auditorium the biggest influence there ever was and always would be on Prince's soul and music—an obsession lasting his entire life. Not James Brown, Joni Mitchell, Stevie Wonder, Sly Stone.

It was Muhammad Ali, who, when Prince first saw him on a

closed-circuit theater screen was still Cassius Clay, the 7:1 underdog twenty-two-year-old challenger set to get destroyed by the invincible heavyweight boxing champion Sonny Liston, a fearsome and illiterate ex-con, and Mafia headbreaker.

Young Prince was not alone in finding Ali a source of inspiration. Spike Lee explained Ali's mesmerizing, motivating effect in *When We Were Kings*, the 1998 film about the boxer that won the Academy Award for best documentary: "He was a *specimen*," Lee said. "A fighting machine. He was handsome. He was articulate. He was funny. Charismatic. And he was whuppin' ass too."

From age five on, Prince would try to live up to the example set by the man variously known as "the Black Superman" and "the Greatest." The match never left him, or those Prince was trying to tutor to be just *so*.

Prince, like Ali, determined from his first memories that he would be a handsome fighting machine who danced, danced, danced; he may have had his own color, but not even Prince had a dance step named after him, à la "the Ali shuffle." He never suffered fools with Ali's bonhomie, but his self-conscious silences said more than he could ever have gotten across by yakking. And he would be funny and charismatic—because he *was* funny and charismatic—and, most important, Prince knew he, too, would whup ass on whatever stage he chose.

Duke Ellington came in second as an inspiration, with Joni Mitchell fading as fast as a horse that stumbles at the finish line. Every other hero he'd had, he swore, had let him down.

James Brown, down. Miles Davis, worse. Sly Stone, waste. He didn't really know Stevie Wonder, he said; he loved his work but had absolutely no interest in anything personal about him. He quizzed me, though, on what I thought Stevie Wonder's favorite hotel chain was. I didn't know. "Holiday Inn, man," Prince said strenuously, seriously. "They've only got four different room designs; it makes sense, yeah?"

Of course.

But Ali, whom Prince had loved since he was still "Skipper" and Muhammad still Cassius, never let him down. He would fly to Ali's home and mow his lawn if the champ wanted, Prince told the press.

He was charmed that my four-foot-ten-inch mother's hero was also Ali (I'd taken her to see *When We Were Kings* for Mother's Day and arranged for Ma to get her picture taken with him, as well as get a personalized autograph on a Black Muslim pamphlet).

But before all that, Ali had to beat—impossibly—Sonny Liston, the bully, Goliath, the heavyweight champion with no élan, no personality, and who couldn't dance, dance, dance. A BBC announcer called Liston, as he entered the ring the night Prince's father took Prince to the theater, "the most frightening man in the world."

That night and that fight changed Prince's life forever. Watching on close-circuit televison in Minneapolis, Prince said he actually saw, and I half-believed, Clay miraculously strip Liston of the heavyweight championship, but also taunt him into giving up his very soul.

Days later Clay would announce he was changing his name to Muhammad Ali to honor his new station as a member of the Black Muslims: "I don't have to be what you want me to be," Ali said to reporters, almost all of whom would continue to call him Clay.

That fight, and Ali's attitude before, during, and after destroying Sonny Liston, would provide Prince a template for showmanship that would allow him to effectively hide behind his own shadow for his entire life.

I'm not sure if Prince was telling me the truth when he said he saw the fight live, at age five. His father said he didn't remember; his mother said: "What did he say? That he and John saw the fight? Well, then, I believe him!"

But even if he didn't see it live, he watched it and showed it to so many other people so many times—I'd bet hundreds—that he might as well have been there.

"Welcome to Miami Beach and the giant convention hall for what may be the richest heavyweight championship title fight of all time," begins the BBC broadcast of the film, which Prince owned on videotape, and which I would watch with him at least a dozen times. Prince would watch along—insistently.

"It's the details," he would say, slowing down the punches. "Everything that's me is in the details."

I didn't need much convincing. In college I'd written my senior thesis on Jack Johnson, the first African American heavyweight champion, at the turn of the twentieth century, whose purported utter "badness" every which way led for the famous call to find a "Great White Hope" who could win back the black man's title.

"And into the ring now comes the somber and menacing figure of Charles 'Sonny' Liston," continued the British announcer. "The champion, aptly [nick]named 'the most frightening man in the world.'

"Not for Liston the claptrap of his opponent Cassius Clay," the BBC man went on. "Liston, one-time convict, is a man of action. He'd looked on Clay's antics with contempt. Clay looks pretty confident; despite what everybody said at the weigh-in when he was fined twenty-five hundred dollars—that's about nine hundred pounds—he shouted, he raved, he taunted Sonny Liston.

"Cassius Clay, fifteen stone and a half* [217 pounds] now comes for him—the moment of truth. For months he's taunted Liston, he's said what he's gonna do, he predicted. Now he has to make his fists do what his mouth has predicted."

It would be a slaughter. As Salman Rushdie recalled what was supposed to happen in the ring: "We remember Liston, the terrifying hulk, the killer, the wordless monster of whom the young Clay should have been terrified and mysteriously was not. We remember the sports writers unanimously worrying that Clay might actually be grievously, perhaps even mortally harmed in the fight."

During their eight rounds Clay took away Liston's heavyweight championship, his manhood, and his basic will to go on. Six years later, Sonny was found dead in his Las Vegas home from a heroin overdose.

"What Sonny Liston got to complain about?" Prince asked. "He was a chump and a bully. His only reason to exist was for Ali to

---

* A stone—14 pounds—is an obsolete unit of weight still used in the United Kingdom, especially in reference to people.

show the world he was a bully. How he entered and left the ring was how I want my bands to leave other bands. You see how big Sonny Liston was walking into the ring before the match? You see how tiny he looked when he left?"

He paused and drove on, looking at the sights of Plymouth Avenue.

To Prince the fight was more than a favorite scene of combat, one he'd watch and rewatch hundreds of times over the years as an instruction manual on how to perform, entertain, outrage, show complete domination, and prove the potential power of crazy over his opponents.

Some of my very favorite of his practiced routines were the prefight scenes he'd reenact, both to entertain and to practice his own onstage attitude. Later, when he was tutoring Morris Day on how to play the character "Morris Day" in *Purple Rain*, he showed him the same scenes of young Ali over and over, as always, until Morris got it just the way Prince wanted.

"You just been to see Sonny Liston?" Prince began his spot-on re-creation of one of the prefight interviewers, as Ali is questioned. "Ain't he ugly? He's too ugly to be champion, a champion should be pretty like me!"

And then Prince would launch into some of the doggerel young Ali had used to taunt Liston before the fight.

"Who would have thought"—Prince began, his Ali imitation better by a power of 10 than, say, Billy Crystal's—

> When the time came to the fight
> they'd witness the launching
> Of a human satellite
> Yes, the crowd did not dream
> When they laid down their money
> That they would see
> A total eclipse of the Sonny!
> I am the greatest!

"Liston walked into the ring looking twelve feet tall, and left about six inches high," Prince reiterated. "He was *through*. Somebody should have told Sonny he was good as dead. He may have called Ali 'Faggot,'" Prince said, "but I guess Sonny already knew."

When Prince met Ali in 1997, he asked the Champ what his greatest thrill was in life: bringing the word of God to billions; becoming the most famous person in the history of the world, his name ringing out from European castles to sub-Saharan huts; going to countries that considered the United States their enemy and getting American political prisoners freed; the hundreds of millions of dollars he'd given away and raised for charities?

No, Ali whispered back to Prince. His biggest thrill, he said, remained beating the unbeatable Sonny Liston for the heavyweight championship of the world in 1964 when he was twenty-two.

"I could barely hear him," Prince remembered a month later. But he remembered, he said, what Ali had told him. As Ali had earlier recalled to a reporter:

> The only time I've been frightened in the ring was when
> the referee was giving Sonny and I instructions in the middle
> of the ring right before the bell, and he was just staring at me,
> silently. After all the mischief I'd bring down on his head, he'd
> told me, "I'm going to have to hurt you, faggot," and I knew he
> meant it. That first round we fought—no one had survived
> more than a round or maybe two with Sonny—was the most
> frightening three minutes of my life. I know that other stuff
> is more important, it's God's work, it's God's will—but as a
> weak human being, I must say that was my biggest thrill.

Prince had pressed Ali. What about his poetry? How about the fact that he was credited as having the shortest poem—two words—in *Bartlett's Familiar Quotations*? In 1975, while speaking to a group of Harvard students, Ali had offered the spontaneous poesy, first pointing his palms to himself, then outward to his audience: "Me? We!"

And that, said Prince, "is what time it is."

7

"THE PROBLEM FOR SUPERHEROES IS WHAT TO DO BETWEEN PHONE BOOTHS"

> Hi, Bruce Wayne
>
> I've tried to avoid all this, but I can't
>
> I just got to know . . . are we gonna try 2 love each other?
>
> —"Batdance," 1989

> The problem for superheroes is what to do between phone booths.
>
> —Ken Kesey

Ken Kesey, author of *One Flew Over the Cuckoo's Nest*, was referring to the failure of many of his fellow 1960s counterculture icons to compose second acts for their lives when he said that the problem for superheroes was how to kill time between gigs saving Gotham City. Kesey would have known: He'd already written his last good book by the time he said it.

The origin story necessary for the creation of the superhero named "Prince" actually *was* a phone booth, located on the Plymouth Avenue main drag. When summer riots hit America's ghettos in the mid-1960s, it was Plymouth Avenue that burned.

Four years after Martin Luther King was shot, Skipper Nelson was already fourteen, and that phone booth was where the teenager sobbed for two hours. According to Prince, his father had just kicked him out of the house for good. He'd just been denied a roof, let alone shelter from the psychic storm, by John Nelson.

After that two-hour sobbing spell, Skipper never cried again, Prince said, punted from that phone booth with the paternal order not to bother to come home, which he never did. When he arose from his crying jag he was a new creation: *Prince.*

He pinky-promised me that he was dishing me the printable truth, which he was, except for the slight detail or two he was leaving out. Still, prospects were dim back then, to say the least, for Prince Nelson, a penniless, homeless, pint-size, and often bullied African American kid in his early teens.

And so, the creation myth goes, Prince Rogers Nelson, stranded in the then whitest metropolitan center in the country, with nowhere else to go, finally got up after two hours outside that phone booth; never ever wept another tear; and just walked on, reincarnated as "Prince."

Forty-two years later he would die inside Paisley Park, his bigger, better phone booth, where he could hide, hide out, and change personalities with nobody watching.

In 1976 Johnny Wakelin recorded a popular novelty song about Muhammad Ali called "Black Superman." The lyrics tell the story as much of Prince's future as Ali's past:

> This here's the story of Cassius Clay
> Who changed his name to Muhammad Ali
> Sing Muhammad, Muhammad Ali
> He floats like a butterfly and stings like a bee

Prince assumed his origin story was akin to Ali's, whom the song dubbed "Black Superman."

The why of how Prince came to need superpowers simply to survive is more closely related to the story of Bruce Banner, the fictional physicist who would be the Incredible Hulk. Those who have seen only the Hulk of film may be aware simply that he is a green rage-a-holic in ill-fitting clothes who has two sides—mad and madder—and let's just be happy he's fighting for the forces of good.

What's left out of the movie narrative but is in the comic book—how Bruce Banner came to his superpowers and became the Hulk—tells a more nuanced story, a tale that mirrors in some ways exactly the circumstances of how Prince Rogers Nelson got up off his arse and out of that telephone booth, with the powers of Prince.

Until he was a teenager Bruce Banner, like Prince, had universal, identifiable, actual human feelings. *More* than human feelings. Perhaps *too* many human feelings. It was then that Banner tried to rescue a boy from a mega-testing area for chemicals, where an explosion turned him into a rage-filled monster.

Well, that was certainly a worthy creation story. Of course, in the making of his own saga, Prince had to . . . *sweeten* a few details.

It was June 2018, and the truth of one particular story Prince had told me, thirty-three years before, was nagging at André Cymone. André didn't know Prince's phone booth saga, and if the tale wasn't true, I would no longer be able to believe anything I'd ever thought I'd known or figured out about Prince's "story," the narrative that made some sort of sense out of Prince's life.

The events in question were central to any understanding of Prince I'd had since the first day we really talked, back in 1985. After all, in my head it was his creation story, the traumatic happening that transformed him from the pubescent with an Afro as tall as the kid was short into a superhero.

From the beginning I told Prince that his tale about the phone booth across the street from McDonald's, on Minneapolis's Northside, was *his* creation story.

I told Prince, "It's your Rosebud!"

"What?" he asked. "Rosebud?"

"You know, *Citizen Kane*. Orson Welles. Rosebud."

"What?" he repeated.

"You know. Lost innocence. The end of the beginning. The end. *Rosebud*!"

"Relax," Prince had said. "Okay, 'Rosebud.' I'll find out." (Boy, did he find out, five years later!) Prince thought it flattering, when he'd come to learn all about *Citizen Kane*. I'm not sure when he saw it for the first time, but it became one of his favorite movies. By then he was a cinephile, as well as the much-mocked star of the film *Under the Cherry Moon* and director of the popular howler *Graffiti Bridge*. His favorite director? "Woody Allen—because he has final cut." (It was the 1990s.)

Either André or I brought up the phone booth tale—and its veracity—every single time the two of us talked over the next several months, from our first meeting at Minneapolis's Sebastian Joe's coffee shop, a few hundred yards up Franklin Avenue from Rudolph's barbecue joint. For decades Rudolph's had served as Prince's favorite local restaurant, or at least the preferred gathering spot for his troops, however large or intimate that night's battalion was.

I didn't want to try to convince André that the anecdote was factual. I hoped he could figure out the equation that would render the story more than plausible, more than likely, but *accurate*. *Emphatically* accurate. The story wasn't just a fact that I'd either gotten right or wrong, that Prince had either fibbed up or been straight about.

From *Rolling Stone*, 1985:

> *We used to go to that McDonald's there. . . . I didn't have any money, so I'd just stand outside there and smell stuff. Poverty makes people angry, brings out their worst side. I was very bitter when I was young. I was insecure, and I'd attack anybody. I couldn't keep a girlfriend for two weeks. We'd argue about anything.*

Cymone hadn't heard this story when it ran in *Rolling Stone* in 1985. And he wasn't surprised that he'd never heard it from Prince himself, because the tale began not long before the adolescent Prince moved not just into André's house, with his mother, Bernadette, and five siblings, but into André's *bedroom*. Soon transferring to the basement, Prince stayed for four years.

"I just don't know," André said upon hearing the story retold. "Something isn't right."

And then, on the phone with André at his home in Los Angeles, I mentioned for the first time that the McDonald's was not far from where my grandparents had lived, and I'd often visited. Oliver, right off Plymouth.

"Oh, the McDonald's that's *north*, on Plymouth. I thought you meant the McDonald's in South Minneapolis, where we all used to go. There wasn't any phone booth across the street from the McDonald's South."

"I tracked this one down," I said. "They tore the North Minneapolis McDonald's down in 1995."

"Oh," André said. "Well, that changes everything. I know what you're talking about. Never mind. I get it."

Thank you, God.

"Except a couple things Prince maybe . . . altered a bit."

Oh no.

"His father didn't kick him out," André said. "He got sick of living at his mother's house, I don't know why. She was so nice. I liked his stepfather, too, he gave Prince anything he wanted, let him play his piano as much as he wanted, unlike his own father. All that nasty stuff he said about his stepfather? He made that up. He *always* blamed the wrong people for everything."

"And . . . ?" I said warily.

"He wasn't broke; his father gave him a ten-dollar-a-week allowance, and his stepfather helped him out, too."

Later, I listened to a podcast featuring Susannah Melvoin, Prince's former fiancée. The interviewer asked Susannah about Prince constantly running away as a child, supposedly homeless and with nowhere to go. Susannah, whose stories have remained consistent through every interview she's ever given, laughed heartily.

"He could have gone anywhere. He had his pick of families that would have taken him in."

I believe that when Prince died, André Cymone clocked in as his last authentic friend, in all the traditional senses of the word "friend." André Cymone disagreed with that notion in person, when we finally met to see if either of us trusted the other long enough to keep talking, after months of wrangling, officiated over by his wife, Katherine, to check each other out.

Their friendship would fall apart as Prince's star rose and he made André less a comrade and tried and failed to make him more of an employee. André would have none of that. He wasn't built to be anybody's underling, let alone the guy with whom he'd always co-conspired about their paths through life. Prince had reconciled with his old buddy by the end. And by the very end, André tried to reach Prince, tried to not let him be left alone, to save his life. He hadn't been able to get through.

Before meeting Cymone, I expected he'd probably be the bitterest soul I'd meet as I revisited and investigated the whole Prince megillah. Perhaps the saddest sack of all would be John Nelson, Prince's father, who had more bile built up against his famous son, but that was his own damn fault. As a purportedly devout and God-fearing man, John Nelson was supposed to honor his children as much as they were commanded to honor him.

Yet of all the people who'd been seemingly betrayed and abandoned by Prince during his lifetime, no one, it seemed to me, had *earned* the right to be more eternally, infinitely bitter then André. John Nelson abused his son, and the son, I'd believed before I met André, passed on the legacy to the closest thing he had.

André met Prince when they were seven or eight years old, singing together in the local Seventh-day Adventist church. Soon separated from each other for several years by living in different neighborhoods, André and Prince intersected again at Minneapolis's Lincoln Junior High School, now barely teenagers, and immediately bonded over their mutual passion for music, and for their shared position of not giving a fuck what anybody else thought of them.

"By eighth grade we were both outsiders," André now recalls. "That was our bond."

When—as the story goes—Prince was left outside that phone booth without a dime in his pocket or roof above his head because of a stone-hearted father, André talked to his divorced mother, Bernadette Anderson, a community activist well known throughout the Northside, about the plight of his pal.

André asked his mother if Prince could move into the Anderson home and share his room. Bernadette said yes, though her household on Russell Avenue already held six of her children with her ex-husband, Fred. (It wasn't until Prince moved in and recognized a photograph of a jazz combo that included André's bass-player father that either of them realized that their fathers had once shared the bandstand as members of the Prince Rogers Trio.)

Once ensconced in the Andersons' home, Prince, disgusted by what he took to be André's slovenly ways, soon moved to the basement. For four years the two friends jammed on every instrument they could find and decided that music was their shared destiny.

Ye olde story—they vowed to each other that whoever made it first would take the other one along for the duration of the ride. During those formative years, Prince also, in effect, swiped most of André's onstage outrageous bad-boy shtick.

Painfully shy in front of strangers, Prince had always been an excellent student prodded to excel by his do-your-homework-hectoring mother, Mattie. The outspoken André, by contrast, had the neighborhood reputation, both real and affected, as the street tough who boosted cars for joyrides, stole with impunity, and settled beefs with his fists.

Prince, meanwhile, relied on his nimble, lacerating wit to chop down bullies, André remembers. His cause was aided and bravery made possible by the strength, size, and not-to-be-fucked-with protective instincts of Duane Nelson, thought to be Prince's half-brother. (In a game of domestic genetics too complicated to be worth explaining, they weren't.) And if Duane wasn't around, Prince's blinding speed made for an effective volley of wicked jibe, followed by a quick getaway.

André, who punched first, second, and third, saved his streetwise bon mots for *after* anyone showed disrespect and had been properly laid out supine, didn't teach Prince the art of the sucker punch. André punched straight on. From André, Prince learned the pimp swagger; the power of building your own mystique; and the necessity of never letting an opponent sense weakness.

"Okay, I admit it, I didn't fight fair," Prince told me. "But where I lived, there was no such thing as fair. You just go and do what had to be done. You couldn't hesitate, and I swear, I never got my ass kicked, let alone lost." Ronin Ro quoted Bernadette Anderson's assent: "[Prince would] hit and run," she recalled, "but he'd get even."

André and Prince played in the same bands, André favoring the bass. He appeared in see-through pants with The Revolution during Prince's infamous *American Bandstand* performance, where Prince responded to Dick Clark's questions with hand signals and facial contortions instead of words. The host famously never forgot the incident, considered at the time an ungodly faux pas. Clark recalled it time and again over the decades, turning a seeming debacle into a public relations coup.

As André had taught him, Prince knew how to strike in unique manners, when least expected. He also demanded that Cymone relinquish to him his watch-me-perform-in-my-underwear look—a guise a designer girlfriend had created for André by making several pairs of the see-through slacks.

Then, on Prince's fourth record, *Controversy*, the star neglected to give his friend credit for "Do Me, Baby," allowing Prince to keep the hauteur of the auteur who wrote every note and played every lick of every instrument on every song. As an introduction to Cymone, I'd emailed him an audio clip of Prince discussing the mid-1980s incident, in which Prince blamed his reputation as a believer in the ethos of all-for-me on a misunderstanding. In the clip Prince said it was all a mistake, "that that misunderstanding all came about because of a typo error, and my bass player, André, not getting a credit."

I realized too late it was a hurtful, idiotic clip to send. Prince had insulted his best friend, who'd literally sheltered him from his life's storm by referring to him as merely his "bass player," a hired gun, and not a best friend. And so, their friendship would rupture when Prince offered André a salary to tour with the Revolution like any other hired gun—and didn't ask, André thought, the way a friend needing a favor would.

Prince also patently lied, I think, about the credit on the album. A typo would have meant misspelling his friend's name on the album. Leaving his name off altogether seems more intentional.

In not too much time, André tired of being treated by his not-long-before adopted blood brother as just another member of the band, and left. Cymone forged a successful career of his own, and eventually forgave.

And today he doesn't seem bitter in the least. "I've got six kids and a wife I love," he said. His first child, a son, was with his ex-wife, singer Jody Watley, for whom he produced and wrote the number-one single, "Looking for a New Love." Accomplished, yes, but not to the heights of his friend. And yet, he says quite convincingly, "I'm satisfied with my career. I've released four of my own albums, won my own Grammy [for best new artist], had my own number-one hit ["Do Me, Baby," credited to Prince] on the rhythm-and-blues charts."

Now fifty-nine, sitting in a Minneapolis coffee shop, under a black beret and behind sunglasses, André still looks like the coolest cat in the room by a factor of 97. He also looked like the most satisfied and content person I'd seen in a long, long time.

He paused, stared into space, thought about his old friend's odyssey, smiled, and said:

> The thing about Prince and his ascension to fame is that it is actually a beautiful story. It really, really is. It was harsh at times. I know, I was right there. I know what he went through. But in the end, it was worth it. But he had the chance to show people who didn't believe in him that you can rise above your circumstances. That is a beautiful story.

And then André was quiet, and reached for his wife's hand. I think it pays to grow up in a happy household.

As a full-time employee of Honeywell, Nelson was paid a relatively munificent wage—that is, compared to the financial prospects available to most African American males in Minnesota in the late 1950s. And yet there was never enough money to adequately share with his multiple families.

Not with the crisp and dapper suits and ties John Nelson bought, making the real-life plastics molder look as if he was always two seconds away from taking the stage. Not with the payments on that 1966 Thunderbird convertible. Not with the dead presidents he was shelling out nights he was playing the Hennepin Avenue strip joints.

Even though her husband was now a nine-to-five Square John, Mattie continued to call him Prince. "She was mocking me," John Nelson later told me.

Prince's half sister Sharon, whom he didn't meet until he was in his teens, was one of the two members of the family who took a guess as to the what and why of her brother's favorite color: She said his actual preferred hue was orange. Tyka, his full sister, said he chose purple early on because the color was regal, downright—well, *princely.*

At the time he hardly seemed to care about the meaning of specific colors. Elsewhere he remained Skipper, though in some locales the teenager was known as Roger or Rogers.

Prince's story is festooned with often-stranger-than-truth true facts. The tall tales of Prince's childhood and adolescence are well known, told often, and quite frequently written about with great intellectual and/or funky insight.

Unfortunately, sifting the facts from the fabulist fictions written about young Prince is impossible, a quagmire of conflicting stories.

For example: Seventh-day Adventists? Well, I mean, it sounded like hokum to me, and I couldn't find any hard evidence.

Neither Prince nor his mother or father ever mentioned the Adventists, and on a sunny Sunday afternoon in 1985, Prince drove me by a Baptist church in North Minneapolis and said he used to go there growing up. There a photographer in a black tuxedo took pictures of a beaming bride and groom, as well as their platoon of all-decked-out attendants. There were so many in the wedding party, in fact, that several were photographed on the curb outside the church.

"Well, look at that," Prince said with a pleased and casual familiarity. "I wonder who's getting married?"

Besides an utter lack of proof that Prince had grown up a Seventh-day Adventist, I stumbled upon an LP of *Sign o' the Times*—hmm, sounds familiar, Prince-wise. The publication of the Seventh-day Adventists was *Sign of the Times*. On its front page, published the week he died, the glossy magazine mused about whether he could, indeed, have been one of them. If anybody had any information, could they contact the paper?

Just before I hung up with André Cymone, I asked him: "What about all this Seventh-day Adventist stuff?"

As the Australian musical polymath Nick Cave once said: "Who knows? My life could be quite interesting if you ask the right fucking questions." (Then again, with Prince, the trick had always been to shut up and let him pose and answer his own questions. You'd better have a sound retort; he did not easily suffer toadies, but rather made toadies profoundly suffer.)

"Oh, yeah," said André. "We both used to go when we were seven or eight. I don't remember Mattie going, though she might have. It was John, his father. He was religious. I don't know if any of us actually joined the church, but we were all looking to belong somewhere, you know?"

As for other religions Prince is credited with following, I also couldn't find in the Jehovah's Witnesses' own weekly update on the apocalypse anything resembling an ethos or custom that seemed to indicate that it was customary to hoist Prince's cremains up into Paisley Park's ionosphere for the touring masses, where, only two years before Prince died, the Chanhassen police, responding to a call, noted that Prince was the only person who had a key or free access to the building.

I was aghast. I'd been sick-joking in the couple of weeks after

Prince died, saying members of his family were as unendingly avaricious in their quest for Prince's *gelt* after he was gone as they'd been conditional in their love when he was alive—or at least before he became rich and famous. If they could, I said, they'd probably put his remains on tour: I bet they could sell out Madison Square Garden for eight shows by simply placing a coffee can filled with his ashes—he loved the scene in *The Big Lebowski* where Steve Buscemi suffered that fate—on a rumpus-room high-backed bar chair, and blast over the loudspeaker a used, scratched, 3-disc copy of Prince's *Best of* collection, purchased on clearance at the Electric Fetus record store in Minneapolis, his favorite.

8

BALLER

I might be small but so is dynamite.

—Prince, "Data Bank," 1990

It certainly will be interesting when Prince's blood kin—to whom I mean no disrespect—find the will Prince had buried somewhere on the grounds of Paisley Park. I wrote the document, a kind of last testament, that accompanied it. Also to be included, Prince informed me, was a copy of his unpronounceable latest record that came to be known as the "LoveSymbol" album. The album, along with the will and the document I wrote, would be buried together in what Prince called a "time capsule."

Why am I so sure? There are several reasons. But for people who knew him, perhaps the most convincing argument is that the check cleared. Indeed, he paid me five thousand dollars for a seven-page narrative that explained what he was doing; it was the only money I ever took from his chuck wagon. And what he actually paid for he intended to use.

Maybe I'm totally wrong.

But it's there.

Or maybe it's not.

But it's there. I'm sure of it.

But Prince's check cleared. They always cleared when he was do-nating to a charity, but five grand for seven pages? And I got paid immediately?

It's there.

The document I had written in my own voice was a kind of sum-mation of his life Prince. Not that he planned on dying anytime soon, though he did want the "story" I was to interview him for and write up—his declaration, among other things, of why the man who had been known as Prince was indeed dead, replaced by a human being thereaf-ter to be known as an unpronounceable glyph. The only other person who knew was his ex-bodyguard-turned-manager, Gilbert Davison.

The document was also a critique of what the unpronounceable glyph thought of what he saw as the general wreckage of the music business of the 1990s, the horrors in specific of a hip-hop movement where a superstar needn't know how to play a single instrument or sing a single note on key, how he was the most talented man in the industry and deserved to be paid as such, and the desperate straits of the black man in twentieth-century America.

His mother, Mattie, remembers Prince banging out rhythms on the rocks in her garden when he was around a year old. I will leave it to future retro- or neocultural critics to make something of the fact that at the exact moment the infant Prince was drumming melodies in his mother's Minneapolis garden, Bobby Zimmerman was a freshman at the University of Minnesota.

Zimmerman's home was 915 University Ave SE, a ten-minute drive from Prince's childhood home at 539 Newton Avenue S. Dylan was living at the Jewish Sigma Alpha Mu fraternity (now occupied by Alpha Chi Omega), and when he refused to stop his atonal bang-ing on the frat's parlor piano at midnight, he was summarily given the boot. He landed on his feet as Bob Dylan, bound for New York and Woody Guthrie.

Dylan had to leave Minneapolis, go to a scene, and make it there. Prince had to make his own scene, in the middle of nowhere, where no one had ever before made one. He tried to leave a few times, predicting he'd be gone as soon as he could, when he gave his first interview ever, to the Central High School paper in 1976.

As soon as graduated high school, he moved to New York to try to get a record contract. No luck. A couple of times in his career, he tried to move to mansions he bought or rented in Los Angeles, Toronto, and Spain, but it never took. He even tried Las Vegas.

Prince always came back to Minneapolis, the scene of the crime.

My grandparents, peasant immigrants who never learned English, seemed to me to be the last two white people on Minneapolis's Northside. They lived in a pleasantly peasant-size, spackled gingerbread house on Oliver Avenue North.

My grandmother had refused to be swept up in the white flight that followed the city's seven riots in 1966 that chased from the neighborhood—once a mixed working-class community of African Americans, Jews, and Slavs—almost all its ivory-hued inhabitants to the suburbs.

"I walked across Russia to get here," my father translated my grandmother's declaration about her travels a half century before. "And I'm not moving. We stop here."

My grandfather, a retired truck driver, sighed, and grew tomatoes and cucumbers for pickling, and brewed his savage Shabbos wine, which earned him the moniker "the Wine Jew" as he distributed it freely in Mason jars to his neighbors. That designation guaranteed my grandmother and him, both octogenarian foreigners, safety and popularity in the neighborhood.

Years later, Prince shared that our first encounter took place when I was twelve.

We met one door down from my grandparents', in front of a Dairy Queen ice cream shack at the corner of Oliver and Plymouth avenues. I remember the day, Prince later recalled to me, exactly: It was the weekend my grandmother booted me out of the house for taking bites out of her wax fruit—I believe an orange and a banana, which tasted like candle—and leaving teeth marks in it.

I was only following the orders of my idolized brother, six years older, who suggested my grandmother would think it funny if I took bites out of her wax fruit. She didn't, and before you could spit out a *"Feh!"* I was being led out the door and sent a few yards down the block.

A dozen African American kids were hanging out at the Dairy Queen, and I wasn't sure if the immunity granted my grandparents would also be given me. It was; what wasn't was any attention, and I melted into the crowd to watch a pickup basketball game starring kids several grades older and at least a foot taller than I was. At one point an extra ball rolled my way, and I reflexively began spinning it on my right index finger.

I was no baller. But the only two things at which I've ever felt truly competent were (1) working the French-fry station at the Uptown McDonald's the summer I turned sixteen, and (2) spinning basketballs and performing dribbling tricks I learned through careful study and practice of the Harlem Globetrotters, the comic basketball team I saw every year at the Metropolitan Sports Center. When I was ten I sent away for the .45 of the Globetrotters' theme song—Brother Bones's 1939 version of "Sweet Georgia Brown"—to which I'd seen Meadowlark Lemon, Curly Neal, and the rest of the team work their magic with brain-boggling tricks of ball spinning, handling, and shooting.

All I remember of my early years in junior high school is the incessant repetition of these tricks, practiced in front of the mirror until I'd mastered the art of keeping a basketball spinning on one finger; then moving the rotating orb across eight fingers; and then, if a backboard was handy, I could—three out of four times—bounce the ball off my head and through the hoop.

Prince remembered the wax-fruit/spinning-ball incident. "That's the kind of thing that Prince would have taken note of," said André Cymone years later, with a laugh.

I don't remember Prince.

A few years after he and I met as adults, as we drove through the streets of the Northside, I recalled that day at the Dairy Queen, wondering aloud where I found the chutzpah to draw attention to myself, alone in a crowd that sunny afternoon, more than a decade before. I recalled to him how, weekend after weekend—each time we visited my grandparents—I'd repeat the performance.

"I know," Prince said when I finished. "I was there."

I distinctly remember thinking at the time that he was bullshitting me. I figured he'd merely had to spit back the facts I'd just told him. I was further convinced he was lying when he had to add a little more to the story, make it better, even flatter me. When Prince wanted to flatter, he would flatter.

"We called you Casper," he said, as in the Friendly Ghost, as in "white boy."

Casper. I love that. I only hope it was true. Ever since he told me, I've tried to make childhood memories where Prince is in the background with his monster Afro. (I had one, too—an Isro, aka a Jewfro.) Here he is admiring my ball-handling tricks. There we're talking wrestling, Mad Dog Vachon and the Crusher. Here I am doing the evil Dr. X's figure-four leg lock. Now, a generation later, I can see it.

The first time we took a ride through Minneapolis together, touring the streets where he'd run as a kid, Prince was starting to explain the difference between the Southside of Minneapolis and the North. I interrupted him. I have it on tape.

"Oh, I know," I said. "My grandparents lived down there." I pointed toward Oliver Avenue N. "And there," I said, pointing at Wirth Park, "is where I used to go sledding."

"Me too," he said, disbelieving, and I believed him when he said he didn't know I was from Minneapolis. He added, "Our sleds probably ran into each other."

"You still owe me a Flexible Flyer," I replied. Then, in passing, I told him about my great-uncle Augie, former owner of an eponymous sleazy strip bar on Hennepin Avenue. I didn't yet know that Augie's was one of the places where Prince's own father, John, had performed years before, under the stage name of Prince Rogers Nelson. Prince, though, didn't say a thing.

And then came the moment I knew was *it*.

It. The moment when I *had* Prince. Every reporter knows that feeling, when they are trusted by an important source and the agenda isn't necessarily all "the story." It is a moment I always warn friends about when they're getting interviewed.

As we drove past Wirth Park, I mentioned its grisly history as the dumping ground for the corpses of those who crossed the once powerful Minnesota mob. The Minneapolis police hated working Wirth Park body drops, I said, because they were usually professional hits, and oftentimes the guy who got killed was worse than the killer. Minneapolis cops, in the old days, would sometimes drag a corpse several hundred yards, across the city limits, into Golden Valley, a first-ring suburb. Let *them* deal with the paperwork!

Prince looked over at me from behind the wheel of his 1966 Thunderbird. He was smiling. It was the smile of gotcha. The smile of *it*.

Prince was funny, he was fast, and the girls liked him as far back as junior high school. It was then that Prince began alchemizing his personal philosophy of "sick." It had nothing to do with illness, nor necessarily bad taste. Rather, it was an existential outlook that if someone else had done something, it needn't be done again in any recognizable form—and that if no one had done something before, it was worth a close look to find out why, and maybe try it.

By junior high Prince was already, seemingly, on his way to becoming a brother from another planet. And doing what hadn't been done before—and not looking like a shmendrick or simply trying to be weird for "sickness'" sake were prime in his mind: "In junior high I saw the need to be noticed," he said. "That while I couldn't erase all the loneliness at home, I could act out whatever part I wanted during the day and nobody knew if I was performing, being me, or just being sick."

The just-released "Raspberry Beret" video was where he first showed me his concept of sick. Kneeling in front of his VCR, he cued up the tape. The pretty-as-peonies song begins with Prince clearing his throat in a prolonged guttural rasp of the kind I emit when forced to eat mayonnaise. And why?

"That's it, that's what I'm talking about," he said, "I just did it to be sick, to do something no one else would do." He pauses and contemplates. "A lot of my peers make remarks about us doing silly things onstage and on records. They don't understand the simple idea of sick."

Please explain. "What kind of silliness, exactly?"

"Everything," Prince said:

"The music, the dances, the lyrics. What they fail to realize is that is exactly what we want to do. It's not silliness, it's sickness. Sickness is just slang for doing things somebody else wouldn't do. If we are down on the floor doing a step, that's something somebody else wouldn't do. That's what I'm looking for all the time. We don't look for whether something's cool or not, that's not what time it is. It's not just wanting to be out. It's just if I do something that I think belongs to someone else or sounds like someone else, I *do* something else."

In junior high he could still publicly display his talents at basketball. He was remarkably good, almost unbelievably good, given his diminutive size, but good no matter what. He was the sixth man on Bryant's ninth-grade team, and he expected to make varsity his first year in high school, even though he'd be attending Minneapolis Central High School, one of the top teams in the state every season.

Soon he found another man to hate as much as his father. His name was Al Nuness, a member of the University of Minnesota Athletic Hall of Fame for his exploits as an All–Big Ten guard—and Central's varsity basketball coach when Prince was there. Nuness had his own ideas about the plausibility of a five-foot-two-inch sophomore, no matter how talented, ever playing for one of the best high school teams in Minnesota.

And while Prince may have hated his father only every other day, and sometimes not for years at a stretch, he would come to hate Al Nuness every second for all the years of his life. "I hate him," he told me, "even when I'm not thinking about him."

———

"Hack!" Prince yelled in exasperated rage as I intentionally slapped his wrist, connected to the hand that was dribbling the basketball right past me toward the hoop at the Paisley Park basketball court. When not in use, the court was sometimes used to rehearse dancers.

"No hack," I said, breathing heavily. "I was being sick. I was doing what I wasn't supposed to be doing, namely hacking you."

"That's not sick, that's silliness," Prince said disgustedly. "Sick is doing what's never been done, and making it work. Not cheating."

"You're just mad 'cuz you can't call me on it," I said.

Indeed, he couldn't call foul in our game of one-on-one, or he'd have to call foul virtually every time he took the ball. In the ethos of the playground, that would mark him as a crybaby weenie, no matter how blatant my on-court felonies. I didn't play dirty by choice, but as a strategy of survival I'd developed in ninth-grade basketball, when I'd stopped growing (I'm five foot eight) and was barely third string on my junior high basketball team.

"Hack!" he yelled again, this time calling out not just my foul, but me, personally, as a noun, a hack, at least as a basketball player, possibly as a writer, and definitely as a human being as well. He was pissed like I'd rarely seen him—except, that is, every time we played basketball.

He took my continuous, relatively effective, no-other-recourse style of cheating personally—he'd beaten hundreds of people who were thousands of times more talented than me, and at least a foot taller.

"You want to play like a basketball player," he asked—saying "basketball player" with the reverence of a reverend saying "God"— "or like a no-account hack?" He enunciated that final word in a manner that somehow came out sounding like "Satan."

It became shtick for him to play ball in platform shoes with journalists, who spread the tale that that's the only way he played. In an interview with *GQ*, I mentioned that he always wore basketball shoes with me. I wasn't saying the others were lying, just that I never saw the myth turn into truth. Sure enough, within weeks, I'd collected three or four pictures off the internet of the adult Prince shooting the ball in basketball shoes.

And he was so good—really, I can't emphasize how good he was, with no qualifiers—that we can only thank bad karma and small-minded coaching for derailing his court ambitions. He was good enough, he was smart enough, and doggone it, he had talent.

As Richard Robinson, Prince's ninth-grade basketball coach at Bryant Junior High recalled, he was not only a gifted playmaking guard, but the guy to get the ball to for a last-second shot at the game-ending buzzer. He was the proverbial player, in all senses of the word, who not just wanted, but needed, the ball when it was hero-or-goat time.

"When we needed to kill something, we'd give the ball to Prince," Robinson said. "He could dribble like crazy. He's a real good athlete—he was quick."

And, off the court and on, Robinson said, "He was really smart. He didn't have to study too hard to do junior high work; he'd do it once and he had it."

Indeed, Mattie saved his report cards, and showed them to me in 1997. Half or two-thirds As, half or one-third Bs, that's as close as I can remember. I wasn't taking notes that morning, I was eating a bowl of Raisin Bran Mattie had fixed me while Prince asked if the workmen who had been called to her place to fix the gutters had shown up.

Jimmy "Jam" Harris, Prince's longtime friend, later to gain fame as Jimmy Jam, remembers his old pal's court skills vividly. (Jam, producer with his partner, Terry Lewis, of Janet Jackson's biggest hits and many others, is less enthused to talk about when asked why Prince fired both him and Lewis in 1980 from The Time, a talented, albeit prefabricated Monkees-of-funk side project for Prince, fronted by his old chum Morris Day. Jam and Lewis were fired after a freak snowstorm left the neonatal producing pair stranded in Atlanta, where they'd been producing the SOS. Band. They missed a show for The Time, and as a result, soon were "Time"-less.)

"Prince was short," Jam/Harris said, "but he had confidence

because he was a heck of a basketball player—a point guard who could distribute, had great handles, and could shoot the lights out. Steph Curry reminds me of the way Prince played, literally. He'd run up the court and girls would scream, 'Ahhh! Prince!' It was crazy. Where we lived," Jam continued, "if you could play, people respected you."

My basketball skills were infinitely worse. I'd peaked in sixth grade in both on-court talent and poise, and who knows what else. I grew at the rate of a bonsai tree. By ninth grade my only real duty on the junior high team was to scrimmage the first team starters in preparation for their play in the next game. Besides being oodles more talented than I, the first team was also made up exclusively, it seemed, of pretty-boy show-offs, albeit pretty-boy show-offs who could drive by and shoot over me with a skill and precision that brought instant and constant humiliation.

The only way to slow them down was to hack. To cheat. Perchance to foul, hitting the pretty boys' wrists just as they arched a shot; to step on their feet to impede their progress as they dribbled by; to hold the back of their shorts when they were calling for the ball to begin another ritual of shaming me.

"Hack!" the pretty boys would yell in protest, but I had no alternative. Girls, cheerleaders, were watching. When I wasn't hacking, I was on the bench, even during practice. I backed up my ever-diminishing skills with a terrible attitude, a combination coaches at all levels love.

So I practiced and practiced on the sidelines: spinning basketballs on my fingers, bouncing, spinning balls off my head and into the basket at the other end of the gym from where the real team was practicing half-court drills, and learning how to dribble the ball a half inch from the floor and between my legs.

Coach Winter wouldn't have cared if I'd been practicing the cello, let alone basketball tricks. At the end of the season, my career in organized basketball was as justifiably ended as Prince's had been unfairly brought to a close the year before. And the only reason Prince continued to play against me, in spite of the fact that he was so much better?

Those tricks. He could spin the ball on his finger—but I did it better. He liked to watch me move a spinning ball up and down all the fingers on both hands, and to roll a ball ad infinitum around my chest and arms, joined in an O.

"You suck, but that's cool," he said.

After he died, on my Facebook page's "Featured Photos," I put a picture of him spinning a basketball, looking intense, right next to a picture of me, also spinning. I was about thirty when the picture was taken. I was wearing shades and a look of terminal blasé. I took the pictures down after a week, even though, side by side, they were the only time in our shared history where I looked like I was even in the same solar system of cool. I am what I am, but I knew I was never that.

Come sophomore year of high school, Prince got fucked over by the game itself—a game that does not treat five-foot-two-inch guards with respect, no matter their talents—and by Coach Al Nuness.

If he'd gotten not a break but his due at basketball, Prince might have been spared some lifelong social dysfunction. Perhaps he wouldn't have needed to choose, develop, or automatically default to indulging his mythic monomania for music in order to achieve popular acceptance and critical hosannas.

Unpossessed by the demons and/or angels who urged him ever forward in music, toward wherever his intuition led, his place would seemingly still have been secure in any roomful of contemporary famous songsters. True, his not utterly developed music skills if he'd been able to keep playing ball might have limited his time on the top as a rock star to a few years instead of his entire adult lifetime. But in his time, whatever chair he sat on would be a metaphoric throne; and wherever he sat would be considered the head of the table.

His skills with instruments and song came so easily, and so seemingly fully formed, that maybe his almost pathological hyperdose of single-minded perfectionism wouldn't have been necessary if he'd been also able to focus on basketball. Using the professional wrestling term he used for making it big in the music business, he would have "gotten over" anyway. Like Wayne Gretzky at hockey, William

Shakespeare at drama, Superman at superheroing, or Albert Einstein at physics, he wasn't just preternaturally gifted at music. He was better than his chosen field itself.

So perhaps thank Yahweh, or the genetic shuffle, that brought him to a peak height of five foot two, with a motherfucker, in his eyes, as the varsity basketball coach at Minneapolis's Central High.

Albert Einstein once said, "If I were not a physicist, I would probably be a musician. I often think in music. I live my daydreams in music. I see my life in terms of music." If things had worked out a tad differently vis-à-vis Einstein's vocational choices, would the world have gotten either a musical genius or the theory of relativity?

In pinball game terms, Prince would still, I'm quite sure, have succeeded in turning over the machine he was playing, beating the game at its own game. Indeed, if he'd been distracted by two different passions, he might have not scared so many people.

He could possibly have been even more than just liked by his peers and fellow humans. By watering down both his skill at leading people to follow his will and his talents at making folks both laugh and think, he might have, in *Death of a Salesman* Willy Loman terms, been downright well-liked.

Who knows, he might have gone beyond even idolized, worshipped, and deified. He might have been able to indulge in the simple pleasures of being a human being, instead of choosing virtual solitary confinement in a prison where he chose to be not only the prisoner but his own guard and warden as well.

And his Howard Hughes–like behavior, he said throughout the last several years of his life, when he had ostensibly "opened up" to the world, wasn't a result of his going Howard Hughes–style cuckoo. He was doing the world a favor by walling himself off from humanity, he said, because no matter whom he was with, he said not far from the end, "I make them feel small."

True, historical judgments would probably have stopped short of the comparisons to Mozart that were commonly made throughout Prince's life, and postmortem. Yet, say Prince had just paid proper attention to the natural genius he'd been granted and watered it with just enough practice and standard doses of professional ambition, motivation, and self-discipline to not self-destruct. I still believe that would probably have placed him in the ranks of widely admired musicians and funksters and/or pop stars like Eric Clapton on guitar, James Brown at funk—whatever and whomever at whichever instrument or three (not thirty) he picked.

True, playing basketball remained important to him. David "DVS" Schwartz, a songwriter/rapper/visual artist who worked with Prince in 2000 and toured as a member of the Funky Bald Heads on Prince's 2001 USA Hit n Run Tour, said:

"We would be at Paisley recording songs. I'd be watching them rehearse, or we'd be rehearsing for the tour. He had a basketball court right in the middle of Paisley next to the studio. I didn't really know he played. He just came through one day and just started picking up games. We must have played over a hundred games during that year or two out there. It was fun. He was good.

"We'd go out there knowing we were probably gonna play. If we were gonna record, basketball was always implied. We always had extra gym clothes in the car. We would take a break after a few hours of recording and rehearsing and play for like an hour, then go back to work.

"He was a trash-talker. He would try to make you miss every time he would shoot. Obviously he wasn't tall enough to swat you, so he would say weird things, make a weird noise, or he would run around you in a circle—anything he could to distract you. It worked for a while; then I got used to it and ignored it."

By fifteen Prince had stopped living with his parents, forever; had formed his first band, Grand Central; formed his second band, Champagne; learned virtually every instrument in existence; was loved by girls; was already affecting signs that for better *and* worse, he lived in another dimension than his peer group. And most brutally—and mournfully—Prince had already played by tenth grade his last organized league game of basketball.

Going quietly might have been the correct career move for Prince. Still, surrendering basketball left a wide and deep scar that remained fresh for the rest of his life.

He could play, everybody knew that, and still Nuness wouldn't let the five-foot-two-inch point guard try out. Prince bore the snub as an existential wound. It was as if he were told he couldn't play the guitar because his hands were too small, or if he lost access to all pianos because his arms weren't long enough.

Simply say the name "Al Nuness," and Prince would shoot you the stare that looked like it could stop a sundial.

"Fuck Al Nuness," Prince would say for the rest of his life. Perhaps he was projecting the rage he felt toward the abusive John Nelson onto another would-be father figure. While Nelson refused to let him play his piano, the great Al Nuness wouldn't let him play his game. For the rest of his life Prince used him as one of his primary substitute Great Satans.

"Nuness played himself by not playing me, ya feel me?" Prince asked. "We would have won state all three years if I had been running that offense. Al Nuness owes that school some trophies, and me a lot of playing time."

9

HIGH SCHOOL

Prince was fourteen when he, along with sundry surrounding personalities, formed a band of many monikers. They played under the name Soul Explosion, then Phoenix, then Grand Central, and then finally Grand Central Corporation. André's mother, Bernadette, a pillar of the community, began booking the group at the local community center.

The principals included Prince playing guitar, André on bass, André's sister Linda on keyboards, and Prince's cousin Chazz Smith on drums. André's pal Morris Day soon took over for Cousin Chazz, who was unceremoniously disinvited from the band. Everyone blamed Prince for the betrayal; Prince blamed André. LaVonne Daugherty, Morris Day's mother, enthusiastically took over managing the band, and Prince got his first taste of playing in a recording studio at age seventeen, via a band, East 94, that included a fellow named Pepe Willie, one of Prince's cousins' beaus.

The first paragraph in the profile that ran in the Minneapolis Central High School student newspaper was cogent and clear. It was also 100 percent true, unlike many of the stories labored over by battalions of reporters, including me, yet to come.

Student reporter Lisa Crawford's article began with a straight-forward quote from the subject himself: "'I play with Grand Central Corporation, I've been playing with them for two years,' Prince Nelson, senior at Central, said. Prince started playing piano at age seven"—when his family broke up—"and guitar when he got out of the eighth grade."

The headline above the first article ever written about Prince is hauntingly prescient. The title of the story was "Nelson Finds It 'Hard to Become Known.'"

Within a couple of years, he had a recording contract with Warner Bros. Records. That pact was hyped as the richest for a new artist in music business history.

There were no hints in that first article on his later, often unrequited love affair with his hometown. "I think it is very hard for a band to make it in this state," the story quotes Prince, "even if they're good. Mainly because there aren't any big record companies or studios in this state. I really [think] that if we would have lived in Los Angeles or New York or some other big city, we would have gotten over by now."

In the picture accompanying the piece, Prince seems to be exhaling an impatient are-we-almost-out-of-here "*Harrumph*." "Threaded up," as his hero, New York Knicks guard Walt Frazier, would put it, Prince is wearing a wide-collared, button-up shirt, a frown, and an Afro "as big as the Ritz," to borrow from F. Scott Fitzgerald.

The ants-in-his pants look is genuine: The caption reads: "Prince Nelson takes time out to get his picture taken before he starts his daily practicing on the piano."

The story did not, however, reverberate with the sense of entitlement of someone who was already a legend in his own mind. Indeed, he veered within sentences from sounding like a bebop hepcat who couldn't be bothered with learning notes, to a goody-goody lecturing wannabes to practice their notes:

"Prince plays by ear. 'I think I've had about two lessons, but they didn't help. I think you'll always be able to do what your ear tells you, so just think how great you'd be with lessons also.'"

And then comes the Boy Scout: "One should learn all their scales, too. That's very important."

He had a backup plan even then, though it's merely hinted at in the last paragraph. "Eventually I would like to go to college and start lessons when I'm much older," he told Crawford, stating that if he couldn't "get over" as a musician, he'd go to the University of Minnesota and get a degree certifying him to be a high school music teacher.

He gave kudos to his own high school music teacher for two years, Katherine Doepke. Now ninety-seven, she taught in the Minneapolis school system for twenty years, and was at Minneapolis Central for Prince's entire time in high school. She taught him voice and piano his sophomore and junior years; the only course of hers he didn't take was Choir because, she remembers him telling her, "I'd had enough choir going to church growing up."

Doepke's memory is sharp, and she says she remembers a few main things about young Prince Nelson to this day: "He never smiled, and he almost never talked. I couldn't teach him a thing. I just wish I could have made him laugh or giggle or just even smile. He didn't seem troubled—he just wouldn't smile."

Mrs. Doepke was shocked when I told her he'd gotten cut from the basketball team the first year he was her student. "He played basketball?" she said. "But he was so little! Do you think that's why he was so quiet? He never said a word about basketball."

The first day of Voice class, the dozen students taking the course went around the room and announced what their musical interests were. Prince, remembers Mrs. Doepke, said: "'I want to become a rock-and-roll star.' I remember that most vividly of all—how matter-of-factly he said that, like he was saying he wanted to be a lawyer or teacher." She was on the verge of a retort along the lines of "Well, I don't teach rock and roll." And then, she remembered: "I looked at this young kid, so little, and thought, 'Good for you. You should work for it.' And I didn't say a word except 'That's fine.'"

She recalled that "I couldn't do a thing with him. He was so good; he knew how to play amazingly well. He'd have one hand playing a synthesizer and another hand playing the piano. He was just so above all the rest of them."

He was the only student she ever had who asked to study music theory. She was relieved "because I didn't know what else to do with him."

She found a music theory workbook for him. The book was basic: It was about the different values of notes and scales, giving examples of a whole note, a quarter note, an eighth, chords, and intervals. "It was all fill in the blanks," she remembers, "and I gave it to him and he did it in about fifteen minutes, handed it back to me, and said 'Thanks.'"

And finally, Mrs. Doepke recalled, he smiled.

He knew all the material already, she realized. Prince just didn't know the names of the notes. He'd simply picked it all up himself.

I handed her the clip from the school newspaper, the first profile of Prince, and she was tickled at the shout-out she'd received in the 1976 article—as well as by Prince's admonishment in the story to other aspiring musicians. "My, my," she said. "You don't see many high school piano students telling others the importance of doing their scales—especially a high school piano student who tells a class full of strangers on the first day of class he wants to be a rock-and-roll star!"

Katherine Doepke's second-fondest memory of Prince came years after he graduated. She was running one of the competitions at a national choir convention, and wrote to Prince at Paisley Park to see if he might have a memento he would be willing to donate as a prize to the winner. "I guess he remembered me," she said, "and a few days later, I got a huge poster back that was autographed 'Love God, Prince.' I thought that was so special. He was a nice kid, a good kid. I just hope he learned how to laugh."

However, her *fondest* memory came after he asked her if he could take home a synthesizer. That was against school rules, but she figured she could take the synthesizer to his house, and bring it back to school that night. She did, stayed until nine-thirty, and Prince rewarded her by letting his teacher play the maracas and tambourine with his band. At ninety-seven, she positively *gleamed* when she announced: "I can say I played with Prince!"

She paused, making note of what had become apparent to so many who'd had so much less experience with him than she had in two years. "It's funny," she said, "how that can become your identity—'I did this or I did that with Prince.'"

After he died, and reporters came looking for "Prince's high school music teacher," she recalls, "I didn't say a word, and the reporters never found out." Instead of announcing herself, Mrs. Doepke kept as her greatest notoriety and joy going down to the lobby of the senior resident center where she lives, and playing and singing to the other residents. She said with a laugh: "It's a blessing I can play by ear, because I can't see the music anymore!"

And that's who she was at the center, she said. "People knew me for me. I was Katherine, the lady who plays piano and sings every day." And even though no reporters ever found her out, word slowly leaked at the center about her past. "And suddenly," she exclaimed, "I was no longer 'Katherine, the woman who can play 1940s standards by ear—I was Katherine, the woman who was Prince's music teacher!' That quickly became my identity, even just amongst all us old-timers, even though when you get down to it I only knew him a little bit, a long time ago."

André Cymone knows the phenomenon of people who only knew Prince a little bit, a long time ago grandiosely inflating what they knew well. "As soon as he was gone," Cymone says, "people realized they had a new lease on how they could present the relationship they had with Prince."

But let André talk for himself:

> Now, they could rewrite history. For example, he has this cousin who used to almost brag about how he hadn't talked to Prince for so long. I don't know if he'd always bring it up so you'd feel sorry for his cousin, or feel that Prince should be ashamed of himself for not

being closer. But he used to always say things like, "Man, I haven't even talked to him since 1986." But if you asked him since Prince passed about their relationship, he'll say: "Yeah, we were so close, man, I talked to Prince all the time."

I'm always kind of distant. I didn't make friends easily, I still don't, and I definitely don't trust people. And for some reason—he was asking for a piece of paper or something, and I gave it to him. Yet with us it was an instant bond, an instant kind of trust. We were so close we'd be finishing each other's sentences. My mom would tease us about being so close.

There's no question that a lot had to do with music. You'd see that closeness when we were playing together. We'd call it Funk Face, where we'd just be staring at each other. It was the seriousness with which we took it all. We'd always look at each other like we knew each other from somewhere else, like we were related.

I really don't know what was behind that bond. I can only assume it was because he was kind of an outsider, and I was kind of an outsider. And that might have been it. You recognize that someone is like you.

And then there's the closeness of coming of age together. You know each other's first guitar, first bass, first girlfriends, you're in your first band together, you go on your first tour alongside each other, his first album is your first album. You're together for the first of everything, first guitar, first bass.

And you know, I get really sad because this is somebody I really, really, knew and was really close to. And then, obviously, through the years, things happen, things change, and people do what they do. And you realize that only a handful of people really know you.

I just try to be honest. I remember. I have a very good memory. I know what exactly happened and what didn't happen. I know who's making up stories and who's telling the truth. I know who to talk to and who not to talk to. Sometimes I wonder if I know a little too much.

And I understand, people want to exploit things—and I try not to get in anyone's way, because it's really not my place to rain on anybody's [parade]. But I do feel a responsibility to telling the truth

about what was, because I know he would do the same. I feel a responsibility for his sake, for his fans' sake, for people who really
deserve to know what kind of person he really was. I could just let it
go, but the reality is, he and I were so close, around each other all the
time for ten years. I literally had to move in with a girlfriend, just to
get away from him for a while, because it was a bit too much.

It makes me feel really bad [what happened at the very end],
because I think he was really trying, in his own way, to reconnect.
Through the years he had reached the height of popularity, stardom,
and all the things that come with it. And some of those things aren't
positive, and you don't know who you can trust. [And in the end] I
think he realized that we were both the same people that met way
back when. We were absolutely the same guys. Felt that whenever we
got together, it was like we were never apart.

When I was in town, Prince would call and say, "You gotta come
out to Paisley Park." And then when I would see him, he would say,
"You gotta stay a long time." And I'd say, "Dude, I've got to get up in
two hours and take my kids to school."

My life had become so completely different, and he was so disap-
pointed. We used to talk about how one day when we get rich, we're
going to come and we're going to do things for the community.

The last time Prince reached out to me wasn't by text, it was
through Bobby Z [Rivkin, drummer in the Revolution.] I had heard
about what had happened [in Moline], and I just didn't feel right. I
felt like, Okay, something isn't right, so let me see if I can get ahold
of him. I'm going to tell him I'm homeless and I need some place to
live. I had been talking to [my wife] Katherine, and we were talking
about some conversations Prince and I had recently had, and how it
seemed he was trying to tell me something.

But I always thought of Prince as being extremely healthy. He
never did drugs, and he never really drank. From way back he would
always make me feel bad about smoking weed or drinking wine. I
used to get into all kinds of crazy stuff, and if it weren't for him, I'd
probably have spent a whole lot of time in jail. So, I always thought
of Prince as being at the top of his game. So when he'd say stuff the
last couple of months of his life about having health issues, I never

thought of it in terms of anything serious. Almost every other time we ran into each other he'd mention that he wasn't feeling great.

The next time I saw him I'd say, "You good now?" And Prince would say, "I'm better now!"

So when he was telling me things, it just wasn't registering. I was thinking he had a cold or something. But when I heard about [Moline], it all came together. So I thought, I need to reach out and find out what was it that he had been trying to tell me all this time. I tried to get ahold of all different people, and no one was getting back to me.

I finally got ahold of Bobby Z and asked him, "You usually talk to Prince, what is going on?" And Bobby says he said he talked to Questlove, who said Prince was okay. But Bobby hadn't talked to him. Then I talked to [Prince's sister] Tyka, and asked her to let me know what was going on. Then I got a text from Prince that basically said, "Ya, I'm OK. It's crazy. We'll get together when I come to California."

And that was it, that was the last time I heard from him. I knew something wasn't right. I totally didn't think he was going to die. It never crossed my mind. But it sounded like he needed somebody with him. I started putting it all together, all the times we had hooked up. I thought I should have made myself available, and I told Katherine, if I hook up with Prince, you may not see me for a while. When you jump into Prince's world, it's a constant.

When he passed, I felt extremely sad. I just walked around my neighborhood. All these different conversations in my head, all the cryptic messages he [was] trying to pass along.

But I realized it's not like when we were kids anymore. For someone in his position, I had to step back and let that go, and let that part of his personality go.

There was so much that was left unsaid between [us]. Some of the most important times of my life, and I assume his, we needed to address and talk about. We left so many things unsaid about when I left and how I left. We always assumed it would happen.

We were starting to see [each other] more and more, and every time we'd see each other we'd hang out a little longer. It was less and less forced, and more natural. We'd always say we gotta get together. Even the last time, I was kind of clowning around with him like I normally would, teasing him about stuff.

When Prince and I were growing up, we were both very, very competitive. It's interesting because Prince and I had done a documentary in 2003. We had interviewed different people in the band—Morris, William, Terry.

All their stories made it sound like Prince did everything, like he put the band together, he picked the music, he put them in the band, and all that. And that is something that always bugged me. I mean, Prince was a shy dude. I'm not a shy person. I'm the person who goes out and says, "Hey, listen, it should be this way . . . you need to be right here."

So there is this part [about Prince's legacy] that would kind of get under my skin. Like, what I said earlier, when people weren't there, when things happen, and people hear it a certain way, they assume it happened a certain way. And when it comes to Prince, well, it just ain't always so, what people hear, or said they saw, or actually saw.

Cindy Stoewer was a student Prince's age at Edison High School, where his mother was a counselor and social worker. Stoewer also worked in the school office an hour a day, and got to know Mattie Shaw's occasionally visiting son, whom she knew as "Roger Nelson":

I just knew him as Mattie Baker's son, Roger. Not Prince. Mattie was proud of him, I felt that. It very much felt like, "This is my son." I felt like he was her gem. It wasn't just, "My son had to tag along over here today, or my son this, or my son that." She always seemed pretty dang [sic] proud of him.

But I was just this little confined Northeast Minneapolis girl, back in the day, in a very white community. And so, I thought it was pretty cool, talking to someone of another race. I respected him a lot because he was Mattie Baker's son, and I really liked Mattie. He had a giant Afro. So not only had I not been around a person of the black race, but I had never really seen an Afro close up. And I remember staring at it while I was talking to him. He probably wondered what I could possibly have been staring at.

He told me he was a musician. He told me he played the guitar. He told me he was a singer. He talked about it a lot.

I thought he was really nice. He was just so shy and quiet. And you'd meet him, and you'd talk, and you'd have a nice time.

He seemed very sure of himself, not cocky sure, not conceited sure. He just seemed very confident in this big record deal happening. He seemed very confident and the fact that he was going to L.A. and something was going to happen. Even though I thought it was bullcrap, I didn't think he seemed like a sucker. I don't remember thinking someone was pulling the wool over his eyes.

The last time I remember talking to him in her office, he said, "I have this really, really big music thing happening. I think I may have to go to Los Angeles. I think I'm going to become really famous. I think this thing is really going to make me famous."

What's really weird is that even though every ounce of me grew up in the Prince era, I didn't know Prince was Roger from Mattie Baker's office. I didn't know that the Prince that I was crazy about, that I watched filming *Purple Rain* downtown—I just didn't put it together. And now that he'd become a star, he looked different than the little ragtag kid with the great big Afro sitting in Mattie's office.

And then someone said to me, "Well, that's Mattie Baker's son, right?" And I said, "Mattie Baker from Edison?" And they said, "Yeah." And I said, "Her son's name is Roger." "Yeah," they said, "that's Prince."

10

THE TEENAGE AUTEUR

How could he not make it? He didn't need to get lucky and get a break; a record company had to get lucky and catch the break and find this teenager and give him whatever he wanted. Luckily, life is sometimes a meritocracy, and the right people find each other.

For a while, at least.

And so, Prince, Mo Ostin (pronounced "Austin"), chairman of Warner Bros. Records, and Lenny Waronker, president of Warner Bros. Records, found one another, and it was the beginning of a beautiful friendship.

For a while, at least.

And they believed. When Prince's first movie was about to be kiboshed because the producers couldn't find the last million they needed to finance the filming of *Purple Rain*, Mo went to the highest powers that were at Warner's and, as a personal favor to one of the corporation's most beloved nabobs, got them to hand over the last dough needed to green-light this dubious-sounding project.

Mo and Lenny had *the* strategy, encouraging their talent scouts to lead with their guts, and the results were often stunning. Robert

Lloyd, a reporter who's written extensively on the history of Warner Bros. Records, described Ostin's overall plan as to "sign the original and most extreme exemplar of any contemporary trend." It was the perfect home for a teenage musician with an already highly honed notion of the righteousness of "sick." Lloyd continued: "No one in pop was more apocalyptically heavy than Hendrix, more psychedelic than the Dead, more soul-searchingly sensitive than Joni Mitchell, or more authentically strange than Tiny Tim."

Further, Warner's acts were given time to develop. Joni Mitchell's 1968 album peaked at only 189 on the *Billboard* charts, while the Grateful Dead's entry that year made it just as far as 87. Meanwhile the Kinks' *Something Else* reached but 153. That was all fine by Mo. He believed in each of his acts or he wouldn't have signed them. Warner's could wait.

And while he waited, Mo proved he could deal with difficult personalities without getting himself soiled—people who made Prince, this teenager from Minneapolis, as headstrong as he was unknown, seem like an easy-to-please lapdog. Mo, after all, had begun in the business as Frank Sinatra's accountant; by the early 1960s he was president of Sinatra's boutique record label, Reprise.

As for dealing with the difficult, well . . . in 1962, for example, Sinatra, Dean Martin, and Sammy Davis Jr. all agreed to sing at the opening of the Villa Venice, a Chicago nightclub owed by the city's Mafia overlord Sam "Momo" Giancana, a homicidal psychopath who would eventually be executed with six bullets to the face so he couldn't have an open-casket funeral.

But that was later.

For the Villa Venice gig, neither Frank, Dean, nor Sammy would be paid, but Sinatra had received permission from Giancana to record the threesome's performance for release on Reprise, also home to Martin. The album, it was jocularly whispered, would be called "The Mafia's Greatest Hits."

A week before the show, Sinatra dispatched Ostin to Chicago to oversee the musical arrangements; Mo himself would produce the record. However, by then, Giancana had grown furious with Sinatra and his prima donna act. Apparently, the last straw for the

Mafioso was when Sinatra demanded that the don commission a private train to transport Martin and himself from California for the performance. Giancana was apoplectic with rage.

Somehow, however, the low-key Mo Ostin simultaneously soothed the outsize wounded egos of both Sinatra and Giancana. The reformed CPA also capably oversaw the technical aspects of recording the Villa Venice show. Though the live album was never released, Mo had proved he could deal with the vainest stars and toughest businessmen. Within a year he would be running the latter half of a merged company called Warner/Reprise.

By the time Prince came along fifteen years later, Mo's power and reputation for rectitude and honesty were so entrenched that many in the music business referred to him simply as "Chairman Mo."

So when Mo decreed giving the kid what he wanted, the kid got everything. A teenager who wants to produce his own albums? Okay, soon enough, Mo decided—though it came about sooner than either Lenny or Mo expected, as in essentially Prince's first record.

And so what that he was a teenager who wanted not just to produce—and to play all the instruments on—all his records? Prince was also kept on the books after he booted Lenny and Mo themselves out of the San Francisco studio where they'd gone to observe their much-vaunted-if-still-totally-anonymous new signing.

Prince loved them, for besides not being typical record company weasels, they seemed to get him. Lenny quickly came to understand Prince's production priorities and wants, and whenever the youngster visited Warner's headquarters in Burbank, his first stop was Mo's office to sit and simply talk about—whatever. Momo Giancana and the unreleased "Mafia's Greatest Hits."

Both Mo and Lenny, Prince thought, had "it." They had also agreed to start him off with a three-record deal when no other company would pony up more than two. But most of all was "it."

And having "it," for a record company executive, was the equivalent of having an "ear" for a music-business talent scout. "It," an equation nobody has ever been able to spell out in the history of the recording industry, "it" involves a record company executive being able to balance the innumerable variables of the talent (who usually act like children), the competition (who usually act like thieves) and the consumer public (who, when properly stimulated, can respond like sheep).

And no one, *no one*, had ears like Mo and Lenny. Chrissakes, Waronker had been Randy Newman's producer's when the *Toy Story* composer was still considered the best singer-songwriter on the horizon.

So, Lenny, besides being president of Prince's label, wasn't simply flexing his corporate muscles when he and Mo went to visit their rookie record his rookie record in San Francisco, and he questioned Prince's production priorities while playing back "So Blue," a mellow acoustic number that showed how far across the musical spectrum Prince could stretch. Waronker, Prince said, asked: "Where's the bass? I love the song, but where's the bass?"

Prince didn't want bass. This was exactly what he meant when his parting words to Waronker after he signed with Warner were: "Don't make me black." With its jazzy, acoustic inflections, "So Blue" was the exact kind of vehicle to show the spectrum of the commercial possibilities.

So, with that, twenty-year-old Prince ordered Mo and Lenny—men he liked and respected—out of the studio. Owen Husney, Prince's manager, told the Minneapolis *Star Tribune* that he thought the name "Prince" would be heard no more in the halls of Warner Records.

Not so.

Mo was impressed by the kid's chutzpah. Not even Sinatra had tried to kick him out of the recording booth.

Lenny had, in Yiddish, *sechel* (SAY-chel)—wisdom that went beyond his ears. "It's fine, it's fine," Waronker told Husney, worried that his charge had blown his career before he'd even begun. "I understand what he's trying to do," Lenny told Husney. "I'm on his side, and don't worry."

Lenny understood that Prince was underscoring his central demand—"Don't make me black." And if Waronker couldn't see that Prince could easily perform funky ebony-focused songs, right next to dewy-eyed acoustic-ivory-perfect-for-crossover appeal to white folks in the number of seconds it took to finish one song and begin another, well, then, he should just get out.

Lenny and Mo understood. They got out of the studio, but stayed with the kid.

AUGUST 20, 1983

Debate continues to this day whether Prince stole or destroyed the show the night he joined James Brown and Michael Jackson onstage at the Beverly Theater: Did he kill or did he bomb? remains a live question depending on one's reading of a grainy YouTube upload of the event. Did Prince outdance the masters, or were his steps stilted? Was his guitar playing peculiar noise or inspired jamming? As New York Yankees announcer Mel Allen used to say: "You make the call!"

Jackson wowed the crowd with some dance steps, then asked Brown to call Prince out of the audience as well. Brown tentatively shouted out Prince's name several times, and Prince finally appeared moving toward the stage on the back of Brobdingnagian-size body-guard Chick Huntsberry.

When he was strapped into his guitar, Prince, to many eyes, proceeded not to make a magic moment of spontaneous collaboration, but to sabotage a would-be history-making jam of the generations. He would not be summoned, according to this line of critique. even by Mr. James Brown, *especially* since Mr. James Brown seemingly did not know who he was.

It was 1983, and James Brown didn't know who Prince was? Unthinkable, at least to Prince. And so, goes the lore, the Godson of Funk wrecked the Godfather of Soul's set, with random, erratic guitar playing, time-wasting shenanigans, and stunts like bending a fake lamppost that was part of the stage set to the point where it popped off into the audience. Instead of a magic moment, the meeting of the trio was reduced to a less-than-legendary YouTube clip.

(Prince, goes one theory, showed his contempt for Brown for putatively disrespecting him by only calling him out of the audience at Michael Jackson's urging, while apparently having no idea who "Prince" was—never mind that his "Delirious" had entered the Top 10 that week, his third Top 20 hit of the year, along with "Little Red Corvette" and "1999." The Godfather of Soul had called Michael Jackson to join him onstage from the audience, which he excitedly, dutifully did.)

"Don't meet your heroes," he warned me when I was thirty, and headed off for an assignment to write a magazine piece on Willie Mays, forever perched in my personal pantheon. "James Brown," he concluded. "James Brown. Except for Muhammad Ali, every hero has let me down."

He loathed Michael Jackson, ridiculed Michael Jackson, and laughed off Jackson's management notion in 1987 of pairing His Royal Badness with The King of Pop for "Bad," where the first lyric would be Michael singing to Prince: "Your butt is mine"

Prince was not amused. He relished telling the story of when Michael Jackson agreed to play Prince in Ping-Pong, a game he'd never before attempted. Instead of it being a probably apocryphal event that would be embarrassing to most celebrities, Prince loved telling the story—even if it wasn't true—imitating Michael Jackson flailing helplessly at the ball.

"He looked like Helen Keller!!" he'd end the tale every time.

And Prince didn't even want to see Miles Davis, never mind his public pronouncements. His flattering remarks were true—he could separate talent from the person—but that still didn't mean he wanted to be in the same room with said person.

"Prince and I did a song ostensibly for Miles Davis, called 'Can I Play with U?,'" saxophonist Eric Leeds remembered in Mobeen Azhar's *Prince*. "They were considering it for Miles's first Warner Brothers recording, *Tutu* (1988.) There were people in Miles's camp who were very interested in it, for the cachet of having a Prince song.

"Miles dubbed trumpet on it. I said, 'Oh boy, it gets me into the Miles Davis discography!'

"Prince asked me about it, but I think it was a *fait accompli* and he had already decided that he didn't want to [be on Miles's album.]"

Not that Miles was known for his generosity to other artists. In a 1958 issue of *Downbeat* magazine, Davis reviewed a recording of "Caravan" featuring Duke Ellington, Max Roach, and Charles Mingus. "What am I supposed to say to that? That's ridiculous," Davis said upon hearing the three collaborating. "You see the way they can fuck up music?"

And so, it went, down the line. Miles Davis and James Brown were also known not to particularly like each other—Miles seemed to like no one. And yet: "Miles Davis and James Brown, who [had] similar reputations for being cantankerous and outrageous, seemed so much alike," according to James McBride in his incisive biography of Brown, *Kill 'Em and Leave*.

"Each admired the other from a distance," McBride wrote.

> Those who knew them describe them similarly: hard men on the outside, but behind the looking glass, sensitive, kind, loyal, proud, troubled souls working to keep pain out, using all kind of magic tricks, sleights of hand and cover-up jobs to make everyone think "the cool" was at work when in fact that cool was eating them alive. Keeping the pain out was a full-time job.

And it was a harder gig for James Brown, from America's South. "You cannot understand Brown without understanding that the land that produced him is a land of masks," declared McBride, who could just as easily have been writing about monolithically opaque Scandinavian Minneapolis.

"The people who walk that land, both black and white, wear masks and more masks, then masks beneath those masks," McBride wrote. "They are tricksters and shape-shifters, magicians and carnival barkers, able to [metamorphose] right before your eyes into good old boys, respectable lawyers polite society, brilliant scholars, great musicians, history makers. . . . This land of mirage produces outstanding talent and popularity—Oprah Winfrey being the shining example."

Minneapolis is also a land of mirage, of what appears really isn't, and Prince was the shining example.

The musical part of the music business was easy for Prince. Besides being able to play any instrument alive to death, he also proved an intuitive prodigy at the "show" part of show business.

After all, he'd been pretending his whole life. At first, taking up permanent residence in make-believe land was self-defense. It was a necessary coping skill for Prince. He was also adept at personifying a boy who took perverse delight in growing up with a virtual whore of a fictional mother, not the dignified, personally and professionally sparkling woman—and battered wife—Mattie Shaw actually was.

But why all the bullshit all those early years, I asked him at his house a couple of years later? Why had Prince kept taking journalists "knee-deep through the big muddy" that separates true facts from fiction when he was the hottest new thang on the critical block?

He didn't say he was "lying"—he said he'd been "teasing" reporters—just as he'd once described boxing promoter Don King not as a blowhard con man, but a showman whose "trickerations" could be excused because "he made" everything seem like a big deal, even when it wasn't."

So why all the prevarications with adoring critics from the beginning? "I used to tease a lot of reporters early on because I wanted them to concentrate on the music," he told me for *Rolling Stone*. "What was important was what came out of my system that particular day. I don't live in the past. I don't play my old records for that reason."

Well, of course they'd concentrate on the music of a budding new talent! What else would music writers care about? "On me coming from a broken home," he said. "I really didn't think that was important."

Such prolonged, omnipresent reliance on dis- and misinformation—because he came from a broken home? It hadn't exactly been a Northside scandal when John and Mattie Nelson divorced in 1968.

But I realized a few weeks after that conversation that Prince had not been talking about his parents' divorce but about his truly *broken* home—a toxic, dysfunctional, and violent potpourri of madness under one roof.

Forget Machiavelli's quote in *The Prince* about the wisdom of—
for power's sake—occasionally feigning craziness: "Sometimes it is a
very wise thing to simulate madness." By 1962, in his tome *Thinking
About the Unthinkable*, futurist Herman Kahn argued that to "look
a little crazy" was potentially an effective method to get an enemy
to blink.

Richard Nixon called it "the madman theory."

The problem was, Prince had been pretending forever. Who was
Prince? I'll bet my whole baseball card collection that no one really
knows or knew—including him. Prince had an entire philosophy on
the power of shock and awe for shock and awe's sake: the same old
same old *sickness*, whose point, of course, was to not be the same
old anything.

Meantime, Prince's real religion, throughout his life, was not
Seventh-day Adventist, Baptist, Methodist, or even the Jehovah's
Witnesses.

It was "kayfabe."

Kayfabe, pronounce it how you wish. It comes from early
twentieth-century carnies and conmen, later passed on to professional wrestlers. One pro wrestler, after Milton Berle, probably the
most famous television star of the 1950s, Gorgeous George, was so
influential that Muhammad Ali, James Brown, Little Richard, and
Bob Dylan all pointed to him as perhaps the most major influence on
their careers. Sound ridiculous, again with the professional wrestling?

Kayfabe—the art of never letting down the pretense to the
"rubes"—as they were still officially called in professional wrestling
circles—that what they were watching was a simulation, an entertainment. Under the laws of kayfabe, disbelief must never be unsuspended.
Never.

"Kayfabe," writes Mike Edison, is merely holding up the professional wrestling "illusion that everything you see is real," continuing,

It's maintaining the gimmick at all times, meaning the sadistic Marine
Drill Sergeant you see on television battling the Russian Heathen is

actually a sadistic Marine Drill Sergeant in real life, and the Russian is without equivocation our biggest threat to losing the Cold War. And, after they are done working, they do not go to parent-teacher conferences or mow the lawn, and they especially do not have drinks together at the hotel bar.

And so, by necessity, Prince lived a kayfabe life. By all accounts he was *always* dressed as if he could step on stage in two minutes; never carried a phone; believed he'd been cured of epilepsy as a child by the swift intervention of God. He always insisted on giving lovers bubble baths and would just as soon take strychnine as a recreational or even potentially addicting drug.

And his father never hit him or his mother. All of that. Which might have been true most of the time. Except when it wasn't. Which it wasn't, as everyone who actually knew Prince knows.

Prince was intrigued by the fluid drama of kayfabe life, going from working babyface to heel and back again. Heels could not be seen in public partying with babyfaces. It was called "breaking kayfabe."

And kayfabe, the concept, was not limited to the wrestling ring or to Prince—it extended to anyone who lived their life by pretend, where the illusion was never to be dropped, where the eager-to-please little man behind the curtain pulling the levers to project the monstrous image of the all-powerful Wizard of Oz was never to be seen as actually the weak Professor Marvel.

Mickey Mantle lived a kayfabe life as the eternal All-American boy; Rock Hudson, as the embodiment of heterosexual masculinity, was so kayfabe it was tragic; Franklin and Eleanor Roosevelt had a kayfabe marriage. For that matter, "Morris Day," the character, versus Morris Day, the teenager, then the man? Kayfabe.

The occupational hazards of living by the rule of never letting on you were living a make-believe life could be fatal. People could make a joke out of themselves by buying into their own version of kayfabe.

Mike Edison explained, using Hugh Hefner, the by-then-antique founder of *Playboy*, as a pathetic example: "When Hefner made his splash on reality television in 2005, at the age of seventy-nine, with *The Girls Next Door*," Edison wrote, "a farcical view of what life in the mansion was like for his flock of 'girlfriends' (which numbered as high as seven at one time), he outed himself as a cynical and feckless relic who had fallen hopelessly in love with his own kayfabe." He was, in wrestling parlance, a "mark for his own gimmick." I believe that Prince, too, was a mark for his own gimmick, and that in the end, it was part of what killed him.

He eventually came to believe what everybody had been saying about him. And to my way of thinking, when the kayfabe becomes realer than what's real—when you can't tell the kayfabe from what's authentic in your life—you're already dead.

On April 7, 1978, Warner Bros. released Prince's first album, *For You*.

A relative bomb as a crossover, the album never cleared number 163 on *Billboard*'s pop music chart, though it placed nicely on *Billboard*'s soul chart hitting a not-bad number 21. Still, *For You* had underachieved sales expectations, and burst budget boundaries. Around 150,000 copies sold in the United States.

Prince had put into professional practice not just a lifestyle, but a way of being. He began by freaking out reporters, not because he was insane but because he didn't want to talk. He lived a perfect pretend life.

Grudgingly, over time, Warner *de facto* gave in to Prince's demand to produce himself when he was barely able to vote, during the months of preplotting for *You*. Like so many other things he wanted, for better *and* worse, he simply wanted to be left alone.

And the money? Was this the biggest deal ever for a new artist? Who knows—there is no bigger game played in Hollywood than "How to Lie with Statistics."

And Mo Ostin, chairman of Warner Bros.?

"Mo is good, he tells good stories, and he tells the truth," said Prince, fifteen years after he signed his first contract.

"Prince reminds me of Frank," Mo told me in 1993. (Mo never gives interviews, and I am positive he thought I was Prince's PR guy when I was granted ten minutes of his time.)

Mo liked Prince, "the kid from Minneapolis," and the kid from Minneapolis liked Mo. The kid also liked Lenny Waronker, Mo's trusted lieutenant, both sharing truly deserved reputations for honesty, decency, and probity, not easy qualities to find in an industry crawling with reptiles and motored by small men seeking big revenge for everything from everyone.

Mo and Lenny were considered industry-wide to be the very best of souls. Critically, both also knew talent when they heard it (in Prince, Madonna, the Talking Heads). And Warner knew how to alternately coddle, cajole, and create an environment in which artists could produce their best work.

Lenny had brains, and he knew not to take umbrage when the talent, especially those with actual talent, made demands or asked favors.

Ya gotta believe!

Bob Merlis, the head of publicity for Warner Records during Prince's early years, remembered when the musician was doing an early interview with a woman at *Record World*. "They talked about whatever," Merlis recalled. "Then [Prince] asked her: 'Does your pubic hair go up to your navel?' At that moment, we thought maybe we shouldn't encourage him to do interviews."

And then he creeped out Dick Clark. In 1980 his band was invited to play on *American Bandstand*, where Prince gave the host the silent treatment. Dez Dickerson, his guitarist, remembered, "Dick Clark came into the Green Room and did his cordial thing. He's everybody's friend and puts everybody at ease. After he left, I saw that look on Prince's face that meant: Uh-oh, something's coming. He said, 'This is what we're going to do. When Dick Clark talks to you, don't say anything.' My heart sank. But it ended up being considered pure genius."

Meantime, things were getting weird in Minneapolis. Prince had turned from peer to king.

And Prince's career proceeded. In shorthand, perhaps, because it seems 1,219 separate pages on Google have the exact same information:

The second album, *Prince*, October 1979, a number-one soul hit, "I Wanna Be Your Lover!"

American Bandstand, Dick Clark, fuck you!

Lisa Coleman in on keyboards.

Dirty Mind released October 1980.

Controversy, October 1981.

Prince needed Morris Day. They were fighting for the championship of themselves.

He also knew that he needed what Walter Sobchak—played by John Goodman in *The Big Lebowski*, a demented bowler and Vietnam vet with the worst case of PTSD in the history of the syndrome— termed "a worthy fucking adversary."

Prince instinctively knew that to be great, and remembered as great, he had to vanquish a worthy fucking adversary. Just as the Beatles needed the Rolling Stones and vice versa, as the Hatfields needed the McCoys, Cassius Clay needed Sonny Liston then Muhammad Ali needed Joe Frazier, Superman needed Lex Luthor, so Prince needed an adversary, and since he was Prince, proclaimed a genius by the international cognoscenti, he would have to fight in a vacuum against himself and use kayfabe to find someone who could at least pretend they were worthy enough to be a true opponent.

He had to create a "Morris Day."

Day, a character so brilliantly invented by Prince, and portrayed by the real Morris Day in *Purple Rain*, is described in the film's screenplay this way: "Morris Day stands in the shower, steam whirling about his face. He's twenty-two years old, matinee-idol sexy with large, dark, bedroom eyes. He headlines a slick techno-funk group called The Time which sports gangster suits and wide-brimmed hats.

He's gifted with a wealth of self-laudatory humor which he uses like a knife, moving through life with a calm but ruthless grace. He breaks into a wide grin. Hair standing up like Don King, he wipes off a hand mirror, regards himself unabashedly as he brushes his teeth.

"He doesn't just walk to the curb," the screenplay soon continues in vivid style, "he slides—his promenade punctuated with a dip at the knees you could snap your fingers to."

11

PURPLE RAIN:
"DANCIN' IN THE DARK"

The book on *Purple Rain* has already been written, several times, and several times written well. If there were only one, I'd say it's Alan Light's *Let's Go Crazy*. It's a great book.

Still, I envy not the true accomplishment of Mr. Light, the former editor of *Vibe*. Because even better than writing that book, I was retroactively given a credit for working on the film. Not as a creative force or even a contributor. Rather, I am credited as the dolly grip, one of the technical crew responsible for pushing the camera dolly around.

Very funny, Prince. And very flattering, Prince.

When Prince told me I'd been granted a retroactive credit on the film, I told him that was the single greatest personal honor I'd ever been given.

Damn right I'm proud.

Just as I plan on being proud after I claim legal screenwriting credit for actually working with Prince on something that I did actually do but he *didn't* give me credit for: writing the story of the just plain awful rock video opera, *3 Chains o' Gold*.

So that's what I have to add to the saga of *Purple Rain*, beyond what Alan Light and a host of other writers have contributed to our understanding of the moment when Prince and the Revolution seemed to be the Beatles, and Minneapolis actually seemed to be the center of the hipster universe. I got a fake credit for not shlepping the camera dolly around.

Simultaneously *Purple Rain* was the number-one film and album, and bore the top-selling single in the United States, "When Doves Cry," a feat accomplished previously only by Elvis Presley and the Beatles. The soundtrack displaced Bruce Springsteen's *Born in the USA* for the number-one spot in album sales and remained there for twenty-four consecutive weeks. As of 2018 it has sold more than twenty-five million copies worldwide.

As they used to say in old Hollywood, that movie sold popcorn.

For Prince the moment signaled both the end of the beginning. He'd achieved his goal, a crossover star had been born, and he'd served as his own *Idolmaker*, like Ray Sharkey in one of Prince's favorite movies. Unlike Sharkey in the cult classic, Prince sculpted *himself* into the idol. He turned himself from a true nobody into a true somebody.

Purple Rain was also the beginning of the end—for the old Prince, the overly bossy boss, perhaps, who still had recognizable friends, ambitions that seemed of this planet, and a sense of showmanship devoted more to keeping the customer satisfied than himself.

Baby, he was the star, and thus it would ever be.

Except not.

Oh, Prince would ever after be a star, a superstar no less, even at his lowest ebb, but for long stretches of time it seemed he wasn't sure at what. He'd been a genius at playing every instrument imaginable and singing in every key possible; he'd worn each of his kayfabe personae with apparent sincerity, seamlessly moving between a polymorphously perverse magician in a raincoat, bikini underwear, and ejaculating guitar into a snakeskin-suited or plush-velveteened dandy who could alchemize all sounds into a never-before-heard beautiful noise that worked, whatever his look and personality of the moment might have become.

The days surrounding the opening of *Purple Rain* were swell, and for those hours, at least, all seemed well if not downright perfect, right down to the premiere at Grauman's Chinese Theatre (now officially known as TCL Chinese Theatre) in Westwood. Mattie looked proud as punch, appearing with the heartily welcomed Hayward, Prince's stepfather. John Nelson had also waved broadly at the flashing bulbs as he walked up the red carpet and into the theater.

By Monday morning the numbers were in. *Purple Rain* had earned $7.7 million in its opening weekend, replacing the effects-laden *Ghostbusters* as America's top-grossing film.

Prince later told *Paper* about that first Monday after what one might have expected to be a triumphant weekend. "We looked around and I knew we were lost," he said. "There was no place to go but down. You can never satisfy the need after that."

He was right. Prince was an artist, and to begin imitating himself as some sort of shtickmeister would be the equivalent of death. And yet the first law of show business is giving the people what they want. He had, and it'd been hard enough to figure out what they wanted. Now he had to figure out what *he* wanted, which was not necessarily, not even probably, what the fans who'd made him rich and famous wanted. Never again would he hit the popular heights of *Purple Rain*, the point at which many millions would only remember him by, even in death, thirty-two years later.

Prince had no choice, and no obvious answer to who he was. No longer was it enough to define himself simply, as Muhammad Ali had, by what he wasn't: "I don't have to be what you want me to be."

Ali also said: "I know where I'm going, and I know the truth, and I'm free to be what I want." Prince knew where he was going, he thought, but only for the moment; he knew the truth, but only for that second; and even if he could wriggle himself free from all contractual, cultural, and interpersonal bonds that tethered him to earth and to others, he still had to deal with himself—and in his kayfabe lived life, who was that?

And yet he had no choice: Not to decide what he'd be next was to decide. The easy decision—stay what made him boffo box office around the world—would probably result in him becoming an oldies act before he was old, germinating into essentially fronting a cover band, covering the songs that originally made him famous.

Jim Carrey explained it well in the documentary *Jim and Andy*, an exploration of the melding of characters that happened when Carrey—who grew up broke and homeless with an embittered, failed showbiz father—played the late Andy Kaufman, who was later the subject of the biopic *The Man in the Moon*. In the documentary Carrey recalls how Kaufman became famous on the sitcom *Taxi* as "Latka Gravas," the odd mechanic with the Foreign Man accent most commonly heard intoning, "Thank you very much."

He was rich. He was famous. Kaufman could have spent the rest of his life saying "Thank you very much" in his funny accent. Kaufman, a notorious professional wrestling fan, was dedicated to making his audiences decide whether he was playing kayfabe in his most out-there performances or playing it straight.

Kaufman almost destroyed his own career in a quixotic, questionable attempt to make a point, whether serious or not, about gender differences in the professional wrestling ring. His campaign went up to and included getting the crap kicked out of him by the genuine ring specimen Jerry Lawler, but it was to be expected, in retrospect—that was Andy, no?

Just as Carrey pointed out, the things he was doing at the beginning of his own career threatened to destroy him: "Every [successful] comic that gets a catchphrase like Andy's 'Thank you very much' [and] goes crazy with it, it's like their signature," Carrey said:

> Ultimately that kind of stuff that drives them [insane] is the very thing that made them famous. After a while, you're going to have to either *let* that creation that made you famous go and take a chance on being loved or hated for who you *really* are—or you're going to have to *kill* who you really are—and fall into your grave grasping onto a character you never were.

Prince, though not enunciating it with such clarity, reached a similar crossroads that Monday after the opening of *Purple Rain,* when he realized that over the weekend he'd become an international sensation.

"Where did this character come from?" Carrey asks in the documentary, that Andy Kaufman, he, Prince—one could name a dozen celebrities—had ridden to stardom?

"What is the dirt that the pearl is built around?" Carrey continues. "The pearl is the personality you build against that thought, 'if they ever find out that I'm worthless, if they ever find out I'm not enough, I'll be destroyed.'"

What Carrey was talking about was falling in love with your own gimmick: believing, like all the rest of the rubes, that the kayfabe the person (say, Prince) was enacting (say, in *Purple Rain*) was a reasonable version of his real reality. It was profitable, but it would have spelled the end of him as a person, an artist.

It had already begun infecting others in the troupe; people were beginning to buy their own gimmick: We're part of the Revolution, or closely aligned with it. We're with the band.

Among the more benign and understandable phenomena were the inflated senses of self among the corps that temporarily took flight in the wake of the film's unexpected success, the musicians' unprepared-for stardom, and the arenas that greeted Prince and the Revolution every night, twenty thousand fans shrieking their names and numbers.

Prince, from back in the pack, had been launched into the stratosphere of superstardom. Was it the kayfabe hubris of the Crusher and Ali, or just his opinion, when he said he just didn't like anyone else's music besides Joni Mitchell's, it seemed, and by the summer of 1985 was saying: "I never liked popular music, I never really did. I liked what I heard as a little kid." He hadn't changed by the mid-1990s when he told me, "I feel like I finish everybody's sentences when I hear the beginnings of a song, and snap [makes a turn-off motion]."

The Beatles? Cool for the time, he said, "but I don't know how that would hang today."

Bob Dylan? He played dumb astonishingly convincingly: "I don't know too much about him," Prince said, which is exactly what one can see Dylan saying in 1965 about . . . anyone. He came to Dylan sideways, via Jimi Hendrix's version of "All Along the Watchtower." Though he didn't know him at all, Prince said, "I respect his *success*." *Rolling Stone* changed that to "but I respect him *a lot*."

Big dif. But if it's Jann Wenner's paper in 1985, Dylan would not be disrespected.

As for Hendrix? Prince performed the difficult-to-land simultaneous double disrespect of both Dylan and then (gasp!) Jimi. "They only compare me to him because I'm black. That's really the only difference. . . . Santana was a much bigger influence."

Not that Carlos Santana was shown any more respect. When Prince visited his home in San Francisco while recording his first album in 1977, he intentionally tracked mud through Santana's domicile, seemingly marking his territory for . . . God knows what.

Is there *anybody* he respected?

"Bruce Springsteen," he said once with earnest admiration. "I'm not too into his music, but that is the one man whose audience I could never steal." He said the word "steal" with wonderment, because Prince's take-no-prisoners approach meant not only beating your band but *owning* your band.

But one thing more than any made the Boss for Prince—the fact that he was such a *boss*. Prince was backstage at his first Springsteen concert, and Bruce's band "started going off somewhere, and Springsteen just turned and took one look and you can bet they got on it!"

They became friends, exchanged notes; when Prince died one of the most rerun tributes was Springsteen opening a concert with "Purple Rain." Still, even with a possible compadre, Prince had to fuck around with Springsteen.

According to Wendy Melvoin, speaking to the *Minneapolis Star Tribune*: "Unfortunately [Prince] would kind of screw with people, especially big famous artists who would come up. If he sensed they were a little bit lost, he'd try and expose that: grab a guitar and do a blistering solo in their face. There was a certain amount of, like, straight-up competitive humiliation. But he thrived on that, like, "I know I'm great."

Lisa Coleman agreed, especially when it came to Springsteen. "With Bruce," she recalled in the *Star Tribune*, "I remember Prince being a bit of an imp and trying to throw him off. He was giving us his secret hand signals while Bruce was trying to play a guitar solo. There was a little cat and mouse going on. I never knew if Bruce knew Prince was doing that because there was a bit of giggling, but *we* knew and were like, 'No, don't do that, it's so mean!'"

Prince was reveling in it. It was his goal to tower over everybody in a lot of ways. To this day Springsteen hasn't had a number-one hit single; he was trapped at number two behind Prince's "When Doves Cry" from the *Purple Rain* soundtrack, with "Dancin' in the Dark."

Prince loved that. Even those he admitted to his pantheon of peers he couldn't stop publicly fucking around with. Springsteen was at the Forum in Los Angeles to see Prince on the *Purple Rain* tour. According to singer Paul Peterson in the Minneapolis *Star Tribune*, Prince brought Bruce up and gave him a guitar to play a solo. Then he took the guitar over Bruce's head and played a little bit, pretending it wasn't working right. He gave it a little look. And then he gave it this look like, It's fine now that I'm playing it. He was giving Springsteen the attitude.

Prince had to change or die; or change and die. He had wanted desperately to cross over, to not be pigeonholed as black, as he'd ordered Lenny Waronker while making his first record. But that did not mean he wanted to sell out his funk credentials, even using as his amanuensis The Time, and the frustrated, empty vessel that was Morris Day.

He had willfully turned Morris into a monster for his own purposes—the monster who had stolen *Purple Rain* out from under him with a brilliant comic performance as the all-time vainglorious performer—a fact Prince was grateful for. "I wanted Morris to steal that movie. I needed him to," Prince said to me a couple of years after it came out, watching Morris weave his *Purple Rain* magic through the VCR.

That it was jive didn't matter, that "Morris Day" wasn't Morris Day, that Prince showed him how to sing every note didn't matter. Cassius Clay had his *bête noire* Sonny Liston; Muhammad Ali had Joe Frazier. Observing the third brutal championship boxing match between Ali and Frazier, sportswriter Jerry Izenberg was moved to write: "They weren't fighting for the championship of the world, they were fighting for the championship of each other."

With Morris, and the Time, a band he still proudly proclaimed was the only group "I've ever been afraid of"—Prince now had the worthy fucking adversary he needed to prove his ultimate greatness—but greatness at what?

Things changed immediately at the beginning of the *Purple Rain* tour across America. And a critical variable in Prince's simple social functioning was irrevocably destroyed.

Most hurtfully, he was abandoned and then sold out by Chick Huntsberry—the bodyguard built like Paul Bunyan by way of the Banditos outlaw motorcycle gang—a giant whose very presence had served to separate Prince from his people—the people who knew him and cared, as well as the people who knew and didn't give a shit beyond what he could do for them.

Prince no longer rode on the same bus as his band once the film came out and he and the Revolution began their triumphant tour of arenas that roared every night like the Thunderdome. His companion on the bus was Big Chick, and the behemoth guarding his dressing-room door served to keep even his bandmates at bay.

Even there there was trouble. Prince said:

> Chick has more pride than anyone I know. I think he feared for his job. So if I said something, he'd say, "What are you jumping on *me* for? What's wrong? Why all of a sudden are you changing?" And

I'd say, "I'm *not* changing." Finally, he just said, "I'm tired. I've had enough." I said fine, and he went home and left the tour. I waited a few weeks and called him. I told him that his job was still here and that I was alone. So he said he'd see me when I was in New York. He didn't show up. I miss him.

Chick's adventures in cocaine were changing him. Mid tour, he took off, in kayfabe talk, for parts unknown. Prince kept him on salary, didn't hire a new bodyguard, and waited for him to return. He spoke to him on the phone, and Chick agreed to meet him on the New York leg of the tour; but he never showed up. Instead, the next thing Prince knew, Chick had sold his story for coke money to the *National Enquirer*, telling his tale as the world's biggest babysitter for apparently the world's biggest baby.

It was an interesting piece of infotainment that Chick shared with the world. It painted Prince as a superstar whose megalomania dwarfed his elfin physique. Meantime, the depths of *that* sociopathy, Chick told the tabloid, needed to be multiplied several times to approximate the psychological dimensions of Prince's wall-to-wall fetish for Marilyn Monroe, whose image, Chick went on, virtually obliterated the innards of Prince's entire purple house.

Still, Prince kept Huntsberry on the payroll, choosing to overlook Chick's treason and blame the medium he chose to deliver his message.

"I never believe anything I read in the *Enquirer*," he told me for *Rolling Stone*:

> I remember reading stories when I was ten years old, saying "I was fucked by a flying saucer, and here's my baby to prove it." I think they just took everything he said and blew it up. It makes for a better story. They're just doing their thing. Right on for them. The only thing that bothers me is when my fans think I live in a prison. This is not a prison.

No one had asked about whether he was living in a prison. But *again* with the prison. That he protested at all simply reinforced the notion: This twenty-seven-year-old international icon lives in a prison, in Minneapolis, Minnesota.

And so he did.

And so he died, thirty-one years later.

Alone in a prison where he was his own guard.

Meanwhile, even as it seemed the Revolution might have been planning to spend their lives as the Revolution, Prince was already getting ready to move on.

Months after *Purple Rain* broke, Prince was still calling Wendy Melvoin and Lisa Coleman his sisters. Belying his reputation as a control freak, he gave them virtual carte blanche in the recording studio to go nuts with their visions, individual and collective, and send them on to him from Los Angeles via tape. It seemed like it was going to last forever.

"We don't want to leave and start our own thing because this is our own thing," Lisa Coleman said backstage one night at Los Angeles's Universal Amphitheatre, preparing for a show in 1986. "I don't feel like we're just hired musicians taking orders. He's always asking for our ideas."

Wendy Melvoin agreed. "This band is going to be together for a long time," she said. "I'm sorry, but no one can come close to what the three of us have together when we're playing in the studio. Nobody."

Live, it was pretty good too. Delicious.

It was April 1986, and it had only been last year that Prince had announced that he and the band were through playing live. That night, at the Universal Amphitheatre, the silence was going to be broken by a surprise appearance by Prince and the Revolution following a Sheila E. concert.

Lisa and Wendy, waiting for the afternoon sound-check call, tried to describe their relationship with their fearless leader. An aide walked in and announced: "Prince wants you onstage ASAP." Lisa walked down the stairs and through the door and said: "I nicknamed Prince 'Fearless,' as in 'Fearless Leader.' As in Rocky and Bullwinkle."

On the stage Lisa and Wendy strapped and plugged themselves into position—Lisa back in her dark corner with a little smile and her head cocked slightly; Wendy in front with a wide grin, next to Prince in the fully lit, empty auditorium.

Gone were the days when Fearless Leader put his friends through all-afternoon sound-check jams that could last as long as that night's concert. Clean-cut, dressed in a resplendent black suit and a white ruffled shirt, Prince faced the band and ordered up a tune. The Revolution began hammering.

"Okay," said Prince, "Sheila comes in here." Cut. "Is Sheila here yet?" he asked. Momentarily Sheila E. strode in, stage left, in sunglasses and a trench coat. She and Prince huddled for a second, then the maestro barked: "'Controversy'! Ready!"

The band was pounding again. "Come on, stay in beat," said Prince. "I'm listening." Perfection is found in a few measures, and the band carried on with the song.

Prince then announced: "End of 'A Love Bizarre.' Check it out." He jumped offstage and ran up an aisle, both listening to the sound and practicing an audience run he would perform that night.

"Can we lose that low range somehow?" he asked. "Let me hear the bass out." Perfection again, then into the Revolution's new number-one single, "Kiss."

Prince paused. "I think finger cymbals would be better. Now, when we film videos tomorrow, we're going to drag it out so everybody will get their chance to be in it." With that he headed offstage. Wendy unstrapped herself from the guitar, Lisa unplugged from the keyboard, and they headed back upstairs for dinner.

This was how life was to be, and it was good. But by October 1986, seven months after the three of them had appeared on the cover of *Rolling Stone*, Prince called the band together to tell them the Revolution no longer existed.

What he found did exist inside him, while on the *Purple Rain* tour, is what in ancient Jewish kabbalism was known as a *dybbuk,* a devilish spirit that inhabited the bodies of living souls and created much mischief. Only the dybbuk Prince felt inside himself was urging him on to disaster.

By 1990, it had been four years since Wendy and Lisa appeared with the boss on the cover of *Rolling Stone*, billed as "Prince's Women." From not just out of left field, but from the satellite parking lot behind the parking lot behind left field, he'd fired everybody in the Revolution, except keyboardist Matt "Dr." Fink, and the reverberations of bad vibes could still be felt.

By 1990, when he next talked for publication, Wendy and Lisa had put out their debut eponymous album—and Prince was quickly on the record, profoundly unimpressed. So far, Prince said, the two women hadn't listened to the few tidbits of advice he'd offered. For their first video, Prince recommended that they try to announce themselves by making a splash, by "doing something like jumping off a speaker with smoke pouring out everywhere. Something."

When he saw the video, however, Wendy was sitting in a chair, playing her guitar. "You can't do that when you're just getting established—kids watching MTV see that and they go click," Prince said, miming a channel being changed. "They'd rather watch a commercial."

Prince seemed genuinely flummoxed as to why and what for. "I talk to Wendy and Lisa, but it's like this," Prince said, moving his hands in opposite directions. "I still hear a lot of hurt from them, and that bothers me. When I knew them, they were two spunky, wonderful human beings. I honestly don't know what they're hurt about."

Still, Prince's pronouncements seem proffered more in mourning than in malice. "Wendy and Lisa are going to have to do some more serious soul-searching and decide what they want to write about," he said sadly, and shook his head. "I don't know what Wendy and Lisa are so hurt about. I wish I did, but I don't."

Still, I owed Wendy and Lisa the biggest solid of my career. "Don't you think," I asked—adding a silent, 'you fucker'—"that you've been kind of a dick to them? They were your *sisters*."

He then asked the most unexpected question, it almost sounded as if it were a non sequitur; maybe it was. "What if everyone around me left? Then I'd be left alone, and I'd have no one to fend for me but myself."

It was 1990, and his European *Nude* tour. His band, the New Power Generation, was a much broader array of African Americans than the Revolution had been. His drummer, Michael Bland from Minneapolis, was my favorite. A corpulent nineteen-year-old with the fearsome look of an All-Pro defensive tackle, he actually still lived with his mother and sang in his Baptist church choir. He was also a bona fide autodidact. Once, backstage a couple of hours before a show, I caught him reading a copy of *The Portable Nietzsche*.

I asked him about it, and his reply remains my all-time favorite quote from anybody in Prince's entourage of musicians and . . . folks. "Nietzsche's cool," Bland said. "But Schopenhauer"—he continued, giving a shout-out to the father of nihilism—"now, there's a brother with no *hope*."

Prince, meantime, was still as maniacally churning stuff out as when his head hurt from too many thoughts. Now, in the middle of a frenetic concert tour, he was also editing the film *Graffiti Bridge* from VCRs in hotel rooms across Europe

Once again, the bandmates around him didn't realize that they were as expendable as the Revolution turned out to be. In Lucerne, Switzerland, after a concert, a gaggle of hundreds of fans were rocking the band bus following a concert, and Michael Bland was waving wildly and smiling broadly at those rocking. "We're the Beatles!" he yelled to his mates in the bus. "We're the Beatles!"

But they weren't.

Now it was apparent that Prince probably wasn't going to repeat his *Purple Rain* success soon. His two follow-up films, *Under the Cherry Moon* and *Graffiti Bridge*, won Prince three Razzies (Golden Raspberry Awards) for worst actor, director, and original song ("Love or Money"), and he was nominated for "Worst Actor of the Century" in 2000.

His succeeding albums had done nothing like the business of

Purple Rain. Around the World in a Day, his follow-up album, sold only three million copies, despite sporting "Raspberry Beret," which hit number two on the Hot 100 chart. He'd just read some rave reviews of *Lovesexy* and was peeved because he was again being compared to Jimi Hendrix.

"You can't compare people, you really can't, unless someone is blatantly trying to rip somebody off," Prince said. "And you can't really tell that unless you play the songs."

> You've got to understand that there's only so much you can do on an electric guitar. I don't know what these people are thinking— they're usually non-guitar-playing mamma jammas saying this kind of stuff. There are only so many sounds a guitar can make. Lord knows I've tried to make a guitar sound like something new to myself.

The nineties were now beginning to creep along, though, and making something new that would score would have little to do any more with the guitar or any particular instrument for that matter. Prince would discover this—most thought at the time too late. "They paved my art," he said, disgusted when he realized what had happened and paraphrasing his beloved Joni Mitchell, "and put up a motherfucking parking lot."

12

IN THIS LIFE YOU'RE ON YOUR OWN

The center would not hold for Prince come the 1990s.

In April 2016, on the day Prince died, *Rolling Stone* had a special edition on the newsstands titled "The Nineties," featuring a picture of Kurt Cobain on the cover. Twenty-five groups and solo acts had their names planted alongside his picture, but not Prince.

Mention of him was briefly made in the issue's introduction, where it was matter-of-factly declared: "Prince went off the deep and changed his name to the Artist Formerly Known as Prince. Unfortunately, he was soon just the Artist Formerly Known, setting into a routine of haphazard albums."

Somehow Prince had missed being one of the vanguard who spurred the birth, growth, and maturation of hip-hop and rap, probably the most important development in popular music since Ike Turner arguably invented rock and roll with "Rocket 88" in 1951. Actually, Prince didn't exactly miss the hip-hop revolution.

He just dismissed it. For a bit.

But it was a bit too long. And for Prince not to be way ahead of the curve, ahead of his time, reaching for the limits of expression—seemed at the time to seat him in the public imagination in the nosebleed section in the arena of cultural relevance. What good was Prince— commercially or artistically—as a *follower* of trends?

It happens.

Take Frank Sinatra (like Prince, himself a Mo Ostin project, albeit in quite different ways) back in the day Sinatra had opined that "rock and roll is the most brutal, ugly, desperate, vicious form of expression it has been my misfortune to hear."

Frank's blind spot was rock; Prince was initially sightless to hip- hop. In March 1987 he released "Dead on It," a single telling of him listening to the radio in search of music and finding it . . . lacking, to put it mildly.

He went on in the song to poke fun of Brooklyn, one of the world capitals of the new genre, in favor of the music coming out of Min- neapolis.

"'Dead On It' was an embarrassment and proof positive that he didn't get it," Prince's glory-years engineer, Susan Rogers, told bi- ographer Alex Hahn. The party was over, she sensed, and with his recorded attack on rap the impetus, Susan left his employ before the lights came on.

Prince would be playing catch-up with the cutting edge of popu- lar music for most of the decade until the end of the century. He did okay with rap and hip-hop, sort of, paying his respects, eventually, but in his mind the entire music game had been ruined because the music no longer mattered. For those along for the ride, not just Su- san Rogers, it was mortifying to watch.

"When I had come into this I realized Prince has a lot of hard- core fans who don't give give a damn about rap," said New Power Generation dancer Tony Mosly, whom Prince had asked to inject the new beats, sounds, and raps of hip-hop into his music. Mean- time, Mosly said, most hip-hop fans didn't "give a damn about Prince."

By 1993 I was through writing profiles of Prince, though I'd worked on a few projects for him that I thought wouldn't shatter my own independence. Though I'd like to think it was my profound need to run my own life that made me keep my professional distance,

I couldn't help but notice that there were few second acts for many people who got too deeply involved with him or his creations.

Since my last *Rolling Stone* cover story on him on 1990, I'd written for Prince the libretto to a rock opera he called "The Dawn," later released straight to video as a disjointed kind of rock video opera titled *3 Chains o' Gold*.

Still, I wasn't quite finished working with him. In the winter of 1993 I got a call from Gilbert Davison, the very nice and soft-spoken fellow who had risen through the ranks from Prince's bodyguard to head of his business operations. Was I available, Gilbert wanted to know, to be in Los Angeles yesterday to interview Prince?

For whom? I asked, meaning for what publication, and wondering why unknown publication wasn't contacting me directly so I could turn down the chance to burrow deeper into the pigeonhole I'd never wanted.

"For Prince," he said.

"For what?" I asked Gilbert.

"A time capsule," he said. "Prince is going to bury a time capsule under the grounds of Paisley Park."

"I see," I said, not seeing.

"He wants to explain some things about changes he's going through, and have you write it up," Gilbert went on. "He'll explain," he continued. "He wants to change his name."

"Good," I said. "Fine. To what?"

"He'll explain. A time capsule," Gilbert reminded me. "He's going to bury what you write up—for history. At Paisley Park."

Okey-doke, you betcha, as they say in Minneapolis.

———

Days later, Prince was waxing profoundly irate inside his Los Angeles mansion. He was shredding major recording stars in general who couldn't play, sing, or dance, but were charting when he wasn't. Loops and samples, he said, had taken talent out of the equation of who makes it to the top of the music business.

And then he said: "Prince is dead."

Huh?

"Prince is dead. That's the point of this time capsule. Put that up top. This is for history. He's done. There's nothing more I can do. There's nothing more I can add. I'm not needed."

Oh, and he was also changing his name to an unpronounceable glyph that was emblazoned on his latest, seemingly untitled, effort. That record would be come to be known as the *Love Symbol* album. He wore that glyph, seeming to combine the international generic icons for male and female, on a necklace and held it out for me to inspect.

For the next couple of hours, he tried to explain what it all meant.

It was one of the most astonishing displays of psychological fragmentation I'd ever seen. He seemed to be fracturing—not breaking down, but splintered in his desires of what he wanted. I'd always thought he'd had more contradictions in him fighting to get out then I'd ever witnessed in another human being. But usually there was a refractory period between the contradictions that lasted longer than the time it took him, like now, to reach his next breath.

Within seconds he could sound brilliant or like an idiot. Like many autodidacts who'd largely schooled themselves via books that looked interesting in the library, he bore vast tracts of ignorance and misinformation, as well as deep springs of knowledge redolent of surprising existential pondering.

In explaining why he was changing his name to a moniker no one could say, he would begin by talking with a hypothetical air verging on that of a philosophy professor lecturing about the nature of one's existence, and how to change oneself to fight the powers of the universe once one's essence had been compromised.

Continuing to play with the necklace bearing his new name, he said, looking down, "I think it means 'the dawn.' I never knew what 'the dawn' was before, but now I do. It means peace, perfection."

That riff ended, and without transition, he then began cackling like a street-smart-brute Iceberg Slim about how his motivation for no longer being known as Prince was so that he could weasel out of his contract with Warner Records. The timbre of his voice went from one leading a college seminar to a man of the alleys ready to play anyone before they could play him.

And then he was arguing his case for cultural history, pitting him-self artistically against past and coming centuries of talent. He knew his Mozart trivia, and he was in the same league, he contended. That's why he needed this time capsule, so future generations would know what had gone down musically.

But then a breath, and he suddenly said he was only playing for the moment, and the dollars.

"I always made money," he said. "Put that in. I always had top ten songs. Warner's always knows I will get sales every time I put something out," he said almost angrily, though no one else was there, and I wasn't disagreeing with him.

And the top of his record company? Lenny and Mo? Here came the Iceberg Slim cackle again. His recent negotiation with Mo—one that resulted in a putative contract for one hundred million dollars for ten albums—had been a no-contest, no-fuss, no-mess battle with a mere bean counter. "I said: 'Mo, I'm the best, so pay me the best or I'm hitting the road."

And with that there was jive. Even though under his new contract he'd have to sell five million copies of his last record before he got merely an advance against royalties for ten million dollars, he insisted against the rules of arithmetic that he'd outsmarted those old suckers always plotting against him: Mo and his henchman Lenny Waronker.

And then, again, without being posed a question or offering a transition, his voice would grow softer, and he'd speak of his two bosses with a respect just short of "Sir."

"They know I could change a few chords on 'Purple Rain,'" Prince said, "and get another 'Purple Rain' without people saying I'm pla-giarizing myself. But Mo and Lenny respect that's not what I want to do. And they do what's right."

His goal? The pantheon of all-time great talents, he'd say one minute.

His goal? The riches of Croesus, he'd say the next.

His goal? A clan of his own living inside the Minneapolis city limits on Lake Harriet—not the rich people's lake in town, but the *family* lake with a bandshell where the Fire Department's band plays and strawberry ice cream cones are sold in summertime.

Would anything else go into the time capsule?

Just two things, Prince said. The *Love Symbol* album—and his will.

Of all that he'd talked about that night, the one thing I least doubted him about was that will. He'd been talking not just about death but his *own* death, and his legacy, from virtually the first second I'd remet him since childhood (when I was twenty-six). He cared too much about charity, and gave too much money away anonymously to good causes, to let the government take a bigger bite than necessary from his estate.

He knew a will's importance. He'd made the disposition of a will the central plot point in *Graffiti Bridge*. I never had any doubt he'd be leaving instructions on what was to be done with whatever he left behind, from the recordings in his vault, to the gold bars he'd been investing in when everybody thought he'd end up broke.

His will, okay, hidden somewhere beneath the hundreds of acres encompassing the grounds of Paisley Park. That will would be this preternatural joker's final joke, I just knew immediately, one that would set off upon his death a Keystone Kops treasure hunt proving that even after he was gone, Prince had gotten the last laugh.

But perhaps the joke will be on him, for perhaps there will be nothing left of his estate by the time his will was found, I thought at the time. His mind was so scattered when he mentioned his will—his thoughts so disjointed, his brain holding such opposing viewpoints he ostensibly held at the same time—that perhaps he hid it too well, forgot to leave a proper clue, or was too clever by half in his plotting.

Parcels of his property have already been sold at this writing, and sometime in the future, I imagine, heavy earth-moving equipment will be uprooting ground for perhaps the last subdivision across the hundreds of acres encompassing Paisley Park Condos, or the like.

And there it will be. And like so many of his jokes, it will be misunderstood, not understood, or thought to be just crazy. Whatever. It will be a fitting episode in an afterlife that has proven just as tangled as the life he lived.

13

THE CRACK-UP, ACT 1

In 1996 Prince broke.

He'd been breaking all his life. While unknown and then famous, while richer and poorer, in all shapes and forms, for good and bad, sometimes good *and* bad simultaneously, only time would tell.

The year Prince broke got going beatifically. Minneapolis in January once again proved somehow bearable, and then, on February 14, 1996, Valentine's Day, Prince married Mayte Garcia, in a hush-hush ceremony in Minneapolis, at the Park Avenue United Methodist Church. (He didn't invite John Nelson, who he despised again, though the father continued living in the son's purple former house.)

Prince was thirty-six, Mayte was twenty-two when they wed; she was a professional belly dancer—a real one, a great one, not a give-the-boss's-chick-a-tambourine member of his onstage retinue. Mayte had known Prince since she was a jailbait teenager, and they'd fallen in love. Satisfying his priapic needs elsewhere and everywhere, he mindfully kept his hands off her until she was legal—and well-practiced under his tutelage for a perhaps profoundly successful professional dancing career.

As far back as 1993 he'd known he wanted to marry Mayte; three years before the actual I-do's, he'd asked me to write up a piece of fiction, as per a general storyline he'd concocted and provided me, that he said would be part of a wedding present to her.

The tale would be called "The Dawn," what he called a "rock opera," and would be about a princess of the desert being rescued by a strange—ahem—prince. The prince would be Valentino-like in his moves and his smoothness, only much more mysterious.

They were still in love three years later when they finally got married. Vows were exchanged, white doves were released outside the church, what happens happened, and Mayte was soon pregnant.

He went from love to rapture—a monogamous, can't-wait father-in-waiting, a man in control of everything, it seemed to him, on all fronts, soon even to be finally free of the onerous Warner Bros. Records. He had valid points to make about the strictures the record industry used to constrain all musicians, be they famous and rich or unknown and starving.

Unfortunately, the optics and timing sucked. He looked like a cartoon asshole when he'd appear in public or performing with SLAVE etched into his beard or drawn on his cheek with mascara. And frankly, he seemed like a cartoon idiot asshole when he invoked the chimes of freedom as he inveighed against his Warner's slavemasters.

Only a few years before, Chairman Mo had shackled him with unbridled artistic freedom and a ten-album record deal that, Prince falsely crowed at the time, was the most munificent in history. His hubris had been an embarrassment, all the more so because he was adamant in believing it.

But Mo Ostin and his chief adjutant, Lenny Waronker, had been gone since 1994, lost in a Hollywood corporate coup. Mo and Lenny—the two most authentic, honest, and artist-friendly record-company executives of their generation, men Prince respected and liked.

Lenny and Mo had never said no to Prince. They weren't angry, but personally hurt at him for waging war against them, especially when cast as the villains in a campaign Prince was leading to do right by the black man.

"Maybe at one time they could get Little Richard for a new car and a bucket of fried chicken," Prince slurred his bosses, famous industrywide for their probity, honor, and devotion to their artists. "We don't roll like that anymore."

Prince had loved Lenny and Mo, and I'd admired both of them mightily. I was reminded of the love Prince had long evinced for Wendy Melvoin and Lisa Coleman, whom I also always had on my Mount Rushmore of respect—and then the switcheroo he pulled.

In 1990, five years after describing the dynamic duo as his soulmates, he had already long disbanded the Revolution, critiqued their first album and video with a viciousness that was so clinically cold, cruel, and dismissive I couldn't believe we were talking about the same people. I loved Lisa and Wendy for their spirits, personalities, hearts, and talent, never mind that without their advice to Prince to "talk to this putz," I would never have interviewed him in the first place.

As he continued attacking them, I interrupted Prince. I never interrupted Prince, and I interrupt just about everyone. I wasn't afraid of him, it's just that I knew that whatever he was about to say was probably more interesting than what I was going to say.

He seemed stunned by my stopping him midsentence, but if I didn't stick up for Lisa and Wendy, I would—suck. So I shot back to Prince what he'd said to me in 1985 about the days around the time of *1999*.

"I was very angry back then," he'd said. "I was expert at cutting people off, turning my back on them, and never seeing them again. I think I'm a much nicer person now."

Prince looked at my tightened eyes and lips. We were in the middle of an interview.

"Next question," he said, as if I was just some shmuck from *Rolling Stone*.

"I don't have a next question."

"Well, see ya," he said, and got up to walk to his hotel room down the floor in Nice.

"Wouldn't wanna be ya," I whispered aloud, though under my breath.

I wrote my story.

I had no idea if I'd ever talk to him again. He was pissed. I was pissed.

Two months later he called me in Minneapolis.

Three years later I tried to understand how he could go to battle against Mo and Lenny, the two most important allies in his career, who respected his art, his craziness, saw the artist and his peccadilloes were a matched set, and were always willing to pay top dollar to get both, neither sure if it was his art or his craziness that made him a genius whose likes they'd never seen before.

So why'd he do it? Why'd he go to war against Lenny and Mo? Even though the duo had been gone for two years by the time Prince's battles with Warner's wound down in 1996, he gave me virtually the same reason he'd given me years before about dropping Wendy and Lisa from his band, his life, his influences, and, at that moment, even people he understood.

"What if they left me first? I'd be all alone. Who would be on my side? I'd have to fend for myself. I'm too old to fend for myself."

"You're talking about declaring war against Lenny and Mo, I'm talking about you leaving them, attacking them like they're captains of some slave ships."

"I gotta call my wife," he said, getting up.

At the end of April 1996, he and his attorney, L. Londell McMillan, handed over the last two albums owed on the contract: *Chaos and Disorder* and *The Vault: Old Friends 4 Sale*.

Warner's executives loathed both albums and saw them as potpourri from whatever Prince had lying about in his vaunted vault of unreleased music. They no longer cared whether there were hidden gems in that Paisley Park vault; they wanted out as much as Prince did.

It was over. Prince was free. He didn't need record companies anymore.

What would he do? Easy, Prince said when I asked him. He was a happily married man with his first child on his way. That was it.

Not that he didn't pay attention to the rock-and-roll box scores and throw an occasional shit fit. In early 1996, shortly before Prince was off Warner's hook and vice versa, Janet Jackson had just signed a four-album, eighty-million-dollar deal with Virgin Records. Apparently the most lucrative record deal ever, it dwarfed even Prince's 1992 ten-album deal worth a hundred million with Warner's—*if* he hit *Purple Rain*-esque sales figures on each record.

Considering where Prince's mind was musically, and that he'd shown absolutely no interest in selling that many copies of one record again—while making it clear that he easily *could*—he was basically saying he could get a hundred million . . . if he wanted it.

Scott Buccheit, Prince's former personal photographer, remembered the boss "walking around Paisley Park one day muttering 'fucking Janet Jackson! Fucking Janet Jackson!' When I asked the art director, 'What's this Jackson thing about?' he explained that it was because Janet Jackson had just signed the biggest record deal of [all] time."

All that was for Janet Jackson's music to come. Meantime, the virtually unanimous verdict on the Prince music newly out there was that it sucked. In July 1996, Prince and Warner's released *Chaos and Disorder*. Even the devoted, the insightful, and the devoted insightful were bummed. Jim Walsh, for one, who had played schoolyard basketball with Prince as a teenager and forever been an enthusiastic, informed supporter, opined, almost mournfully, in the *St. Paul Pioneer Press* that *Chaos and Disorder* was "an uninspired collection of warmed-over jams, sketches, snatches, and leftovers." Paying homage to Truman Capote's critique of Jack Kerouac's prose as typing, not writing, Walsh adjudged the album to be not "record making but recording."

It was even worse than some recent "tossed-off works," Walsh wrote, "the hastily composed 'Lovesexy (1988)'" or the Batphoned-in *Batman* (1989). "There is a creeping feeling of déjà vu [in Prince's work]," Walsh continued in his critique of *Chaos and Disorder*, "a feeling that even if we haven't heard these particular musings on love, sex, spirituality, human rights and the afterlife, we've heard him do it before. And better."

This was from loyal but discerning allies at home who weren't willing to cheerlead for that which wasn't cheerworthy. *Rolling Stone*'s critique called it sour and jagged: "At its best, the record sounds like a collection of polished demos," read the review, noting that "it's been awhile since (the Artist) has really had anything important to say in his music." Ultimately *Chaos and Disorder* "is the sound of a man repeating himself badly."

The record sold 140,000 copies in the United States, the worst sales figures in Prince's career. I never listened to the album; to be honest, I had no idea that *Chaos and Disorder* had come and gone.

We talked every couple of months, but he didn't mention *Chaos and Disorder* once. He told the press, said Ronin Ro, that the album was "dark and unhappy."

Prince did one interview in support of *Chaos and Disorder,* with Elysa Gardner of the *Los Angeles Times,* an interview about being finished with Warner's: "I was bitter before, but now I've washed my face. I can just move on. I'm free."

There were hints of weirdness, but nothing *too* weird. With Mayte pregnant, Prince collected all the keys from every Paisley Park employee and musician, meaning that either he or Mayte had to buzz them in. The self-made isolation could also be read as sensible security, especially since Prince was planning on making some wholesale personnel changes soon.

One night keyboard player Ricky Peterson rang the Paisley Park buzzer, and a "barefoot and pregnant" Mayte came to the front door, Ronin Ro reported in *Prince: Inside the Music and the Masks.* "It was the sweetest thing," Peterson said. Then Prince descended a flight of stairs by the front door in big bunny slippers.

"'Come on in,' Prince said. He was so happy," Peterson remembered. "I've never seen him happier than when she was pregnant."

All was well within on Prince's planet—except for everything.

Then, on October 23, 1996, Prince broke.

"Of course, all life is a process of breaking down," wrote St. Paul's F. Scott Fitzgerald, in the famous first sentence of his three-part Esquire essay, *The Crack-Up,* his detailed 1936 account of his own spiritual and physical implosion. (Unlike Prince, it took Fitzgerald fifty years after he died, not one day, to become a favorite—no, *beloved*—son of the Twin Cities.)

In the essay the fallen novelist delineated two primary forces of destruction that befall the unlucky, the human, the anonymous, the famous, and even the cartoonishly notorious, which Fitzgerald himself had become, a state into which Prince had seemingly devolved, by the time they both broke, two generations apart.

By the time Fitzgerald wrote *The Crack-Up*, he had, in the eyes of the industry that had made him famous, already and willfully leaped off the peak of real artistry into a moribund, even ridiculous career. Fitzgerald, as he'd prophesied for all America, had gone from an alchemist stirring up great art like *The Great Gatsby*, to a miserable hack, hacking out confessionals like, well, as it was thought at the time, "The Crack-Up," for *Esquire*.

Prince, meantime, the Artist Formerly Known, as wags whispered, had gone from instantly recognizable almost supernatural genius superstar to late-night quip, almost too-easy fodder for even the least hip late-night quipsters. "The Artist Who Formerly Sold Records," Jay Leno called him, to great studio guffaws, during a *Tonight Show* monologue.

But years of worldwide ridicule and shitty record sales weren't the variables that broke Prince on October 23, 1996.

"The first sort of breakage seems to happen quick," Fitzgerald wrote in mapping his own precipitous spiritual and professional descent from a wunderkind literary superstar lapping the pack, to a star running ahead, to a has-been-still-might-be running blindly, to a man running on empty, to a crack-up running in place.

The quick blows he described that caused such inner wreckage were ones that could usually be named, and then faulted, for all that had gone wrong in any "failed" life. "The big sudden blows . . . come, or seem to come," Fitzgerald wrote, "from outside—the ones you remember and blame things on."

The sudden bolt hit Prince and Mayte when Amiir Nelson, their week-old son, died after enough days of hell on earth. He'd been born with Pfeiffer syndrome, a genetic disorder where the bones in the skull fuse prematurely. Sometimes this causes a squished brain; maybe with water on it, maybe not. Perhaps mental retardation, maybe some disfigurement. Still, that was only sometimes, and good, workaday, "quality" lives were lived by many born with Pfeiffer syndrome.

Unfortunately, Amiir had Pfeiffer syndrome 2. The difference between Pfeiffer syndrome 1 and 2 is vast and all bad; as Mark Twain's old saw has it, "the difference between a fire and a firefly." Pfeiffer syndrome 2 turns atheists into God-fearing souls, turns the born-again into doubters and the devoted into the fallen.

The national media descended upon Minneapolis for the grotesque carnival known in the business as a "clusterfuck," and every morning brought a new day of the locust, half of the swarm carrying checkbooks. Prince had declared a news blackout, but hospital staff answering ward phones were unused to the wily ways of sneaky little shits looking for pediatric diagnoses, and with no real news, reporters interviewed one another, tossing gossip back and forth with all the gravity of a Nerf football.

Amiir, whose name had leaked as "Boy Gregory," was born so debilitated there's no reason to get specific. He had several operations in a week and was put on a ventilator to make sure he could get oxygen. The next step, doctors explained, would be to take the baby off the breathing apparatus, give him a tracheotomy, and see if he could take in air on his own.

Or there was another option.

"Ahem," Prince told me the doctor said to him, exactly that: "Ahem." He thought that was strange, very strange. "The doctor said, 'Ahem,' the word 'Ahem,'" Prince told me in a phone call three months after it was all over.

"He's about to ask me if I want to kill my son, and he's talking like a cartoon strip," Prince said to me angrily. It was the most bile he would express about the whole experience, which he related to me just this once, but in great detail, a season after it happened.

Or, said the doctor, Prince told me, they could turn off the ventilator, not do the tracheotomy, and let Amiir go.

It was Prince's call. Mayte is quite clear about that in her illuminating book, *The Most Beautiful Girl in the World*. I was relieved to learn that he at least consulted with her after he made his decision, and made an attempt to at least feign intimacy, to make it *seem* at least as if the couple was making the decision together.

Prince and I had two lengthy conversations in the six months after Amiir's death, but I took very sparse notes at the actual moment Prince said what he had to say. It simply didn't cross my mind to be a reporter; I was listening to a man narrate his own crack-up. Making his account all the more hideous was Prince's affect.

His tone was flat and carried with it all the ain't-that-a-shame emotion of someone killing time by recalling, shot by shot, a very, very bad movie that he'd wanted to walk out of but couldn't. This was one thing he couldn't, as he several times had delineated his favorite coping strategy, "close my eyes and wait to open them until I knew the situation was gone."

Go on, I said, when he was finished with his shit fit about Dr. Ahem.

And then, Prince said, the doctor told him the other option.

And so, he faux-consulted Mayte, but the decision had already been made. Prince was letting Amiir go, which was right and decent. And he never forgave himself.

On this one he came pre-Unforgiven, a state of being as much a part of Prince's fragmented makeup as even just a few of his very real personae: Iceberg Slim Pimp, or Walt Frazier Baller, or the Loneliest Guy in the World, Prince the Depressed, or one of his favorite roles to play, Prince, the brother from another solar system.

Still, until Amiir died, he'd at least always figured he still had a chance to be granted whatever form of absolution he always seemed so hungry for. Prince still hoped to make penance with the apocalyptic biblical God of the Seventh-day Adventists of his youth; the you-talking-to-me? Travis Bickle God who made the ingredients his father used to fashion Honeywell napalm bound for Vietnam; the no-joking-around Jehovah he actually quaked before until his death.

The 15 percent of him that quaked, that is. By that I don't mean he was a devout Jehovah's Witness 15 percent of the time; but that 100 percent of the time he was 15 percent a devout Jehovah's Witness, as devoted to reading the foreboding divine signs of the times as he was to the identity of a Prince-era Walt Frazier, Muhammad Ali, or Malcolm X.

Until October 23, 1996, Prince still thought he had a chance of getting through *this* difficult life—the hardest one he'd had by far, he told me twice in thirty-one years, though he never got specific with me about who he'd been in previous incarnations.

At seven-thirty on the morning that Amiir Nelson died, and Prince broke, the baby was dressed all in white for his death by his nurses. The ventilator was turned off, and a doctor checked the infant's vitals every fifteen minutes.

No, Prince did not want to be in the room to watch his baby die. Instead he called the hospital twice that morning. He prayed for the baby to breathe on its own (he told me); he asked one of the nannies: "Is it done?"

Soon enough.

And though he wasn't in the room, in many ways, he never really left that room—ever. For the rest of his life he blamed *himself* for the death of his son, and he wasn't talking unfortunate genetics. The full-time repentant sinner that was part of his makeup never forgave himself, felt he was being punished for the evil he'd done. He had written and sung "Jack U Off," "Head," "Soft and Wet," "Darling Nikki," and with "Sister," made the topic of incest danceable.

On albums, it was because of him, Prince well knew, that in 1985, Tipper Gore went bluenose and co-founded the Parents Music Resource Center, which begat the Parental Advisory Sticker. Because of Prince parents now had to be *warned*—justifiably so, he thought. In concerts, he'd heard parents *and* their children singing along with him to "Sexy MF," tossing the lyrics back to him onstage with the exaggerated enthusiasm for his music that he'd always craved.

He'd betrayed so many—simply as a for-example, not an all-inclusive list, he'd let go or simply let walk out the door, those he'd truly loved as a life mate and a brother (Susannah Melvoin, André Cymone), and as spiritual sisters (Wendy Melvoin, Lisa Coleman). Alternately, he'd been betrayed by virtually everyone he'd ever loved and dared show his vulnerability (his father; Chick Huntsberry).

He was never the same.

Much of his spirit died the year Amiir died, or at least it disappeared from the core, from his DNA. Gone was a certain brightness in his affect, a pilot light he had kept lit even in his darkest moments. Gone with the omnipresent spirit of onwards, a certain glow of optimism, a life force showing even in the worst of times, a hot coal of hope even in the blackest of his apocalyptic fatalistic musings about existence, other human beings, and his chances of ever going to heaven. You had to look closely—and if you worked for him, nobody looked too closely—and it wouldn't become apparent to many for a couple years that something had altered, unalterably.

He'd never liked a lot of people, and now he liked even fewer. The few in a position to notice, noticed, but no one said a word.

Nothing would bring that Prince back, no matter the major glories that would unexpectedly return to him in the coming years. That said, he still could feel joy, and in the coming years he saw he could lead a generally unhappy life—yet still lead a glorious one.

Immediately upon Amiir's death, though, he was able to will himself into denial just long enough to go on and make the loss another piece of the mythic saga that he dragged around with him forever like a tourist with a half dozen pieces of extraneous luggage. He just pretended, even to himself, quite convincingly, that nothing was wrong, that *his* musical family Nelson was as intact as Ozzie and Harriet's had been.

Narratives about what happened next diverge. In Mayte's book she says Amiir's ashes were delivered the next day and that Prince spent the next three weeks at home in a state somewhere between profound shell shock and a coma. Kim Berry, his hairstylist for thirty years, said Prince left Mayte and immediately took off for Miami with her and a bodyguard for weeks, never mentioning Mayte or Amiir for the weeks they stayed out of Minneapolis. When they returned home, Berry reported, Prince carried his son's ashes around for months. Wherever he was, it wasn't planet Earth.

Denial only flows so far, however, and the distress signals of celebrity secret weirdness kept sounding, and the cacophony of tabloid noise about Prince and Mayte's baby either being dead or hideously deformed did not abate. Three weeks after Amiir died, Oprah

Winfrey, sniffing perfidy, brought her talk show to Minneapolis and Paisley Park.

That show provided some of the most robust ratings ever of her robust career. It also included some of the most horrifying pieces of footage I've ever seen, if one knew what was or really had been going on, true pornography in the guise of infotainment.

Prince, dazed in grief and kayfabe bonhomie, waxed sanguine about family life as he led Oprah on a tour of the lavish, still-fully-intact nursery and playroom he'd had built inside Paisley Park, as well as the new outdoor playground that would have served the needs of several elementary schools. Prince's body was almost lost amid the mountains of toys, the piles of paints, and the seeming acres of no-expense-spared wonderments. "It had everything a perfect nursery needs," Mayte wrote in her memoir, "except for the only thing a perfect nursery needs."

Oprah was impressed when she saw the baby's room.

"Oh. . . . wow!" Oprah said. "*Wow*!"

"Here's my favorite room," Prince said.

"For the children to be," Oprah asked leadingly. "The children to come . . . ?"

"Yes, ma'am," Prince said.

"The child in you?" Oprah continued her interrogation. "Or just the children?"

"Oh, the children, yeah," Prince said.

"It's been rumored that your baby boy was born with health problems," Oprah persisted. "The reports have fans concerned."

"It's all good. Never mind what you hear," Prince countered, looking as beatific as someone who has just discovered the meaning of life, but sounding as stilted as a dummy being handled by the world's worst ventriloquist.

Oprah finally had to let go with one last direct query:

"What's the status of your baby?" she asked.

"Our family exists," Prince said. "We're just beginning it."

He tried to make the truth go away just the way he always did: He closed his eyes until he sensed the unsettling vision before him was gone, then opened them again. It always worked, he swore. Always.

Harold, in Prince's favorite children's book, had needed a magic purple crayon to draw a revised reality; all Prince required for the bad to disappear was to pretend that it just wasn't there, that the bad had never even *been* there. The never used nursery and playroom? It wasn't disassembled and given away—Prince instructed that everything be *burned*.

After Mayte miscarried, only months after Amiir died, Prince finally wasn't able to close his eyes away from reality, the accumulation of tragedies, of the hard blows Fitzgerald had written about that are easily used to easily explain the horrifically unexplainable. His trials seemingly didn't make Prince stronger, weaker, or force him to integrate the horrors he'd experienced into a new sense of existence, for good or ill. He was a gone guy. Even when he was standing in front of you he wasn't there.

The miscarriage split Prince and Mayte apart, as such tragedies do to so many couples. But instead of just divorcing his wife, Prince had the marriage *annulled*: His human child was gone, so was his unborn child; and finally, the romantic pairing that had—through no fault of Prince or Mayte—brought such loss, didn't just end. It was made to disappear, officially, as if it had never happened in the first place. How could it hurt, if it never happened?

A few years later his father died. Prince had been a good son every which way except when he was pillorying his father. He gave his father not just a roof, but pride in himself in the form of profits John Nelson hadn't earned, with song credits he didn't deserve. From 1984 to 1989, Prince gave John full or cocredit for more than half a dozen songs including "Computer Blue" from the *Purple Rain* album and film, "The Ladder" on *Around the World in a Day*, and "Scandalous" from the *Batman* film and soundtrack. Prince didn't look at it as charity; alternately estranged and entangled, Prince still relied on his father for advice, or at least pretended to.

Prince couldn't remove memories of Amiir, or his perceived role in his death.

"It's genetic," he said several times in the coming years. "It came from me. I gave it to him."

"Did they tell you that?"

"No," he said, five years later. "They didn't have to. Some things you just know."

Five years after that, he was watching a rerun of *The Sopranos*, one of the many shows he binge-watched. He brought up Amiir again after describing the episode he'd just seen, when the young son of psychotic Mafia capo Ralphie Cifaretto is seriously injured by an errant arrow shot by another little kid. Ralphie, who seemed to kill for pleasure as much as business, breaks down in the episode, sure his boy is being punished for his sins. "I'm Ralphie," Prince said, hanging up, after briefly describing the episode.

Five years after *that*, Prince was binge-watching *Boardwalk Empire*, the HBO series starring Steve Buscemi that featured actor Anatol Yusef as young gangster Meyer Lansky in the years surrounding Prohibition. Prince had been instantly drawn to the character of Lansky—portrayed by Lee Strasberg as "Hyman Roth" in *The Godfather II.*

He professed to be fascinated by Meyer Lansky either to flatter me, which I doubt, because Prince was not one to flatter, even though I had come to almost fetishize Lansky, the most powerful Jewish gangster ever, while writing a book about the hoods my great-uncle Augie consorted with when he owned the downtown Minneapolis strip club where Prince's father earned the bulk of the money he made as a working musician.

I think what Prince really liked most about Meyer Lansky was that they both were five foot two—and Lansky's underworld handle—"Little Man"—was always whispered with almost mythological respect. He'd read a book on Lansky; after years of name-checking the Little Man, in conversation, with me at least, Prince said the gangster's biography mentioned that Lansky's wife blamed him and his myriad sinning when *their* first child was born with cerebral palsy. He never mentioned the Little Man again.

After 2006, he mentioned Amiir to me only once.

In early 2007 he put on the greatest halftime show in the history of the Super Bowl. Read all about it, everywhere on Google, watch a recording of it live any place on the internet. One hundred million people watched him put on his second performance of a lifetime in two years. He was impressed by the numbers, the sheer number of eyes upon him, but then wondered about the week when Amiir was alive. The operations the baby needed ranged from procedures on his eyelids to his digestive tract, and his mind turned from the billions of eyes watching him at the Super Bowl to the pair belonging to one little boy.

"I wonder if he ever really saw me," Prince mused softly, then, as usual, when he uttered a sentimental line, hardened in a finger snap. "That was bad," he said, and I wasn't sure if he was talking about Amiir's birth and death, or his performance at the Super Bowl.

14

THE CRACK-UP, ACT 2

I saw a documentary, and I saw people calling Ali "Cassius Clay," which was just so disrespectful. And then they called him mean for punishing the people who called him that. You know that fight when he's beating up Ernie Terrell, Tammi's brother? Well, Ernie Terrell wouldn't stop calling him Cassius Clay, and he's a brother. So, all fight long, this is after Liston, Ali just punishes him, yells at him, "What's my name?! What's my name?!" Then, bam bam bam!

What are people going to say to me when I shout, "What's my name?! What's my name?!" I'll answer if they call me Prince, but I may not act too happy about it. Black people can call me Prince. I know they'll call me Prince, they're too smart for my shenanigans. Usually. [Laughs.]

Tales of the Lilliputian Prince, five foot two, as a basketball phenom of immense, virtually mythical talents, had circulated for decades among the Purple Army. But not until prime time February 18, 2004, did the world at large come to know that rumors of Prince's preternatural on-court artistry just might *not* be more of the same-old same-old jive-ass urban Paul Bunyan mythos that had trailed him ever since Warner Bros. Records publicity department swore that their newly signed nineteen-year-old artist was still seventeen.

In the days after Prince died, the astonishing, hysterical, dozen-year-old video testament to his basketball prowess was downloaded on YouTube six hundred thousand times. The seemingly impossible truth, that the pint-size Prince was a legitimate baller, was officially verified in 2004, on the best possible venue for such news to be dramatized and broadcast: *Chappelle's Show*, the crackling and tight Comedy Central sketch-comedy program starring the truly groovy Dave Chappelle.

That night's show featured the second installment of "Charlie Murphy's True Hollywood Stories," a profane excursion into the underbelly of showbiz weirdness that had previously turned whatever remained of Rick James's reputation to rubble, with Murphy telling of the superfreaky night on the Hollywood town when he had to beat the shit out of an over-the-hill, coked-out, misbehaving pathetic weasel that once had been—well—Rick James.

Comedian-actor Charlie Murphy, who died in 2016, was both Eddie Murphy's older brother, and an inner-circle member of his entourage at the height of his super-duperdom. Charlie, allowed to hitch a ride on Hollywood's A+ party list, made a brilliant shtick out of telling and showing what he saw en route in a profane street patois as tough as was allowed on basic cable.

And after Rick James, on Charlie's apparently literal hit parade? Prince.

The musician was portrayed in the skit by Chappelle himself, who, dressed in *Purple Rain*–era plumage, played Prince as a kind of lisping hybrid of Little Richard, Liberace, and a Martian interior decorator. Charlie narrated, beginning the sketch by disrespecting Prince several times with patronizing winks concerning his sexual orientation.

Murphy's narration addressed the night in the mid-1980s when he and his brother's crew ran into Prince and *his* people at a Los Angeles nightclub. "I like your work, Eddie Murphy," minced Prince/Chappelle.

To make cut-to-the-court, then-this-happened, then-that-happened, then the Murphy gang went to hang out and listen to music at Prince's Los Angeles mansion, whereupon the shrimpy host asked the Murphy gang if they'd like to play a game of basketball.

Murphy's group howled; Prince's threesome didn't even bother to change out of their finery, and their leader stayed in his platform shoes. The script read:

> **Charlie Murphy**: [*when Prince challenges them to basketball*] We can call it the shirts vs. the blouses.
>
> [*Prince looks on the verge of tears*]
>
> **Charlie Murphy**: I don't know what he was crying about. He knew where he got that shirt and it certainly wasn't in the men's department.

But alas, Charlie Murphy didn't go on to rub Prince into the ground. Instead he described how Prince, running his team's offense and swarming defense, had demolished Eddie Murphy's team of tough guys in a show of basketball finesse and power downright worthy of history.

"Well, I gotta admit . . . um . . . it was a good game," Charlie Murphy said he told Prince after the game.

"I wish I could say the same for you and your crew of flunkies," Prince/Chappelle replied. "*Bitches.*"

Then Prince made pancakes for all.

Quite a night, Charlie Murphy concluded, and if any viewers ever ran into Prince, they should bring up basketball, and "challenge him, ah-ight?" And then, with an appreciative nod to the master, he finished: "Make sure your crew is there to witness it, 'cuz you might get embarrassed."

Prince loved it. And the legend was sealed.

Years later Samuel L. Jackson posted a picture of himself on Instagram sitting next to Prince in floor-level seats at a Los Angeles Lakers game. Prince, looking away, does not even appear to be aware that Jackson is sitting next to him. In his description, Jackson wrote that he confirmed with Prince that night at the game that the Chappelle story was real, right down to the fact that he was wearing platform heels, which he termed "church shoes." (In point of fact, Prince told me, he'd changed into basketball shoes to play.)

Prince loved the skit, and so did the world. Another unexpected piece in the puzzle that would serve as his unlikely comeback from the ranks of the celebrity cartoon: He had rapidly descended from the pantheon of artistic geniuses to ridicule in music magazines, only a few steps up in celebrity gravitas from Pia Zadora or David Hasselhoff. Never mind *Purple Rain*—he was the shmuck who'd stricken his name, talent, and life into nothingness.

Prince continued to claim forever that he loved the skit, but the truth was, he came to loathe it within six months.

"It made me too sad," he said not long after it aired, as we readied to play a tame game of 21, the old man's game of accuracy in shooting.

"I wasn't great, like I used to be," he said mournfully. "It hurts too much."

But he loved the legend, Christ, he loved that legend.

Occasionally he'd summon up the grit to play an occasional two-on-two or three-on-three game of half-court basketball, if he felt his manliness depended on a show of wellness. Sometimes he'd play even though he knew he'd pay for it in immediate physical anguish. He loved the feeling of playing the game, being in *control* of the game, too much.

It was the only time, he said, he could get the noise out of his head—make the music stop playing, the dybbuk driving him forward shut up. It was the only time, he said, that he truly felt sane.

The only known footage of Prince actually playing basketball comes in the last minute of an almost-never-seen video of an almost-never-heard song, "Daisy Chain." Though Prince looks smooth, leading in an unusual style with his left hand as he shoots from afar, and driving straight for the basket for an impressive layup, look closely at the camera work. It is fine camera work.

The footage was shot in 2000, though the song wasn't officially released until 2004, the same year Prince was enshrined via Dave Chappelle and Charlie Murphy in the even-cooler-than-you-knew hall of fame.

As Fitzgerald explained when he wrote that "all life is a process of breaking down," he meant to describe two distinctly different forms of cataclysmic breaks.

There are, he began, life's quickly delivered blows—the safe falling from the sky, the drunk driver hitting the stranger, the baby with Pfeiffer syndrome 2—that provide the that's-obviously-the-reason rationales and narratives for why people crack, their souls flattened, forever damaged, especially if they can't bear grieving.

Those blows announce themselves with no warning, just the collapse of hope. Then, for Prince, after the death of his son, came an absence and silence so much more cavernous than even he had ever imagined. So numbing and lonely-making was the grotesque ordeal and stark reality of Amiir's life and death that, in Prince's case, I think his son's death should have been listed as one of the causes of his own.

"There is another sort of blow"—Fitzgerald wrote in the same essay chronicling his own spiritual and physical deterioration—"that comes from within."

Prince, too, suffered that other sort of blow, and it proved just as destructive—a silent, insistent erosion of the spirit that eventually killed him just as surely as the baby's death had. Though "not being able to dance or play basketball without soul-crushing pain" is probably not appropriate to include as a profound contributing factor on a death cetificate, in Prince's case it should be.

"You don't feel [the inner blows] until it's too late to do anything about it," Fitzgerald wrote, "until you realize with finality that in some regard you will never be as good a man again. . . . The second kind happens almost without your knowing it but is realized suddenly indeed."

In the eighteen or so months after Prince's son died, I saw the accumulated, full-force effect of this second kind of blow. Attempts to minimize the abuse to which he'd subjected his body were in vain: He could no longer follow the orders of the devilish dybbuk that lived inside him, forever ordering him on to dance like a funk dervish past James Brown, dribble like a court wizard past Walt Frazier. It urged Prince ever onward, upward, neglecting and ignoring all temporal pain in an attempt to quiet the incessant noise in his head that said, as he first described it in the 1980s, "You'll stop when I say you stop."

Prince addressed his
missives in the scrawl
of a third grader . . .

. . . though he'd been practicing
his florid Hollywood handwriting
since grade school.

"What's lost in the fire is found in the
ashes." Despite Prince's misanthropic
reputation, he knew the value of
friendship, how to say "thank you," and
that he didn't always have to be right.

After years remaining mute, *Rolling Stone* trumpeted, "Prince Talks: The Silence Is Broken." When the magazine reprinted the story after his death, the new headline read, "Inside the Pleasure Palace: In 1985, Prince finally opened up with a free-wheeling interview about God, sex, and his critics."

"Prince's Women," Wendy and Lisa, with the man they called "Fearless Leader," on the cover of *Rolling Stone*, 1986. Only Prince knew it, but the dream was already over.

Prince's last *Rolling Stone* cover story for fourteen years. At the dawn of the nineties, he was beginning to see thieves in the temple everywhere.

A Star Is Stillborn: "The Prince Rogers Trio," with Prince's piano man father John Nelson, a.k.a. "The Fabulous Prince Rogers," leading that night's curiously four-member trio.

Mattie Shaw, Prince's mother, 1976 Minneapolis Edison High School yearbook. Despite what Prince told the press, his mother wasn't a wanton, drug-addled creature who left hard-core pornography around the house. Instead, she was his beloved closest advisor, who worked as a social worker specializing in addiction problems for the Minneapolis School District, and schlepped Prince to his doctor's appointments through high school.

Prince, age twelve.

Prince, age thirteen, Bryant Junior High yearbook. "Poverty makes people real mean."

Prince, ninth grade, Minneapolis Bryant Junior High School yearbook. "I couldn't keep a girlfriend for two weeks."

Sixth man on Bryant's ninth grade basketball team and the end of one dream. He could beat anyone, he claimed, wearing "church shoes."

Community leader Bernadette Anderson's North Minneapolis house. One day her son André brought home Prince—and Bernadette let him stay.

"Grand Central," André and Prince's first band, on André's front lawn, 1975 (l. to r.) Linda Anderson (André's sister), André (Cymone) Anderson, Morris Day, Terry Jackson, Prince, and William "Hollywood" Doughty.

Prince, tenth grade, Central High School yearbook, the year his lifelong rage at basketball coach Al Nuness began.

He's a very kinky boy: Prince's ill-fated first show in front of Warner Records executives, Minneapolis.

Dr. Funkenstein's monster.

"Don't make me black."

"I Wanna Be Your
Lover"—First Soul
Number 1, First
Number 1 Gold Single.

"All the Critics Love You in New York": Revolution guitarist Dez Dickerson, bassist Brown Mark, unidentified, Prince.

The moves: The effect of growing up listening to Grand Funk Railroad and dancing to *Soul Train*?

"You talking to me?"

"I was expert at turning my back on my people, never to be seen again."

No shirt, no flats, praising Jesus.

Apollonia, Prince, *Purple Rain*, 1984.

From *Purple Rain*: Forty-plus years of landing on your heels from speakers and risers = double hip replacement surgery + opioid addiction.

Wendy Melvoin,
Lisa Coleman: "Wendy is
my sister," Prince said.
"Lisa and I are yin-yang.
When I frown, she smiles."

Morris Day stole
Purple Rain as leader of
the Time, "the only band,"
Prince said, "I was ever
genuinely afraid of."

Morris Day does subtle.

Prince, alone.

Prince, as con man Christopher Tracy in *Under the Cherry Moon*. The movie tied for the 1986 Golden Raspberry with *Howard the Duck* for Worst Picture—but the soundtrack went platinum and gave us "It Only Snows in April" and "Kiss."

A New Millennium. "I think I'm a lot nicer person now."

Mayte Garcia, Prince's eighteen-year-old princess bride and mother to their son Amiir—who would die only a few days after being born—all grown up and belly-dancing to her own tune.

Prince, 2009, north of fifty: what becomes a legend most?

"Paisley Park means where you can go to be alone." And so he was, at Flyoverland's Xanadu.

Minneapolis's Electric Fetus, Prince's favorite record store on the planet. In his last tweet, he enthused about the six records he'd just bought, including Stevie Wonder's *Talking Book*, Joni Mitchell's *Hejira*, and Santana's *Santana IV*.

"Baby, I'm a Star"—Prince's gold star on the wall outside First Avenue, the Minneapolis nightclub he made famous in *Purple Rain*.

This was no longer grief. It was despair. Prince now emanated a Grand Canyon of the grief he grew up with, along with the accumulated losses that, viewed close-up, made the workaday blues seem more akin to a bad case of the Mondays than the darkest night of the soul.

"Of course, all life is a process of breaking down": Fitzgerald's words could just as easily have been scribbled atop Prince's medical chart since he first seriously hurt himself, in 1984, on the *Purple Rain* concert tour. Just as he'd reached the mountaintop—it hurt. Then, soon enough, hurt too much.

A decade and a half later, in February 1997, he said casually over the phone in the middle of the night that he couldn't dance anymore.

Well, he *could* dance, but the price had become too steep. He'd hit the tipping point. His hips and ankles had been chronically aching for almost fifteen years, but until 1997, dancing still brought him more joy than pain.

And Prince loved dancing more than he loved playing the guitar, the piano, the drums. He loved dancing more than singing or composing. And the rapturous way he'd always described his ability to move his feet makes me think he even may have liked dancing more than fucking.

And though I truly know nothing about Prince and sex, I stand by that sentence, in all its bad taste. Besides intuitively guessing it's true, I think that in his death, many forget that the inappropriate— along with what was of questionable taste to the stolid citizens who made up the greater population he grew up with—was an important components to Prince's essence. He was a genius, but also a genius provocateur—and though I'm not 100 percent sure of *much* about Prince, I know he wouldn't want *that* forgotten.

Besides, it might really be true. He peddled tales to journalists early in his career about his precociousness at dancing or putting his fingers on the piano keys, at an age even more precocious than he placed himself in his tall tales about his sexual adventuring.

The whopper he told about his stepfather, Hayward, taking him to a James Brown concert in Minneapolis when he was ten, then placing him on the stage in the middle of Brown's set to dance with the master, is still repeated and printed, a sacred saga, a myth so good it almost *deserves* to be true.

The moment when I saw what had happened to Prince—that the silent, relentless blows upon his body had mounted and the bill had come due—came not while he was dancing, but when we were going to play basketball on the half-court he'd installed next to one of his studios, a space he often used to rehearse dancers.

In 1997 I went to play basketball three times with Prince at Paisley Park. I'd never liked going there; the place spooked me before it even existed. He's going to die in there alone, I continued to think, writing it down on one of the four-by-six index cards I always carry with me to take down stray thoughts or remember forgotten errands. I had no conscious notion, when I wrote that down, that dying alone was his greatest fear.

I still feel a shiver when I remember the moment in 1997 when I could see what had happened to Prince—that the physical damage that came with Prince's career had advanced to the point where—no matter how high he might rise again—the twinges he hid from virtually everybody, including me, had already announced their intentions to him. They would turn into pain that knew no bounds and would eventually play a major role in destroying him, never mind whether or not he got a single, double, or no hip replacement at all.

He'd been telling me since 1985 how much he hurt—that he was afraid on the *Purple Rain* tour he would hurt himself so badly that, he said, he "could just die out there, and nobody would notice."

He wasn't as open about it in the twenty-first century, but he was as good as opening his diary by telling me that in 2010 he had indeed had double hip replacement surgery. And there was that voice from 1985, on tape, talking of the dybbuk within, telling him, he said: "It doesn't matter if you're hurt. *I'll* tell you when you're tired. *I'll* tell you when you can stop."

It was nothing, it was everything: I saw that his plate tectonics had shifted, changing *something* in Prince's state of being, that first afternoon in 1997 when he decided he wanted to just shoot baskets, not actually *play* basketball, one-on-one. Huh?

Play the stationary game of 21—picking a spot to shoot from, then shooting—not the running, stopping, hand-checking movement of one-on-one *playing*?

Prince liked to play me for two reasons. First, he was so good that my cheat-to-survive strategies—premeditated for survival in ninth-grade freshman basketball, second nature after decades—playing dirty was simply the only way I knew how to play. Prince didn't mind *too* much; he was good enough to play right past my game, which he called "chop suey."

His superiority duly noted in about three seconds, he could put into action his real motive: putting on a clinic of the shooting, dribbling, and defensive styles of the great shooting guard of the middle of the 1970s, his own glory years of playing basketball. Of course he could have exhibited his skills at personifying the hardwood greats with anyone, but I was of his same exact vintage, and was that special kind of nerd who'd memorized the exact styles of the exact same ballplayers he had studied for news he could use.

I was the only person Prince knew who could tell the subtle difference between Walt "Clyde" Frazier of the great, early 1970s New York Knicks, taking the ball down the left side of the court, dribbling with his left hand, before cutting right and toward the basket for either a quick dish to a teammate or an easy layup for himself.

"Clyde!" Prince would yell gleefully back in the day before everything hurt as he sank the basket without even looking. "Nate!" he'd yell, imitating Nate "Tiny" Archibald of the mid-1970s Kansas City–Omaha Kings, driving past an army of Goliaths so quickly that he, too, could simply drop in a layup.

Did it matter if Prince could reprise exactly the outside shooting style of five-foot-nine-inch Calvin Murphy, the shortest member of the Basketball Hall of Fame and a member of the San Diego (and then Houston) Rockets during the years Prince was newly a teen-ager? No—unless there was someone there who knew what the hell he was talking about, the once-famous, now-obscure names of the past whom he wasn't simply imitating but personifying.

Anybody could feel a bone-chilling guitar lick; who knew the little-kick-of-the-legs-forwards was Dick Barnett of the long-ago New York Knicks, when Prince would shout out his name and per-form his ballet.

He had studied the greats when he still thought he could be one of them, but two decades later, it seemed I was the only one he could show off to. What good was it if Prince, a gifted student of the game, could drive, pull up, and shoot from the hip in precise imitation of "Pistol" Pete Maravich—since no one knew anymore how Pistol had shot, let alone that he got his nickname because he tossed the ball from the side?

Second and third, I amused him, because of the array of ball-handling and finger-spinning tricks I'd taught myself to perform as a little kid. Besides typing—and I don't mean writing, but accurately driving a Smith-Corona—I think it was the only talent on the planet in which I could outperform him

It made Prince laugh—and he wasn't an easy laugh. I'd learned at the same time I hung around with the black kids who congregated next door to my grandparent's tiny house by the Dairy Queen in North Minneapolis, going home to practice to untold gazillion replay-ing's of Brother Bones's 1949 version of "Sweet Georgia Brown," the theme song of the "magicians of basketball," the Harlem Globe-trotters, who did such magical things with the orb that playing the game itself seemed an afterthought, a handy device when one's talent at balling had peaked at age eleven. As a preteen, I'd purchased a 45-rpm record of Brother Bones from a Globetrotters program I'd gotten when my father had taken me to see their just-this-side of a minstrel show—and I was pretty good.

I kept up the basketball trickeration in my twenties as a form of meditation. I stopped in my late thirties, after breaking a leg and being bedbound for six months. My convalescence sapped me both of my need to stay in form, and—even worse—my desire to try.

F. Scott Fitzgerald's life dribbled away as he'd predicted, in one act in 1940, four years after he wrote about the crack-up that had left him feeling like a "broken plate" that could never again "be warmed on the stove nor shuffled with the other plates in the dishpan; it will not be brought out for company but it will do to hold crackers late at night or to go into the ice-box with the leftovers."

"The poor son of a bitch," Dorothy Parker reputedly said, gazing at Fitzgerald's embalmed body.

15

THE CRACK-UP, ACT 3:
A HAS-BEEN IS BORN, 1998

For this reason and that, Prince heard I'd broken five bones in my leg while Rollerblading, and might not walk even seminormally again. For six months I had to stay in bed, though after a few weeks I could hop about my apartment on crutches for a few seconds at a time.

I stared out the window. From nowhere Prince called me out of the blue in the middle of the day, just like real people in Minneapolis do, to inquire about my prognosis and offer his sympathies. We probably hadn't talked in four months, and I was both flattered and curious why he suddenly seemed so interested in me and my woebegone condition.

We talked about this and that, the Twins and the Timberwolves, and—yes, Prince—they gave me an unlimited supply of Percocet after surgery, of course. I was downright shocked when he said he was going to drive right over the twenty miles from Chanhassen and Paisley Park.

This was not in character. It would be no problem at all, he said, to drive over to the once-Utopian Minneapolis neighborhood he'd written about in the 1970s called Uptown, where I had lived forever, and was looted in the wake of George Floyd's murder. Now, I was surrounded by yuppies who lived in condos and worked for Target, or suburban tourists who'd come to the epicenter of Uptown—Lake Street and Hennepin Avenue—not to enjoy the colorful human menagerie that used to gather there, but to go to the shopping center that had popped up at ground zero in 1984, called Calhoun Square. Long ago, "Uptown," Prince wrote in his eponymous song, was his Mecca.

He'd been to my apartment but not for a few years, and for him to shlep so far to pay a little sympathy call felt . . . meaningful.

It wasn't.

He wanted my Percocet, which I'd mentioned I'd been given an unlimited supply of, among a dozen other topics we discussed over the phone that day (it was 1997). I hobbled to the door on crutches when he rang, but I didn't even have time to offer him a glass of water before he spied the white Walgreen's bottle of pills in my living room. Those pills would serve as my little helpers as I healed—that is, until my father demanded I be cut off within a week, when he saw me hobble on my walking sticks directly into a wall.

Prince gobbled a third of the bottle like they were M&Ms, and my heart sank. It was fucking true. I'd heard rumors for years that he'd been off and on heavy painkillers ever since the *Purple Rain* tour a dozen years before; we're talking the fall of 1984.

But no, I'd always bought the company line that he was as clean as a deacon, and I'd been on tour with him when not only doing drugs was a firing offense, but so was smoking a mere cigarette in his general vicinity. I was still a Marlboro Light man the last time I'd gone on the road with him, and I had to be careful to take a shower each time I was about to be in his vicinity so as to not aggravate the star.

I'd heard his patronizing sneers ever since I'd known him over superhero musicians who'd destroyed their lives with drugs—Charlie Parker, Sly Stone; he even looked down on Ray Charles and Miles Davis for their old junkie days: It was *weak*.

And here he was in my living room, looking as eager for my narcotics as Uptown's skankiest panhandler.

He hadn't been around in a couple of years; when I first knew him I would actually *see* him more. He'd never been big on adventures. While in Europe he never wanted to see the sites or museums; he was there—he was wherever—to work. In fact, in all the years I knew him, I think the only "sight" we ever went out and saw was this greasy old Las Vegas cemetery where Sonny Liston was buried.

Though Prince never *seemed* too interested in the world outside his purview, he actually always was, in general (except when he wasn't). Indeed, he liked the world, was once willing to go out, see, and listen. But more and more, being attuned to what was going on simply became less and less important. He was learning less, asking for fewer recommendations from friends, increasingly satisfied with whatever he ran into.

He had once learned all of classical music from Lisa Coleman, marveling that the theme to the movie *10* was actually Ravel's *Boléro*. I couldn't remember the last book I'd lent him because it seemed as if there'd been so many over the years, each redolent of another side of Prince.

He'd loved the book *Homicide: A Year on the Killing Streets*, by David Simon. In *Homicide*, Simon followed the "murder police" for a year—and woke Prince to the problems of Baltimore.

To appeal to Prince's inner con men I sent him *The Big Con: The Story of the Confidence Man*, David Maurer's classic 1940 sociological study of the art, science, and conscience behind the grift, as well as *"Yellow Kid" Weil: The Autobiography of America's Master Swindler*, the 1948 volume that served as the inspiration for the film *The Sting*.

And of course, there was Niccolò Machiavelli's *The Prince*, his 1532 treatise on . . . Machiavellianism.

There was *Pimp: The Story of My Life*, by Iceberg Slim, and to satiate his interest in golems, dybbuks, and the kabbalah, I'd sent him Joshua Trachtenberg's *Jewish Magic and Superstition*, a 2013 reprint of the 1939 classic that included incantations to make your own golem.

I could mention six other books that I sent him and why, but I was never sure what he'd read and hadn't.

I had a lot of *stuff* in my apartment, and he didn't know how I could stand the anarchy of so much . . . *stuff*. Stuff I'd collected, a lot during a lifetime of travels to assorted circuses. From childhood my baseball cards and autographs; from forever a funky T-shirt collection; an astonishingly strange group of bobblehead dolls of African Americans, sold at ballparks in the 1960s for a dollar each, now worth more than a thousand apiece.

I didn't pay big prices, I just got things along the way. I interviewed the artist Mike Judge soon after the launch of his debut effort, *Beavis and Butthead*, on MTV. He drew a picture of Butthead saying "Huh-huh" and signed it; it was free. I collected Holocaust material, material on African American as well as Jewish boxers, and general weirdness. Stuff like that.

My stuff was my version of stocks and bonds.

Wandering my apartment while I stared at the ceiling from bed, Prince was wowed that I had a minibat that had been signed by Tonya Harding, the infamous ice-skating antihero whose ex-husband had arranged to knock out her prime Olympic competition, Nancy Kerrigan, by smashing her leg with—a minibat.

Likewise, he seemed fascinated by the cigarette butt framed in my bathroom.

"What is that?" he asked.

"A cigarette butt," I said. "From either Sam *or* Dave."

"Wha'?"

I explained how in high school I'd gotten an assignment from the school paper to interview Sam & Dave, the great R&B duo responsible for "Soul Man" and "Hold On, I'm Comin'." Rumor had it there were about three separate Sam & Dave duos then touring various parts of the country, but I wasn't going to focus too much on that.

I was seated to wait in their dressing room, wowed by my admittance to their inner sanctum, me all of sixteen or seventeen. And then I spied it—in the standing ashtray, a Newport menthol. It had to be either Sam's—or Dave's.

I plucked it out of the ashtray sand and had somehow managed to keep it for all these decades, this cigarette butt.

Prince moved along the wall. Sometimes I did spend money on stuff; every time I got an advance for a new book, I'd buy something nice. And the nicest thing by far—I think I spent a grand on it—was my autographed copy of Billie Holiday's 78 rpm recording of "Strange Fruit." It was literally a signed record—she'd used silver nail polish to sign the label. Signed, sealed, and authenticated, it was mine.

For the moment.

"Th' fuck is this?" Prince said. "This what I think it is?" he asked, looking at the Billie Holiday–autographed record. "I still can't believe you said my mother sounded like Billie Holiday in that old article. Why'd you say that? She sounded good, but she was too happy a lady to really sing the blues."

"I didn't know any better," I said. "You said she was a jazz singer. My favorite jazz singer was Billie Holiday. All I wrote was she had a 'trace' of Billie Holiday in her voice."

"Don't *you* know?" I said. "You must have heard her sing."

"I never heard her sing," Prince said. "I remember being about five and asking her to sing to me, and she looked at my father and said, real proud-like, 'I don't sing anymore. Not in a long time.'"

It sounded a little pat, a little too cinematic, the "I don't sing anymore," part, I thought. But he was being dead honest: He had never heard her sing. "No," Mattie had told me twice, not seeing any irony, or choosing not to: "I didn't sing anymore." She didn't evince a nubbin of bitterness, but as usual, just pride in her son. "He's the singer in the family," she said. "In the whole world."

I couldn't see him from my bed, but I felt his silence. Billie Holiday, he finally said, had allowed herself to become "wreckage."

"She destroyed herself," he continued, "because she wasn't *listening*."

Well, that was an interesting sentence.

"What do you mean, she wasn't *listening*?" I asked.

But he didn't say a word.

He moved along to the next object: It was a poster for Lenny Bruce's last concert at the Fillmore West before he OD'd on heroin in 1966. "Bill Graham Presents," read the legend on the poster, and Prince's voice brightened, from the other room.

From the bedroom I told him one of my favorite Lenny Bruce routines, one of the ones that got Bruce in such trouble back in the day. It was the one about Jackie Kennedy crawling out of the back of the limousine in which her husband, the president, had been shot.

She wasn't going for help, Bruce said, she was "hauling ass to save ass."

"They always leave," Bruce said in the routine. "They always leave."

"That's the truth," said Prince.

"That's the truth," I agreed.

He looked around my apartment again: the bobbleheads, the baseball cards, the detritus of high and low American culture over the last century. Signed checks of the Jewish Godfather, Meyer Lansky. Signed first editions. Old board games from the 1960s; "Mousetrap" and "Yahtzee."

"How do you ever focus on anything with all this *shit* here?" he asked. "Man, you got to *focus*."

Nineteen years later he died. On almost exactly the first anniversary of his death, my apartment and everything in it burned down in what the fire department deemed an "unintentional electrical malfunction."

I hadn't been home; all I had were the clothes I was wearing and my laptop in my backpack. On that laptop were all the notes and tapes of Prince I'd transferred to my computer. For most of the previous year, trying to start this book, I couldn't bear to look at my notes or listen to those tapes.

Instead, I spent that time reading seemingly every article and book written about Prince.

And then everything burned down. That I was alive was a miracle. That my notes and recordings were still here was . . . something. I was stalling. I was fucking around.

I don't believe in ghosts, and I don't believe Prince was talking to me. And I believe in karma. And twenty years later, a year since he'd been dead, I could hear him say again in my mind's eye, "How do you ever focus on anything with all this shit here?"

I heard him say, "Man, you got to *focus*."

A week after the fire, I looked at the charred bookcase located a couple feet from where I was almost turned into a human s'more. Its contents had been immolated—everything I had kept on Prince over the years, that I'd just put on my computer. Sticking out of the bookcase was a sheet of white paper, burned around the edges, wrapped in flammable plastic.

It was the best letter he'd ever sent me; the only other one I had left was in the scanner at my parent's house. I finally understood the meaning of the old saw, "what's lost in the fire is found in the ashes." Whatever words he said, all I felt, was *start over*.

Or more accurately, *start*. If I believed in the spirits, I'd say he was telling me to write his fucking book.

"So all your shit burned up," I thought I might have heard someone saying a year after he died. "Now focus on what's in *there*." I looked at my laptop. All there was in there was *him*.

"I like Bill Graham," he then said back in 1997 amidst all my *stuff*, including a poster from Graham's old Fillmore West auditorium. "You know, he's the one who got me to come back to that Rolling Stones concert?"

Ah yes, the last time Prince ever opened for anyone, his two-day gig with the Stones, the J. Geils Band, George Thorogood, and Prince. After being metaphorically drawn and quartered, Prince had famously walked off the stage at the end of his set, got in a limo, and headed for a flight back to Minneapolis, never mind he had another date with the Stones two days later.

"What?" I called out.

"Yeah, Mick Jagger called, sorry Mick, and Dez Dickerson called, made some good arguments for coming back, but then Bill Graham got on the phone and just said, 'So kid, you'll be through in this business if you don't come back. No one will hire you. Which is fine, if that's what you want, if you don't care. But what are you going to do? Me, I got it all figured out. This concert-promoting thing doesn't work out, I can always go back to being a waiter in the Catskills. I was very good at that. What are you good at?"

Prince continued: "'This,' I said. 'That's it. I never had no job.'"

"'Well, kid,' he said. 'You'd better come back to Los Angeles and play your gig,' that Bill Graham said. And that's what I did."

I liked when he riffed on his stories, like he did in the old days.

But whether it was boredom with the language, or that the cumulative effects of fifteen years of painkillers had somehow dulled his locution, his words just didn't seem to flow as smoothly, as artfully, as they had when we'd first met.

He could be talking about seduction. Or about a critic: "Not long ago I talked to George Clinton, a man who knows and has done so much for funk. George told me how much he liked *Around the World in a Day*. You know how much more his words mean than those from some non-guitar-playing mamma jamma wearing glasses and an alligator shirt behind a typewriter?"

Yikes, did he ever love fashioning fine-sounding sentences regarding critics: "One time early in my career, I got into a fight with a New York writer, this little skinny cat, a real sidewinder," he once told me. "He said: 'I'll tell you a secret, Prince. Writers write for other writers, and a lot of time it's more fun to be nasty.'"

He could be philosophical: "Nobody can be what they are twenty-four hours a day," he said, "no matter what that is."

He admitted there were limits even to his ego and threw in an intriguing notion. Asked upon the release of *Around the World in a Day* why, for once, he hadn't put a picture of himself on the cover, he said:

> The cover art came about because I thought people were tired of looking at *me*. Who wants another picture of him? I would only want so many pictures of my woman, then I would want the real thing. What would be a little more happening than just another picture [*laughs*] would be if there was some way I could materialize in people's cribs when they play the record.

Twenty years before my fire, I nodded off from the narcotic pre-scribed for my shattered leg. Prince had been looking at my books. I woke up and Prince was gone. The book he'd been looking at, an autographed copy of Walt Frazier's *Rockin' Steady: Walt Frazier's Guide to Basketball and Cool*, had been placed neatly against my bookshelf.

Two months later I opened it to find Prince had underlined in light pencil and written in the margins of the book. It was a kind of manifesto of cool, seemingly ghostwritten by Prince in the voice of "Clyde" Frazier, Prince's very personification of cool when the book came out when he was fifteen.

That was the year that people said that Prince began acting most like an asshole. It was the pills, everybody whispered. He's back on the pills, heavy.

There were three notations bracketing Frazier's notes on what "cool" was.

First: "Cool is having an attitude, too, of how you carry yourself. Especially in pain. That's the time you really should be cool, because if you stay in the game, you don't want the other team to know how hurt you are. They'd try to take advantage of it. First I try to get under control. I know it's painful."

Second: "Cool is my style. I almost never show any emotion on the court. A guy might harass me, and it might be working, but if you look at my face, I always look cool. So, they never know what I'm thinking."

Third: Under the headline, "CATCHING A FLY WHEN THE FLY IS IN A SEATED POSITION": It's technique, not just amazing hand-quickness like most people think. Most people grab straight for the fly. That's wrong. You have to sort of curl your hand back-ward and slowly circle the fly. Then you come around in front of him. You have to be careful and patient, then move your hand for-ward and he'll fly right into your palm."

Ira Berkow, who won a Pulitzer Prize for his *New York Times* sports columns, had coauthored Walt Frazier's *Rockin' Steady* when he was a young reporter in the swinging 1970s.

Decades later, Berkow wrote how he might ultimately be remembered not for his Pulitzer but for *Rockin' Steady*, which he'd recently learned has been used as an introductory text in a Yale class on the African American experience. The book, Berkow was also tickled to learn, had been selected for the private White House Library collection.

"I happened to meet President Obama at a baseball game," Berkow remembered. "When we were introduced, this ardent basketball fan and player said to me, 'You wrote the book with Clyde.' I said I did. He smiled and said, 'With all the fashion and how to catch flies.' I said yes. He said, 'I bought the book when I was twelve years old.'"

Prince certainly knew the priorities of power.

Prince not only had his own color, he seemed to be in possession of his own year, one that came pre-equipped with its own numerical hook. He had recorded the song and album *1999* in 1982.

By the actual 1998, the coming end of the millennium seemed to promise that rereleasing the single was as close to a guaranteed hit as possible. As Ronin Ro wrote, Warner Bros. Records "reacted to growing fan and media nostalgia" by releasing the song to radio stations as a promotional single. Stations could be expected to keep the song spinning all year, and the voice mailboxes all over Warner's were stuffed to capacity with requests for fresh copies.

"Never," Bob Merlis told Ro, "has the simple servicing of a seasonally appropriate song generated so much press attention."

Indeed, merely showing up on planet Earth in 1999 should have counted as a victory lap for Prince. It wasn't.

Prince bitched, claiming in a statement that Warner's would reap the "bulk of the profits," saying that releasing "1999" again, even as a simple favor to radio stations, was an "absurd concept" that would be, he claimed ominously, "challenged." Warner's no longer gave a

shit and did nothing to promote the song all year—it was just a favor to radio stations. Said one spokesman: "It's our right to do this,
and we're doing it. But we don't begrudge him anything. He's a free
agent; he can do what he wants."

In early 1999 Prince released *1999: The New Masters* on his own
label, NPG (New Power Generation, after his backup band that followed the Revolution). Nobody, least of all Prince, seemed to care.
He was behaving erratically. He talked about rerecording all seventeen of the albums he'd recorded for Warner's, which would have
resulted in two catalogs of identical albums, even if each song was
done completely differently.

Meantime, despite having won his artistic freedom, his mind was
on returning to a major label, the radio, and a lofty perch on the
charts. Londell McMillan, the lawyer who'd helped emancipate him
from Warner's, now went about finding him a new deal with an apparent new devil.

The devil McMillan almost literally dug up wasn't of the ethical
character of the mensch Mo Ostin. Rather, it was the ancient Arista
founder Clive Davis, who'd been fired from his previous job at Columbia for, among other things, charging his son's bar mitzvah to the
company. Forget *mensch*—the finest compliment to another's character one can give. Davis, in Yiddish, was the template for something
worse than even just another record company—a *shanda*, a run-of-
the-mill moral disgrace.

That Davis was such a *goniff*—thief—as to dip his hand in the
company till to pay for his kid's passage into manhood meant more,
culturally, than merely staining his own kid's sacred religious rite.

The men Prince branded pirates at Warner Bros. Records—Mo
and Lenny—had long been viewed by the entire industry as the very
models of Old Testament moral rectitude, as well as executives com-
mitted to a sacred ethos of artistic license. Mo and Lenny spoke the
emmes—the truth's truth.

It was an industry in which statements on the order of "I was lying to you yesterday; today I'm telling you the truth" were deemed
reasonable guarantees of honesty. As Hunter Thompson put it: "The
music business is a cruel and shallow money trench, a long plastic

hallway where thieves and pimps run free and good men die like dogs. There's also a negative side."

Davis was nearing seventy, Methuselah-aged by record industry standards, and didn't bother to consult with his underlings after Prince played him a few tunes for a new prospective album. He loved the songs; Prince was Mozart, yada-yada. He proffered Prince a reported eleven million—plus the masters—for one album.

The result: *Rave Un2 the Joy Fantastic*. Davis had loved the album's first single, "The Greatest Romance Ever Sold," when he first heard it and promised Prince it would rocket to number one across the world. It didn't even make it onto *Billboard*'s Top 75 airplay chart.

The bromance was off, and Davis seemed to blame the artist for misinforming him about Prince's hit-machine possibilities. "I thought you'd be different than what I'd read about you," Ro quoted Davis as saying. "Everyone warned me."

Even before the record flopped, Prince's hardiest fans and supporters were shocked that he was so willing to make a deal—and such a profitable one—with an even worse group of slave masters than the ones he'd virtually sacrificed his career to in a battle to his own artistic and commercial death.

Facts were facts. Prince had released six albums between 1995 and 2001, and not one was a hit. The last, *The Rainbow Children*, a barely veiled, simplistic interpretation of his calling to the Jehovah's Witnesses, peaked at 109 on the American charts, scoring nowhere else in the world.

"Sugar daddy once, sugar daddy again," said Alan Leeds, hired by Prince after serving as James Brown's tour manager, apparently in reference to what Prince was actually looking for in lieu of artistic freedom. Leeds decided he'd had enough and left Prince after years of bringing order, rational thinking, logistical planning, and artistic taste to Paisley Park, Prince's tours, and the running of his label.

"He seems more money driven today than he was when I was working with him," Leeds continued, speaking to Ro. "I mean, Arista steps up with a deal and he runs like a thief. He wasn't broke."

He was, however, fatherless.

———————

John Nelson died old and cranky, still convinced he'd been cheated of his chance by the arrival of his first son from his second family. He was living in Prince's famous old purple house—where his son had recorded much of *1999*, entered the cultural pantheon, and made the rather shockingly unprepossessing-for-a-rock-star's domicile the first living symbol of his own famous self.

There John received, without a loss of face, dubiously earned royalty checks that kept him in snappy suits and self-respect for his questionable contributions to Prince-penned songs. Nicely recompensed, Prince not only paid his father's way, he kept up the kayfabe notion with the song credits that John Nelson had been an undiscovered Duke Ellington, whose failure could be explained away by applying Oscar Wilde's critique, writ large and career-long, that while his work had been great, the audience had been terrible.

He had his home, his pride, and though his Cab Calloway looks had long since withered, John Nelson could keep himself in the elegant plumage with which he'd dandied himself up back in the day when he actually *did* look like Cab Calloway, jived like the swingingest cat in town, and abandoned with impunity wives and children for ever-younger wives and newer children, just as Prince's grandfather had done.

When Prince was in one of his regular periods of rapprochement with his father, he'd cast an approving eye at how expensively his aged father was, as he still put it, either "threaded up" (as Walt Frazier had taught Prince to say as a teenager), or attired in "fine vines" (as Iceberg Slim had schooled him for another version of himself in the street classic, *Pimp: The Story of My Life*).

The estrangements between the father and son, however, came as regularly as the rapprochements: The pendulum swings of love and hate between abused famous son and abusive unworthy father seemed to circle their time together with the precise regularity of the Greenwich Mean Time official clock.

How could they not, with John Nelson regularly engaging in his "shenanigans," as Prince continued to call them, for example appearing without warning on tabloid shows like *A Current Affair*—as he did in 1998—divulging family secrets and even demonstrating at length on a piano how he, the Fabulous Prince Rogers, had in fact composed the song "Purple Rain" when his son was still so young he still had a first, middle, and last name?

How easy to see it as pure Freudian reenactment of unresolved, wholly unexamined trauma, with Prince coming back for more of the same abuse he'd suffered as a child, when his gifts were perceived almost as a threat, his talents seen as weapons by a bitter, unrepentant father. Prince appeared doomed to repeat the past by refusing to learn from it.

And yet he was mindful. He *did* leave an examined life—obsessively, remarkably so—except when obsessively, remarkably, not. He put it into words, into song, he laid it right there and he talked about it

There was that 1995 song "Papa," with lyrics about a father stuffing his four-year-old into a closet, the child bleating apologies that he won't do some unspecified misbehavior again.

And then he'd veer back.

I thought the words he'd used over the years, so telling I asked Prince to put them on the record after we'd finished our 1985 interview and continued tooling around Minneapolis in his father's old mint Thunderbird. He was still living in the purple house himself at that time. In fact, it was the purple house that taught him, he said, about what it means to have an old man who is also living by the beat of music, of jazz, of his bag, man. (Yep, he said it.) Sounded nice in 1985; by the time John Nelson died in 2001, the pendulum had swung dozens of times. Prince could have sold his purple house at multiples of its actual worth—Prince collectors were as devoted as Bob Dylan keepers of the shrines. (Indeed, Dylan's modest boyhood home, 193 miles north in Hibbing, Minnesota, hadn't sold from a listing in the *Hibbing Daily Tribune*, but on eBay.)

Prince preferred to have his old house, now his father's, immediately bulldozed. He did the same to the Toronto mansion he'd lived in with his second wife, Mani, in her hometown, upon their divorce in 2005, after five years of marriage.

Alrighty then (as we say in Minneapolis when nothing more needs to be added).

But he didn't want to knock Mattie Shaw, the *real* Mattie Shaw, down or pretend she wasn't there. He *needed* his mother.

Mattie was talking to John by the time he died in 2001, and she attended his funeral, accompanied by his replacement, Hayward, whom Prince greeted and treated warmly.

Mattie, who'd recently had a kidney transplant, died only six months later. Prince was at her bedside when she died, and he was distraught for months afterward. He'd never stopped asking her for advice and guidance; and she'd never stopped being as proud as punch, as Minnesota's own Vice President Hubert Humphrey used to say, of her son.

No matter the trash he'd talked about her at the beginning of his career; hoo-ha so vile I still can't believe he said it, and she died not knowing—I'm pretty sure—that many of his insane tales had gone into the permanent record. These stories still resonated and were retold. She was a bad woman, a jazz singer, and she abandoned her son, but not before introducing the young boy to hard-core pornography (and the horrors of her non-existent drug addictions).

Mattie Shaw retired after twenty years as a social worker in the Minneapolis school system, where she specialized in addiction issues. But let somebody else tell you about her. I'm biased. I only met her—I'd guess—five times. But she was classy.

Prince was devastated when she died in 2001. By now our relationship took place more over the phone. I still saw him—I lived so near his clubhouse of Rudolph's that when he was looking for company my face was acceptable. But our time together was different.

The century was finally over, and the 1990s had not been kind to Prince. He'd entered the decade as the highest-flying Wallenda on the circus high-wire of show business, art, and culture. By the end of 1999, a year he should have owned, he was, wrote *Rolling Stone* in a quick, two-sentence dismissal of his decade: "Off the deep end . . . settling into a routine of haphazard albums with two or three good songs apiece."

Alas, by 1999, Prince had come to believe his kayfabe life was reality. And when the kayfabe becomes realer than what's real—when you can't tell the kayfabe from what's authentic in your life—you're well on the road to the profound showbiz phoniness, which, say what you will about Prince, he'd never before been party to.

But he'd fallen in love with his own kayfabe. He was a mark for his own gimmick. Prince had a delusion of grandeur; He believed he was, in fact, the kayfabe "Prince," a false construct he'd been building since junior high school.

So mummified was he in the notion of his own particular form of badness that he went so far as to sue to shut down half a dozen fan sites and fanzines. It was an every-hour occurrence to sue one's enemies in the music business—but one's fans?

As the century turned, it was clear that Prince had outsmarted himself. Prince not only had his own color, he owned his own year, and seemingly his own city. If his hometown was fixed in the public eye beyond its own borders for anything, it was usually him. (Alas. Even Minneapolis was kayfabe: by 1999 he'd taken up residence in Spain. As always, he returned.)

Record companies wouldn't dare try to play him to their own advantage; instead Prince played *himself*, the cardinal sin of the streets in his Iceberg Slim–pimp persona.

He was a dick, putting on record willfully ignorant, self-righteous condemnations of such righteous souls as John Hammond, the buzz-cut Yalie, who during a remarkable tenure at Columbia signed the unknown Billie Holiday, Bob Dylan, and Bruce Springsteen.

Geniuses aren't necessarily smart; it's not breaking news. However, Prince was *so* smart that he could make you think that he was the stupidest human being you'd ever met. True, he did, during the course of his thirty-nine-year career, make some of the stupidest decisions in both the show and the business aspects of show business history. But those boneheaded moves Prince made weren't coming from a place of stupidity.

Where those idiocies came from, was, I believe, the exact same place as his genius. Prince could seem, as they say, a few French fries short of a Happy Meal.

He would never be happy again, not really, like he'd once been—*sort* of happy. Call him crazy, but he would not be a joke. He could stand failure as long as he failed on his terms, which were anyone's to guess. But he would not be laughed at. Nor, I found, could I laugh with him like I once could. He was no longer, when comfortable in his surroundings, exceptionally funny. If he were the patient in the "Operation" board game, someone or something was slowly removing his funny bone.

With only his own genius to rely on—and he never doubted *that* he vowed to get back on top, in his kayfabe world, to "get over" again. Still, so what if he never stopped believing in himself, his detractors sneered, where had that gotten him? By the end of the century he was willing to talk to Larry King for a full hour. To perform such necessary chores, which he saw as humiliating—Larry King! For an hour!—he had to believe in something beyond himself, well, at least 15 percent of the time.

He would be a witness for Jehovah.

Denise Matthews, once the Prince protégée Vanity—the very poster child of the libertine life—had long been a born-again Christian. And she thought his conversion to the apocalyptic religion was a function of Prince simply needing to believe—in *anything*.

And so, at the end of his appearance on Larry King's show in 1999, Prince introduced his friend Larry Graham, former bass player for Sly and the Family Stone, who had revolutionized how the instrument was played, inventing the "slapping" style. Prince had never not idolized Larry Graham, even preferring his work in Larry's own Graham Central Station to what he'd done for Sly.

And so, with Larry as a mentor, he began reading the Bible again. On Tavis Smiley's show on the Black Entertainment Network, and other venues, he later dated his true conversion to 2000. He'd been reading the bible with Graham, and finally found "the truth."

For one with such a lifelong devotion to deception—be its motive malevolent, dinking around with reporters, muddying his own history, or just for fun—it was a notable find.

16

THE NEW MILLENNIUM:
YOU GOTTA SERVE SOMEBODY—
JEHOVAH AND BOB DYLAN'S RABBI

Prince had actual human feelings himself, of course. He was deeply emotional; those songs and brilliant lyrics came from somewhere. "I love you now more than I did when you were mine"? ("When U Were Mine") Ouch! "It's been seven hours and fifteen days/since you took your love away." ("Nothing Compares 2 U") Yikes!

The man-child had definitely been stung by forces well past his father. But by whom? When? By what?

Other people's feelings? One reason he had *time* to be a genius was that he didn't think about it, or them, all that much. Or at least the first half of his life.

Prince could always put on a show. The hits may not have kept a-comin' like they once did, but what he somehow kept—a spark of his humanity—was a good deal, at least for those who actually knew him. Sadly, by the end there weren't many—he had multiples more protégés than peers—and most of them didn't know one another. You know who you are, even if you don't know why.

Prince's genius, the gravitational forces of too much abuse, pain, and much talent had put him in a developmental pressure cooker that turned him toward narcissism, first as a survival mechanism, then a lifestyle, then as life itself.

He would really begin to learn, or care, about other people and their needs starting around forty. Yet even then, his multiple personae, kayfabe and real, did battle with how he should best present himself to the world. He gave away instruments and computers. He funded libraries and school lunches. He gave a million dollars a year to the Minneapolis Urban League. And he didn't care that his philanthropic efforts, even though they dwarfed most celebrities', were kept as quiet as if they were his most lethal secrets.

But eventually he tried. He hugged long-lost friends. He talked nostalgically once in a while. And it saved his life, long before an overdose of fentanyl took it. I believe he suicided intentionally or at least passively. Not because he was chasing a high or partying, but because everything hurt too much and he had lost so much of what he treasured. He truly no longer gave a fuck.

But before he got worse physically, he got better mentally. He became a *person*. People weren't *all* beings placed before him specifically to take away what was his and what he'd earned, he let me know, as if it would be as much a lesson for me as it was for him.

Not *everyone,* he'd realized, had bullied him as a kid, teasing him as "the Great Gazoo." Still, there are those troublesome charges from around the turn of the twenty-first century: He'd made homophobic slurs (hard to tell if true, the reporter was not allowed to take notes), and also demanded that Wendy Melvoin renounce her gayness and half-Jewishness and join the Jehovah's Witnesses before he'd consider a reunion tour with the Revolution. Wendy Melvoin hasn't told a tale in her life; she wasn't going to begin *there*.

Except. Except talking to him then, he sounded lost, not found, and he didn't speak with the authority of someone who'd found a fun new bully pulpit from which to command his underlings. He dated his spiritual comeback to the start of the new millennium, and by 2004 he'd won, or fought to a stalemate, or annoyed his enemies so that he could declare he'd won all his battles, and was his own man.

He marveled to himself, friends, and audiences how he'd once been so bad, so naughty!!

He was a long way from authoring little ditties named "Head" and "Soft and Wet," let alone playing a song he titled "Jack U Off," wearing high heels and lingerie.

Yet that was 1981. It was a great gimmick to get over, as pro wrestling parlance has it, and it took only four more years before Tipper Gore and her Parents Music Resource Center, in their battle to get music labeled for age-appropriateness, named Prince's "Darling Nikki," his paean to female masturbation, as the filthiest song on a list known as the "Filthy Fifteen." (He also wrote number two on the list, "Sugar Walls," sung by Sheena Easton and agreed with Tipper Gore that his albums should have labels.)

A lot of milk had been spilled since he was the nastiest lad in the land—a lot, a lot. But in 2004 he would achieve what he thought was his greatest victory.

It wasn't just completing his comeback. After a decade plus mostly spun off into the twilight zone, by 2004, he was back on the cover of *Rolling Stone*, elected to the Rock and Roll Hall of Fame, had the highest grossing tour of the year, clocking in at $90.2 million, and released *Musicology*.

After willfully jumping from the mountaintop, he'd climbed back up. But his biggest thrill, he said, was that in 2004 he disappeared from history.

If only I'd known back when that I'd seen the truth immediately. But alas, I hadn't a clue that being given half of a real peek at Prince and his life had given me all the clues within half an hour of talking one-on-one with him to figure it out—the real Prince story. One would have to have been a nitwit not to have realized one'd just been presented with the true, largely all-explanatory saga when we met, and I was a nitwit not to see it until he'd been dead two years.

I'd been wearing the ruby slippers on my feet as to the "story" of Prince; I was wearing the magic key around my neck. I just didn't know it. All I knew were the dimensions of those thousands of pages of papers in the living room, sorted and re-sorted into logical piles so often they were no longer sorted at all.

Two years after he died, thirty-three years after we'd first talked, I was still lost.

I couldn't stand looking at these pages anymore. I knew he hadn't cheated either history or his story.

Jehovah's Witnesses. I know he could play the modest man known as "Brother Nelson" at the assembly halls where members gathered to pray and discuss the Bible. I don't mean pretend, I mean play, inhabit the persona, personify, the way I thought he could personify an actual friend, say, 15 percent of the time.

He had his swear jar but swore. Jehovah's Witnesses are not supposed to be political, but as he aged, Prince, you might say, got woke. Jehovah's Witnesses are not supposed to elevate themselves above others, but a huge hunk of Prince didn't even really exist until he became famous.

His birthday bashes continued, though observing birthdays in any form was forbidden by the followers of Jehovah. He had double hip replacement surgery, supposedly prohibited because of the blood transfusions the surgery requires. However, I also read of hospitals where certain distinguished Witnesses could go, knowing part of the (expensive) deal was that court orders would be sought by the hospital's administration, guaranteeing the Jehovah's Witness would be "forced" to accept blood products.

No one asked any questions, it seemed, certainly not me, except George Benson, himself a devout Jehovah's Witness, who was recording early in Prince's conversion at Paisley Park.

Ricky Peterson, a member of several of Prince's offshoot bands over the years, told the Minneapolis *Star Tribune* that Benson was not impressed by Prince's fealty. According to Peterson, "[Benson] said, 'I don't know about our boy. I don't think our boy's going to make it.' He couldn't get past the part of Prince cussing and trying to get religious after doing a song like 'Sexy MF.' No one knew what Prince was doing."

I bought his devotion, as much as I bought anything he actually believed in. The part of him that was a Jehovah's Witness was not kayfabe. He couldn't have kept it up even that long if he'd been playing a pro-wrestling character. I've met Larry Graham several times, his wife, his children, and they are delightful. I've heard Graham preach and found him to be real.

I just don't feel qualified to judge any religion but my own. I don't know what I don't know. I spent two weeks studying nothing but Jehovah's Witness putative doctrines—and in the end, I was left no more certain about the meaning of it all than the three words Robert Frost said were all he was sure of after a lifetime of life: "It goes on."

Like all his conversions—and basically every new enthusiasm in Prince's life—I charted his true devoutness to his new calling at about 15 percent of his being. No disrespect meant; that was just as much as his compartmentalized soul could accommodate of anything. The contradictions began immediately, though no one seemed to notice.

By 2003, he was tagging along occasionally as I worked on a book about kabbalah and met with a handful of Hasidic rabbis in St. Paul. "Do you believe in reincarnation?" he'd asked one rabbi with a beard to his chest, a dozen children, and the distinction of being the only Hasidic rabbi to ever appear in "Random Notes," *Rolling Stone*'s gossip column.

This rabbi, as it happened, was responsible for reconverting Bob Dylan back to the Judaism of his birth from his foray into evangelical Christianity. Prince seemed unimpressed that this man, who looked like he'd been animated off a box of Smith Brothers' cough drops, had blown the mind of the mind of his generation.

He said he'd like to visit the old rabbi. His first test question was:

"Do you believe in reincarnation?" he asked, as a tryout.

"I believe you can be reincarnated in your own lifetime."

Prince, satisfied, went on to ask questions during the coming weeks, combing the kabbalah and his own life. Had he, Prince wondered, created a monster in Morris Day? A golem—the monster on which Mary Shelley based Dr. Frankenstein's creation—based on the kabbalistic giant with no soul who destroyed his maker?

And a dybbuk—the dislocated soul with no physical being who haunted the souls of the unlucky. Could that be the voice inside him that had forever been pushing him on to do more, more, more, no matter how tired or hurt he was?

And he wanted to know about fame. The rabbi was a real-deal Hasid, whose outreach and willingness to engage with the real world had brought more than a few celebrities to his door in times of dread. "Why don't you move to Los Angeles, and become a celebrity rabbi?" Prince asked, honestly curious.

The rabbi stroked his beard and stared Prince down—a virtually impossible task—I'd never before seen anyone overpower Prince with silence. That was Prince's shtick.

"Los Angeles is a wonderful simulation of real life," the rabbi finally said.

"Yeah?" Prince shot back. "Well, then what about rabbis in Los Angeles?"

The rabbi stared him down again, this time for seven minutes and seventeen seconds, before saying: "They are excellent simulations of rabbis."

Prince laughed, for what seemed like the first time in a year.

Meantime, back in Chanhassen, he continued his Bible studies with Larry Graham, and lectured everyone, it seemed, within his purview. He left me alone: For the first time the notion that he might be an actual friend crossed my mind—he knew I'd lost 98 percent of my family in the Holocaust, and he seemed to sense, for perhaps the only time I knew him, not to go there.

I am a coward, except when I'm not—such as after I'd heard what Prince had told Wendy Melvoin about renouncing her Judaism. It was repulsive, as awful as his demanding that Lisa and Wendy condemn their sexual orientation. I waited two months for his next call, wanting to know the answer to one question: Was it true?

"Yes," he said softly.

I hung up.

He called back and apologized—only the second time he'd ever said "sorry" to me.

Prince and the Hasidic rabbi stared at each other. The rabbi gently stroked his gray beard, which reached his chest. Prince seemed to be trying to psych out the Lubavitch clergy by throwing faux daggers with his stare. The rabbi seemed very calm.

We'd gone into his study and sat down on industrial-looking gray chairs that appeared to have been bought from a used–office furniture store that in turn had gotten it from a high school principal's office, circa 1971. To the immediate left of the desk sat a fax machine that beeped in newspaper clips, typewritten pages, and scrawled notes, written in both English and Yiddish.

"How have you been?" the rabbi asked. "Have you been reincarnated?"

"I don't know if I'm a good person or bad person," Prince said, ignoring the question.

The rabbi thought a moment, chin in his palm, before saying, "The point isn't whether you're a good person or a bad person— you're a person and we're stuck with you."

Prince laughed.

Quiet and gloom soon descended again upon the room.

"How do I repent?" Prince asked.

"You want to repent? For what?" the rabbi said, lightening the mood Prince had brought into the room. "Laugh. Dance. Make fun of yourself. Make fun of God if you want—in the right way. Don't be too reverent about life. We have enough of that, everybody saying they have all the answers. If you want to make fun of rabbis, do that, too, me included. I do."

"I made a lot of money off the profane and blasphemous," Prince said.

"Just because someone is profane doesn't mean they are not wise enough to have left behind a valuable commentary," the rabbi responded. "Have you left behind a valuable commentary?"

"I don't know what I'll be leaving behind," he said. "That's the thing."

Christ, I hadn't heard him sound this unsure of himself *ever*, and I never would again.

Prince asked him about people coming to the rabbi wanting to kill themselves. "You must have talked to a lot of people who come over who want to commit suicide," he said.

The rabbi nodded.

"What do you say?" Prince asked.

"They come and tell me, 'My life has no meaning, my family counts for nothing, I'm a terrible human, I've accomplished not a thing,' the usual. And I say, 'Why stop there? Why not stick around and at least come up with a full list. You're also boring, unpleasant, sloppy, you're a terrible friend, you aren't funny . . .'"

Prince laughed.

The rabbi noted his reaction. "They laugh, too. That usually gives them the distance to see that the world is not revolving around them."

And then he told the rabbi about John Nelson, the abuse, his inability to write him out of his life. The rabbi launched into a parable.

"A king's son once went astray from his father. The king sent a messenger to order the son to return home. The young man angrily refused, saying, 'I cannot.' Finally the king sent another emissary. This time the message from his father was, 'Return as far as you can—and I will come to you.'"

Pause.

"Would your father come to you, meet you halfway?"

Prince refused to answer. Finally, he changed the subject. "How do you do good if you've got . . . what is that devil inside a person called?"

"A dybbuk."

"What if that dybbuk keeps you from doing good?"

"God needs your good deeds, done your way. It's okay being a schlemiel, if that's what you are. You do good as best you can."

"A schl . . . ?" Prince asked.

"An idiot," the rabbi responded. "What are you?"

"Prince."

"Prince of what?"

"Myself. Of my art. Of my world."

"And you're satisfied with that?"

"Sure."

"Good," the Hasid continued. "The only blasphemy that exists is to say, 'If only'—'if only I were born like this, if only I had this kind of parents, if only I were someone else!'

"God needs you to do good, but do it your way," the rabbi repeated. "That's your purpose. Even if we'd been granted our 'if onlys,' we'd still end up exactly as we are, struggling with the same problems of being good and moral in a world that still needs fixing."

"Look," he said. "There is a statement in the Talmud that the sages took a vote on existence, tallied the results, and decided it would actually be preferable for a person not to be born. Because life is a struggle. So the sages said it would be more convenient if a person didn't come into the world in the first place.

"But now that we are born, the sages said we, each on our own, struggle to be good. The foundation of a purpose of life is the absolute conviction that when God creates human beings he doesn't do it in masses. He does it one person at a time, one face at a time. Every life, every soul, is handpicked. Each person has a mission, a purpose, a function that no one else has. Without that conviction, nothing we say about the meaning of life will have any meaning at all."

Prince nodded his head, in seeming agreement. "So how many Gods are there?" Prince said. "As many as there are ways to pray?"

"Let's say that you are at the airport. Everywhere I go, it's usually on Northwest. So if somebody asks, 'Why don't you take Southwest?' I say, 'I'm sure it's a wonderful airline; it takes you where you want to go, which is Florida. But I want to go to New York.'

"It's the destination we're talking about, and the destination for me is Judaism. Everybody talks about the 'true religion.' As far as I'm concerned, every religion is 'true.' If I were interested in enlightenment, my destination would be Buddhism, and I'd have to fly another airline, maybe switch planes to another hub. If my destination was simply to get to heaven, somewhere safe from Satan, my destination would be Christianity."

Prince said nothing. The rabbi went on.

"I recently ran into a Jewish boy I hadn't seen in many years. He was all grown up now, and I asked, 'How've you been? What's going on?'

"And he said, 'Oh, I've become a Buddhist.' I asked him how come, and he said, 'To get closer to God—isn't that great?'

"And I said, 'Well, that's nice, but how do you know that He wants you any closer? Maybe you're close enough. Maybe you've gotten too close and He needs you to back off a little bit, because you're cramping His style.'"

Prince was getting better and better at showing people he cared. He hugged people. He remembered old friends' names, or at least acknowledged the old friends' presences. The first thing Prince had to do was start over, or at least play nice, or at least show up and put on a little show for the folks. Grammys. He'd had to lobby or at least play the good soldier to get into the Rock and Roll Hall of Fame.

But still there was that ever-present buzzing in his head. "I work a lot, and there's not too much time for anything else when I'm trying to stop the pinballs from pinging in my head."

17

"WHILE MY GUITAR GENTLY WEEPS"

Prince's three minutes of work during the supergroup playing of "While My Guitar Gently Weeps" during the 2004 Rock and Roll Hall of Fame induction? I'm not exactly alone in thinking it remains the single most fantastic example of an entire all-star band being blasted off the stage by a single entity, as well as the most illustrative single example of all the baddest parts of Prince melded together to watch in one.

All these years later, it just doesn't seem to matter that at the time Prince was largely reviled for taking what was supposed to be a three-hankie homage to George Harrison, who was being inducted posthumously—and made the occasion entirely about himself. (Such is revisionist history, which haunts almost all of Prince's career.)

But why? Prince was being inducted as well that year, so doesn't *that* count?

Luckily, a taped version of that performance exists, which as of this writing has been downloaded from YouTube eighty-three million times.

Prince was severely on the outs with the music business in the time before he was elected to the Rock and Roll Hall of Fame in

2004. His election was not a slam-dunk; he had alienated *everyone* along the line.

And of course, George Harrison was inducted posthumously, and of course Prince was included in the grand band assembled onstage to honor the late Beatle with "While My Guitar Gently Weeps." Now, natch, it is considered one of the great guitar performances of all time, but at the time it drew a decidedly mixed reaction, especially when Prince seemed to dispose of his guitar in cavalier fashion at the end.

It was great to be there, to bear witness to the hypocrisy.

It was the first real field trip I'd made—well, not *with* Prince but *because* of Prince.

What we did have instead of otherwordly adventures was *code*, Prince and I had always agreed—using the word itself as a code— aping the dialogue spoken in a particular favorite episode of *The Wire* between Bunk, the lovable, capable, morally ambiguous black Baltimore detective yakking the *emmes* of life with Omar, the somehow-righteous drug dealer whose wares he garnered by rob- bing and often blowing away other drug dealers, but who would never scratch a civilian.

Omar was Prince's, mine, and much of America's favorite char- acter on the hit show, and we'd repeated the dialogue for years after the episode first ran in 2006.

"A man must live by a code," Bunk said to Omar, sitting at the cop's desk, both approvingly listening to a drug lord who *would* hurt a civilian being viciously beaten by frontier justice cops in an interrogation room.

"*Indeed*," agreed Omar.

The code Prince and I agreed on at this point—why I was there— had to be our adoption of his definition of cool. "Cool is when you can walk into any room and not be afraid to look anybody in the eye," he said.

I agreed. And there was one person, an editor, in that Rock and Roll Hall of Fame induction ballroom that I couldn't look in the eye for reasons having to do with what I originally thought was a friend's betrayal, but actually had nothing to do with me. Putz.

So big deal. I dealt with it.

After hiding out for most of the evening I gained admittance backstage and was only several yards away when Prince threw that guitar up in the air, the guitar no one saw come down. It's not that I chose to *believe* that guitar did not come down—it did *not* come down.

It was a kayfabe life, maybe it was a kayfabe guitar. Maybe he was even a kayfabe friend, which at least would be *some* sort of friend.

Not that he acknowledged me beyond a quick mumble of "It's done?" as nonchalantly as if he were Tony Soprano, quizzing a button man if he'd completed an assigned whack, please, no details.

"Yes," I said.

"So you're cool?" Prince said.

"I'm cool," I said.

"Some things call for revenge," Prince said in conclusion, still part dirty street fighter of the sucker punch and quick-run strategy that had kept him alive, dangerous, and relatively unbeaten, even at five foot two on the playgrounds of North Minneapolis.

But those had been different days, thirty-five years back, before the blizzard of guns and drug money had come with the national gangs like the Vicelords and Rolling 666s who'd come north, mostly from Chicago, and set up in Prince's old neighborhood. The predictable quickly rising corpse count of mostly young African American males gave a *New York Times* editor license to plant a headline above a front-page story about the phenomenon by redubbing Minneapolis "Murderapolis."

Not even my late grandfather would have been safe anymore, never mind his status as the neighborhood "Wine Jew"—the English-free peasant white man who went door-to-door on Christmas Eve giving away Mason jars of his homemade juice to his darker-hued Gentile neighbors.

The Wine Jew's secret-recipe Mogen David–like old-country concoction had originally been meant for sacramental wine for his synagogue. It was a happenstance that had earned him a government exemption from prohibitions during Prohibition against fermenting grapes.

The runoff—let's be honest, several illegal batches—had always gone to his Christian neighbors as a goodwill Noel gesture.

But he'd kept making his brew, even when the "MD" the bulk of his patrons now used to compare his wares to meant "Mad Dog," not "Mogen David." By the time Prince was inducted into the Rock and Roll Hall of Fame in 2004, all that was left of the operation was his more-than-a-century-old winepress kept in my father's suburban garage.

When I found his ledgers after he died, the name "Nelson, j." had a check next to it for wine every year.

But who cares? Not with the greatest performance I'd ever seen going on around me. The magazines covered the cover of "While My Guitar Gently Weeps" by the all-star band like the Zapruder film, cutting it down to microseconds.

Altogether, calculated *Newsweek* in its special Prince commemorative edition, his solo took 160 seconds total, "during the Rock and Roll Hall of Fame induction of George Harrison, which cemented his status as one of the best guitarists of all time."

"At 3:23," the cultural website uproxx.com noted, "Dhani Harrison [George's son] looks to the side of the stage and smiles, knowing that *something special is about to happen*."

Time magazine read the moment as: "The full watch draws into sharp relief the fact that a true god is entering your life at the 3:24 mark and doesn't leave it until the video ends."

Time goes on:

• 3:24—"Let's talk about that mark. Prince has been onstage all along."

The entertainment website *uproxx* charted the time at:

• 3:30—"Prince, dressed like a Dick Tracy character, makes his presence known with the first notes of the solo. Eyes closed, head lifted, he is master of the strings. His guitar is weeping. Everything makes sense."

- 3:37—"Prince is getting angry? Something is changing. Prince is still staying within the song and its mortal boundaries, but you can feel the tide coming."

Yahoo Entertainment also had an eye on the stopwatch, and noted that at

- 3:45—"Prince played more slow blues bends that led into a speedy ascending then descending fret run."

Time noted that at:

- 3:56—"Then Dhani Harrison smiles as he looks left, and Prince steps forward. For the next 30 seconds, you're in the Rock and Roll Hall of Fame normalcy zone. Keep going. . . ."

Five seconds later in the performance, *Time* noted:

- 4:01—"Prince does this pinch-harmonic solo that lets you know it is f—king on. These kind of solos are almost always bad—if anyone else were playing over a Beatles song, it would be straight trash. But this is Prince, so it's incredible. Then he heads into these bended notes that echo the original version's solo. It's haunting and sweet and distinct. With that behind him, Prince turns to Petty and Harrison and gives them a look. It's almost like he's saying, 'You have no idea what you're in for.' He's right."

Time goes on:

- 4:56—"During a lull, Prince gives Petty a look that tells us he knows exactly what he just did."

And on:

- 5:05—"Deep down in a finger-tappy, Van Halen–y section, Prince delivers some of history's best guitar face. He is feeling it because everyone is feeling it—and he is everyone."

Picking up the clock is *uproxx*:

- 4:15—"The guitar has moved on from weeping to screaming in ecstasy."

Yahoo's commentary on the moment:
"Even when Petty started singing 'I look at you all' at the 4:18 mark, Prince remained the center of attention, turning more string bends into rapid-fire axe excursions before transcending the conventional and entering the sublime."
Continues *uproxx*:

- 4:29—"This is how Obi Wan felt in his prime."

Time resumes its commentary at:

- 4:33—"He does this move with his guitar that looks like he's reloading a shotgun. I've seen other people do it. I saw Bruce Springsteen do it during "Badlands" in concert. I've seen Slash do it in videos. It's a cool move if you are cool. Prince is the coolest, so no one will ever look cooler doing it than this."
- 4:35—"Prince now has control of the song. It is his, and the legendary musicians are no longer sharing the stage, they are guests of Prince."

Time:

- 4:39—"Every time I watch the next ten seconds, I well up with tears. This is how I see it":
  * Prince, mid-solo, turns to face Petty and Harrison and makes eye contact.
  * Petty, for a moment, looks miffed. Maybe not miffed, but not thrilled. Then he breaks into a smile as he sees what's about to happen.
  * A grinning Dani Harrison suddenly becomes all of us. He is watching Prince play.

Picking up the clock for about thirty seconds is *uproxx:*

- 4:43—Prince falls back off the stage into the arms of his beefy bodyguard without missing a beat. *DHANI LOVES IT!*
- 4:57—"Prince looks at a few people on the stage and smiles, as if he's putting on the show for them, and he hopes they're ready for what comes next."
- 5:07—"Prince is losing control. He knows not what he does. Everyone orgasms. Everyone."
- 5:12—Look away.

Time takes over for forty-five seconds:

- 5:15—"Prince took us up the mountain; now he's going to walk us back down. After nearly two minutes of blistering riffs that would make Steve Vai curl up and die, he enters cooldown mode with a few screaming single-note string bends, followed by weird Jonny Greenwood–style ascending harmonic chords that shouldn't feel right but fit perfectly in the pocket. They are pulling when everything else pushes."
- 5:20—"[Prince becomes] seven feet tall."
- 5:45—Petty, Lynne, and Harrison come back in with the chorus. Prince accents the proceedings with wailing notes, just to let you know he's still in charge.

Time noted that at:

- 6:00—"Prince fires off a final flurry, and the band finishes in unison."

Yahoo!:

- 6:10—"Prince does the coolest thing I have ever seen anyone do. I've seen people post it in .gif form, so maybe you saw it. If you did, watch it again. If you didn't, go watch it now."

18

SONNY LISTON'S GRAVE

Prince, standing, suddenly seemingly a little dazed in front of Sonny's Liston's pathetic, tarnished-brass-looking grave marker in a squalid Las Vegas cemetery. It was 2007, and Prince asked me the circumstances of Sonny's death.

"A heroin overdose," I said. "He died alone sometime over New Year's week 1970. They don't even know what *decade* he died in."

Prince's tiny body sagged. He then gave up a startling admission of his own—startling because he was admitting *anything*. He'd never been big on confessing. He had only one fear, he told me, but it was paralyzing.

He didn't want to die alone.

Unlike Ali, he said, lifting his eyes, he'd feared no person on this planet ever since his father had stopped smacking him around when Prince was a prepubescent who merely wanted to plink away at his dad's piano. Prince resumed looking down a few feet, wearing the thousand-yard stare of a soldier just out of battle, at the tarnished marker that provided only what Sonny Liston's own family and the

Las Vegas police department could *guess* were the actual years of the decedent's birth and death.

He read out loud the only words on the tiny horizontal plaque on the ground. "Charles 'Sonny' Liston,'" he said. "'A MAN.'"

"Well, considering what Ali did to him," Prince said, regaining his attitude, "*that's* self-confidence."

Personally, Prince resumed saying, softly, almost whispering, the only thing he was afraid of was dying alone. It was a shocking admission even the second time around.

Never mind the specific fear: Prince was not one to share personal emotions very often, and he was only extremely rarely a physically emotive man. But he would *never* let on being frightened by any human, life event, or personal circumstance.

He'd been in a pissy mood of assholiness from the moment we'd left that morning from the Rio Hotel—where Prince was in residence in 3121, a theater built specifically for him, to his own precise specifications, for a several-month run at the Las Vegas casino. But something had changed—again, for a third time—the moment we finally found Liston's grave.

"I don't want to die alone," he repeated.

He had on his depressed I'm-telling-the-truth voice, the one he saved almost exclusively for late-night phone conversations when he was so depressed he could barely speak. Emboldened because I couldn't see him, I would offer up a joke to try and leaven his mood during those times.

Indeed, Prince could produce the loudest silences in the world over the phone when he was down, and now I was hearing it for one of the perhaps half-dozen times I ever heard it face-to-face. He explained, in different words, but the same sentiment, as these: "No one should go that way."

Hoping to bring him back to his well-known nothing-fazes-me affect with a joke, I aped Jeff Goldblum's response in *The Big Chill*, where JoBeth Williams wonders aloud if many people would show up at her funeral.

"Don't be silly," I said. "I'll be there. And I'll bring a date."

"Shut the fuck up, motherfucker," he said.

Yes, it was the swear-jar years, but whatever.

"Me, too," I said, truthfully.

"Me, too, *what*?" he asked, almost snarling.

I have many, many fears, but dying alone has always topped the list.

"I don't want to die alone," I whispered. "It says something, some truth I don't wish to be said, something I don't want to be true."

"Th' fuck you talking about?" Prince asked.

I challenge anyone who was around Prince all those years who didn't hear him swear. Check that. I have no idea. I can't imagine him swearing in front of Larry Graham, or his brothers and sisters in the Jehovah's Witnesses, and since there were fifteen, twenty-five, fifty different Princes, each in its/his/her own compartment, what did I know? What *do* I know? I know what I heard Prince say.

"I don't know what I'm talking about," I said, but I did, about me.

I knew exactly what it meant.

"I don't know either," he said, scoffing.

But I knew exactly what he meant. I think.

Dying amid hordes, an audience of the grieving, wasn't a sign of one's importance, like Abraham Lincoln passing into the ages surrounded by a dozen of the most powerful politicians in America. It meant, in the end, that no one came. In the end everyone had left, or you'd chased them way.

We stood there, looking down at the unkempt final resting place of the former heavyweight boxing champion of the world.

"You think you can die of loneliness?" I asked the loneliest person I ever met in my life.

"Shut the fuck up," he said.

"I didn't mean anything," I said, but I did. I was forty-eight, with plenty of false starts but no mate, no children, no nieces, no nephews; a couple of relatives somewhere—more rumor than fact—who never wrote, called, or even sent smoke signals.

He was forty-nine, the same. He was rich and famous, though, so

I assumed *his* relatives called, though Prince being Prince, I doubt he picked up the phone.

"Shut the fuck up," he repeated.

Five minutes before, Prince had been glaring at me as I tried to find Liston's grave in Las Vegas's Paradise Memorial Park, located immediately adjacent on Eastern Avenue to McCarran International Airport's north–south runway. Every seven seconds a jet landed or took off with a decibel level louder than a Cheap Trick concert in 1977.

"Where this mamma jamma planted?" he'd asked, impatient, looking down at the corroding brass grave markers at his feet, shaking his head in disgust at the tufts of sunburned brown grass that sprouted here and there from the hardscrabble dirt that blanketed the mostly denuded cemetery plots.

He didn't like one of his guides to be lost; he also didn't like sightseeing, be he in Rome or Las Vegas. "I don't know how long I'm going to hang," he said, about sticking around and continuing our search. "I promised [Ali] I'd come visit the brother and say what he wanted me to say," he continued, scanning the grounds of the skeeziest, sleaziest, most woebegone graveyard either of us had ever seen.

That promise to the Champ had been ten years before. And the nameplates at the head of every plot were laid horizontally, for cheap, easy, and only very occasional mowing of the dirt here. I think it was probably supposed to be grass.

"But Sonny Liston should be buried someplace *terrifying*"—one of Prince's highest terms for earned grandiosity—"and not here."

Prince looked skyward, distracted by the roar of a jet taking off immediately above our heads. "If you don't know where he's at—"

"You're standing on him," I said, looking at Prince's feet. He jumped back; despite his aches, he still had the combined strength, speed, and balance of a granite halfback and an Olympic gold medal winner in all-around gymnastics.

"Sonny Liston," he said, addressing the marker. "The Champ asked me to come here and apologize."

I'd only heard him apologize once, the first time I went for a drive with him and he put on a cassette tape of his unreleased song about betrayal, "Old Friends 4 Sale."

"Is it too much?" he'd asked by way of apology back then.

"Ali said to tell you he went too far and is sorry," Prince said to where Sonny's head should have been. Ali, as mentioned, counted his victory over Liston as his greatest triumph. But he regretted being so cruel to Sonny back then to psych him out—a twenty-two-year-old frightened kid who'd resorted to shrieking how ugly and talentless and useless Liston was to boxing, and to the world.

When Prince had met Ali in 1997, he not only told the world he "would mow Ali's grass" if he asked, he told Ali. He also let Ali play with his hair—probably the only man on the planet who could do so and live to tell the tale.

Prince had asked Ali if he had any regrets, and he said he wished he'd apologized to Liston for humiliating him so. "If you're ever in Vegas, could you apologize to Sonny for me?" Ali said in his bare whisper. Prince promised. And ten years later, he was making good on it.

Liston had died of a heroin overdose either at the tail end of December 1970 or during the first days of January 1971. He'd been home alone, his wife traveling at the moment of his demise, and the coroner wasn't able to establish an exact time of death, let alone if Sonny's passing had been an accidental OD or, as word had it, a murder perpetrated by a visitor who purposely administered a fatal "hot shot" of smack.

Liston had been a mob-controlled enforcer, then boxer, and after retirement, informed rumor on the Strip had it, he was trying to hustle his way into rackets that weren't his to be had.

Sonny was illiterate and spoke largely in monosyllables, but he came up with one line during his life that was so splendid I still have my doubts whether he actually said it. But those who were there swore he said it in 1960: "Someday," Sonny said, "they're gonna write a blues for fighters. It'll just be for slow guitar, soft trumpet, and a bell."

"I like that," Prince said, keeping his eyes on the legend on the grave marker that said "A MAN." "Say that again."

"So the mob had him?" Prince went on.

Indeed. I then told him a story first related to me by the late, great Harold Conrad. The publicist for the first Ali (then Cassius Clay)–Liston fight had been the only white man both of the boxers trusted.

"I don't trust him," Prince said. "Every other white man had his hand in Sonny's pocket, no doubt," Prince said.

"No doubt," I said, and then told him what Conrad—who when he died in 1992 at age eighty was a contributing editor to *Rolling Stone*—had told me. Apparently the mob had cheated Sonny out of his winnings, and he'd angrily entered the dining room of the Beverly Hills Hotel to challenge Moe Dalitz, the ancient, short, gangster who had gone semilegit, or at least covered his tracks better than in the old days, by setting himself up as a Las Vegas civic leader.

Liston approached the dimunitive Dalitz—the exact same height as Prince—with his mighty fist cocked for action. Dalitz didn't blink.

"If you hit me, nigger, you better kill me," Dalitz said, unruffled. "Because if you don't I'll pick up this phone on my table, make one call, and you'll be dead in twenty-four hours."

Sonny had lowered his fist, and slunk out of the room.

"That is the saddest story I ever heard," Prince said. Then, brightening: "Man, that dude was *short!* What else?"

"Harold wrote the greatest line about him ever," I went on. "His father had twenty-five children by two wives, was a sharecropper, and beat the shit out of Sonny every single day. He never had a chance, and Harold once wrote the line, 'Sonny Liston died the day he was born.'"

"So did I," Prince said without inflection.

"What?" I asked, knowing he was talking about his father.

"I don't want to talk about it," Prince said.

"But that's what time it is," he continued. "Prince Rogers Nelson died the day he was born. And we know who killed him."

Yes we did.

His gloom instantly lifted, and he laughed. "The thing is, maybe my father did me a favor, snatching my life away from me like that, that fast."

"A favor."

"Sure," he said, then paraphrasing Vincent Price's immortal, diabolical line from *The Abominable Mr. Phibes*, one of Prince's favorite horror movies: If he was dead, he couldn't be killed.

I laughed.

"And you know what?" Prince said. "I owe Sonny an apology, too. I learned how to become me watching the Champ take Sonny apart with words and then deed."

To Prince the Ali-Liston fight was more than a favorite scene of combat, one he'd watch and rewatch hundreds of times over the years as an instruction manual on how to perform, entertain, outrage, show complete domination, and prove the potential power of crazy over his opponents.

"Liston was through after that fight," Prince said. "Somebody should have told him, but I guess he already knew."

Boxers never know when they're through, not even Ali. Prince always talked about how he wasn't going to go out like Ali, battered around the ring in a crime against humanity in 1981 at Caesar's Palace in Las Vegas by Larry Holmes, Ali's former sparring partner, still friend, and then reigning heavyweight champion of the world.

Holmes was sobbing in the ring, begging Ali to fall down, take the ten count. Even if he got counted out, he would forever be the champ. But Ali wouldn't go down, and Holmes determined that the only way to save Ali from himself was simply to put him down, raining blows upon him that neither he—Ali—nor Holmes would ever physically or psychologically recover from.

Prince paused then spoke.

"Someone should have told the Champ, 'Ali, it's time to quit.' Someone around him to say: 'No Ali, don't go back in the ring again, it's over.' The man got hit by so many punches he could barely *talk* by the time I got to him. Prettiest talker ever, and he'd whip your ass—couldn't talk. No one said no."

"Well, you got your yes-men," I said. "You need a no-man."

"That's what I'm talking about," Prince said. "Never be without a no-man."

"Who's your no-man now?" I asked.

"I don't know." Prince said. "I suppose that should bother me, but it doesn't. Don't matter anyhow. Everybody afraid of me as it is, this town, these friends, my relatives, they all been afraid of me since I signed my first record contract, proved a nigger didn't have to go to Hollywood or New York to make it, he could do it right from here. When I began, that was terrifying to people. Now they no longer had an excuse for not doing nothing with their lives."

"So who is gonna say 'Pack it in' to me?" he said. It was the only time I heard him contemplate the obvious question; the question never asked; the question whose answer for so many moribund celebrities is "No one."

But as soon as he entertained the thought, it was gone.

"Ah," Prince said, "I'm a musician, not a boxer." He scoffed: "A true musican never get used up. You ever see me used up?"

"No."

It was true, I had never seen him used up, even briefly. This was from a man I'd never once seen sleep in all the years I knew him. Robert Creamer, author of *Babe*, the 1974 definitive biography of Babe Ruth, said after publication that his only reportorial regret was not being able to interview one of the thousands of women—from society grandes dames to street prostitutes—who'd slept with Ruth, who died at fifty-three in 1948.

I'd met *plenty* of women who'd slept with Prince. My reportorial regret was that I'd never once talked to anybody who'd actually seen him sleep, nor had I caught him in the act the many nights I'd followed him around on tour.

This man would never get used up, I thought.

I was wrong.

"All right," Prince said. "Since everybody is afraid to say no, I'm just going to have to live a life that no one has to say no to me."

"No," I said.

"What?" he said.

"No, that's not what you need," I offered, certainly not volunteering for the job, not one he'd ever offer to an acquaintance as distant anyway, I thought, as me.

He looked at me oddly, as though I were an eye chart where he could almost read the letters.

The next day, Prince called me and said he wanted a lift back to Paradise Memorial Park and Sonny Liston's grave. He had me wait about seventy-five yards away, and I saw him mouth some words downward toward Sonny's plaque.

I then saw him take an eight-and-a-half-by-eleven padded envelope he'd been carrying, and place it atop the marker.

"What was that?" I asked.

"You were right. I had someone look it up," Prince said. "Sonny said, 'Someday they're gonna write a blues for fighters. It'll just be for slow guitar, soft trumpet, and a bell.'"

"Did you write it?" I asked, but Prince just kept walking to my rental car.

I wonder what it sounded like. After our Vegas trip, I didn't talk to him for ten months.

19

LAUGHS, LIES, AND LEARNING FROM OTHERS

My penultimate conversation with Prince was one of my favorite encounters with him ever. "Prince had a great sense of humor," people say, but nobody seems to remember many specific jokes beyond his former drummer Bobby Z. Rivkin recalling (early in the days of the Revolution) Prince telling him to turn his shirt down because it was too loud.

His laugh I remember best came at his own expense, as I wreaked revenge on him twenty-four years after he burned me wickedly. The occasion was also the last time I would ever see him alive.

I was sitting in the front room of Rudolph's in 2015, eating a brisket dinner, accompanied by Crystal Gandrud, a friend who happened to be a pretty woman. I looked up, and there was Prince walking past in his kayfabe costume, looking dressed and ready to go onstage in fifteen seconds, accompanied by his posse of BNs—"big Negroes."

Prince nodded toward my high-top, barely, almost imperceptibly and kept walking toward the back room. A chord clanged deep inside me, telling me it was now or never if I wanted to take the

Old Testament revenge I'd been seeking against Prince for a quarter century. It had been forever since he'd made me conduct, sans tape recorder or notebook, an entire batch of interviews for my final *Rolling Stone* cover story on him.

Not funny. I know he knew back in 1990 that I was stealing off to the bathroom every five minutes to take notes, hour after hour, interview after interview, and it had all felt a little sadistic.

Revenge may be a dish best served cold but this was positively Antarctic.

After Prince was settled in the back room, two BNs guarding the entrance, I headed back, having decided to ask Prince for a faux favor for the first and only time in all the decades I'd known him. Crystal was a pal, not a girlfriend, as I would present her to Prince. Indeed, she wasn't even a fan. She was the kind of pain-in-the-ass faux-music snob who thinks Leonard Cohen, not Bob Dylan, should have won the Nobel Prize.

I couldn't even claim credit for inventing the practical joke I was going to try to pull on Prince. Rather, I was paying homage to the late Don Rickles, aka "Mr. Warmth" himself, the insult comic who'd yanked the prank on Frank Sinatra half a century before.

Rickles had told me the story when I was interviewing him in the 1990s while collaborating with Henny "Take My Wife, Please" Youngman on his autobiography, the first book I'd ever worked on. Rickles had known Henny well, and had some filthy stories to share.

But first he told me how, in the early 1950s, he'd been in a Las Vegas restaurant with a young woman he loved to Pluto and back when Sinatra and his beefy entourage of Big Italians walked in. Frank had taken a shine to the virtually unknown Rickles in the prior years, supporting him where he could.

Rickles told me that to impress his date, he'd excused himself briefly, approached Sinatra's table, and was waved through to the sultan. "Frank," Rickles told me he said, "I've never asked you for a favor, you know that. But please, I love this woman. You have no idea what it would mean if you just came over and said, 'Hi, Don.'"

I followed Rickles's script exactly, substituting "Prince" for "Frank"

and "Neal" for "Don." Prince nodded noncommittally when I asked;
I wasn't sure if he'd taken the bait. But after I'd waited him out for
about an hour, Prince and entourage got up to leave. As they were on
their way out of Rudolph's, Prince stopped at Crystal's and my table.

"Hi, Neal," he said, in a stage whisper, smiling conspiratorially.
"How you been?"

I turned to the rock star and spoke brusquely, just as Rickles had
told me he'd done to Sinatra. "Prince, please!" I said, a few decibels
too loud. "Can't you see I'm busy? I'm talking to my special lady
friend. I'll be with you in a minute!"

At that moment I truly understood the meaning of deafening silence. For the first and only time ever, I was the object of Prince's
death glare, a stare so mortifying it could sink a thousand ships, and
scare any musician in the world into getting back on Prince's beat,
and *then* probably make a stop at the dry cleaner's.

In that look I saw the anguish of a grammar-school-age pip-
squeak watching his father beat his mother, trying to step in, and
getting belted himself, then going to school the next day and being
bullied and needled as "the Great Gazoo." I also spied his BNs standing behind him, expressionless, ready to beat me to beyond a pulp.
They had the look of a group who, if Prince said "Jump," would ask
en masse, "On whom?"

"Nice job, maestro," Crystal said to me, as the cold front of silence filled the restaurant.

And then, blissfully, Prince cracked a broad smile.

"Mamma jamma, you got me!" he said, slapping me on the back,
a rare instance of his actually making physical contact.

And *everybody* laughed.

It was very Joe Pesci in *Goodfellas*, very Prince. I have no doubt
whatsoever that if he had told his torpedoes to pummel me, they
would have plinked me with two pinkies all the way to St. Paul.

And Prince had laughed. He had a great laugh, or laughs. This
was his from-the-gut laugh, the appreciative guffaw so different
from his usual weisenheimer sneer. He was funny not because he

laughed at my joke, but because he understood its transcendent meaning.

In junior high school, André Cymone remembers Prince carrying around a special notebook not, as in later years, to jot down prospective lyrics, but to keep track of one-liners he could crack wise at particular kids, especially the bully boys. He'd listen for days beforehand, and try to figure out the bullies' raw nerves.

Then he'd verbally pounce, and usually run away. "Why don't you just punch them in the face?" André remembers asking. "And Prince would say, 'Are you crazy man? That dude's got six brothers.'"

His true comic forte, however, was impressions. No, that's the wrong word. They were so lifelike, so spot-on, they couldn't be called impersonations; they were more like *incarnations*.

And so there was the time teenage Prince fooled Chaka Khan by getting her on the phone, impersonating Sly Stone, and inviting her to come to the recording studio where he was making his first album. She showed up and was infuriated.

He really did seem to inhabit other characters, making even two-dimensional people seem actually human. Once of his funniest incarnations was as Jackie Chiles, Cosmo Kramer's lawyer on *Seinfeld*, a takeoff on the late Johnnie Cochran, O. J. Simpson's smooth-talking defense lawyer who employed the cadences of a Baptist minister as he declaimed, "If the glove don't fit, you must acquit!"

Prince replicated Jackie's pastor's rhythm and style of piling on adjectives until they were in orbit. Actions were, according to Jackie, "lewd, lascivious, salacious, outrageous!" After Kramer got burned by coffee, Jackie said his rights as a consumer were being violated: "It's outrageous, egregious, preposterous."

Rather than take on Cochran himself, Prince preferred to take on the takeoff. "Nah, man, Johnnie Cochran is too easy. That's just the rhythm of a smart church-talking black man. Jackie Chiles is more interesting. He is a loser who tries, and will find a way. He and Kramer are a team, they're in it together, ya feel me?"

I feel ya. He pronounced "team" as if it were a foreign word—a foreign concept; as they said in his beloved pro-wrestling ring, a foreign object.

And then there was his inhabiting the soul of Omar from *The Wire*. Not a sitcom but a situation tragedy.

Prince's Omar was brilliant. He also didn't just impersonate, but *inhabit* Omar, the antihero so street bad, so *anti*, that he made his living robbing the most psychopathic homicidal drug dealers in Baltimore. But Omar lived by Prince's sacred *code*, one set in granite as immutable as that of a proper West Point graduate. Omar reserved his pitiless violence for those who violated his sense of truly humane and just honor, a code as unalterable as the very real scar down the middle of the actor Michael Kenneth Williams's face.

And so, Prince would say, inhabiting Omar's character and character: *"A man gotta have a code. Indeed."*

Ironically Prince took Omar's code to his own street of celebrity.

"The game is out there, and it's either play or be played," Omar said on HBO, and Prince parroted the words (unattributed) on Tavis Smiley's show on BET, speaking of the music business.

"All in the game, yo, all in the game," Omar said, another favorite saying in Prince's argot.

"I got the shotgun, you got the briefcase," Omar said from the witness stand, humiliating the lawyer of a drug dealer Omar had sent to hell, just as Prince drove record-company suits to near madness. "It's all in the game, though, right?"

Or "You come at the king," Omar said, and Prince perfectly mimicked, "You best not miss."

"Mo," Prince had told me he said to Mo Ostin, chairman of Warner Bros. Records, while negotiating the putatively richest record contract in history in 1992, "I'm the best, so you better pay me the best."

"Man, money ain't got no owners," Omar said. "Only spenders." *The code.*

Prince's rendering of his white characters was equally perfect. And they didn't need speeches.

I've never heard a better Fonzie. Or the "Hooooooo-gan" he'd intoned in imitation of Werner Klemperer's Col. Wilhelm Klink on *Hogan's Heroes*.

His Lieutenant Columbo? Pretty good. Excellent actually, a 7.5 or 8 out of 10. "Unhhh, just one more thing," Prince would say, Columbo's white Italian heritage incarnate, virtually the half-white Italian Prince told early interviewers he was.

The only white people he couldn't do were the Brady Bunch. But he loved *The Brady Bunch*. And *The Partridge Family*—like me, he'd been smitten as a kid by Susan Dey as Laurie Partridge, the fake keyboard player who would have a second-act career in the 1990s in *L.A. Law*.

And despite his lifelong battle to stop saying it, he *loved* the word "motherfucker." So much so that he memorized a Don King speech on the majesty the word held for disenfranchised African Americans:

"We're blacks and we have nothing. We don't have expensive suits or big houses, or luxury vacations. We're poor. All we got is the word," he said in exact imitation of one of King's declamations. "Our only invention that belongs to us is a word. And that word is 'motherfucker.' Nobody can take that word away from us, that's our word. It's a black word. It's our heritage. We should be standing on top of buildings, shouting our word—'motherfucker'!"

And there was perhaps his most brilliant: the fire-and-brimstone hybrid of Asian martial arts movies dialogue and Old Testament declamations given to each victim by hitman Samuel L. Jackson, as Jules in *Pulp Fiction*, before dispatching them:

> The path of the righteous man is beset on all sides by the inequities of the selfish and the tyranny of evil men. Blessed is he, who in the name of charity and goodwill, shepherds the weak through the valley of darkness, for he is truly his brother's keeper and the finder of lost children. And I will strike down upon thee with great vengeance and furious anger those who would attempt to poison and destroy my brothers. And you will know my name is the Lord when I lay my vengeance upon thee.
>
> —Ezekiel 25:17 (according to Jules)

In comedy Prince *did* enjoy collaborations, and a cognoscento's view of comedy partners from Laurel and Hardy to the Smothers Brothers. And so he laughed and laughed when we were able to run ourselves the scene in *Airplane!* between two black men in distress who summon a white-as-Wyoming stewardess unable to understand the men's version of what is now known on campus as African American English Vernacular.

Prince liked to begin his version as Barbara Billingsley, June Cleaver on *Leave It to Beaver*, who offers to translate.

Prince would then do a pitch-perfect white girl—Randy, the stewardess, and then perform each of the other characters, one with a falsetto, one with a deep bass.

> Jive Lady: Oh stewardess! I speak jive. He said that he's in great pain and he wants to know if you can help him.
>
> Stewardess: All right. Would you tell him to just relax and I'll be back as soon as I can with some medicine?
>
> Jive Lady: Jus' hang loose, blood. She gonna catch ya up on da' rebound on da' med side.

And he did a fantastic impersonation of James Earl Jones doing a star-turn Voice of God.

Prince claimed to have written the brilliant Abbott and Costello patter in *Purple Rain*. I haven't checked the scripts at the Writers Guild of America, but it sounds like him. And it *is* quite hilarious.

> Morris: Okay. What's the password?
>
> Jerome: You got it.
>
> Morris: Got what?
>
> Jerome: The password.
>
> Morris: The password is what?
>
> Jerome: Exactly.
>
> Morris: The password is exactly?

But my favorite remained Prince's ability to share the many moods of Stanley Hudson on *The Office*.

Stanley, who—when everybody in the office learns they'll have the opportunity to try out for new manager through a series of ridiculous contests—decides that even though he doesn't want the job, he "would rather work for an upturned broom with a bucket for a head than work for anyone else in this office besides myself."

Prince's best Stanley, however, was his angry, shouting Stanley, the one he said reminded him most of his father at home being nasty. His favorite blowup to replay was in a scene where he believed a junior paper salesman was pursuing his eighth-grade daughter.

The ground would shake. The dressing-down Prince was giving to no one but merely acting felt like a scary reality: "That little girl is a *child*!" Prince would bellow, as Stanley, at the young sales associate. "I don't want to see you sniffing around her anymore this afternoon. Do you understand?" The ground rumbled as he roared. "Boy, have you lost your mind? Cause I'll help you find it. What you looking for? Ain't nobody gonna help you out there. Jesus could come through that door and he's not gonna help you if you don't stop sniffing after my child."

And he would play the trickster willing to lampoon anyone. He used laughter as a tool of power, as much as he did the more typical leverage of a well-told lie. As the new millennium revved, Prince even studied lying, as both an avocation, the way he liked reading about con men, and for self-protection, he said, in the famously avaricious music business.

He seemed almost to rue the fact that he'd come of artistic age, growth, and stupendous success under Mo Ostin and Lenny Waronker, famous for their honesty and probity.

"There I was, all ready to pounce on every cat from every label who I knew would just be lying to me," Prince said to me in 2002, "and I get Lenny [Waronker] and Mo!"

Prince was in fact a fantastic liar, the best I've ever met. He knew the fine gradations of propagating falsehood, could tell when a whopper was called for and when a half-truth would do. He knew how to lie by staying silent, and how to lie by merely changing the expression on his face.

In reinventing his history, he knew he could create a proper myth by simply altering a single detail. He judged himself harshly, however, considering himself duplicitous for merely playing the game. After his fall from commercial and critical grace in the 1990s, he was astonished (and pleased) that he was voted into the Rock and Roll Hall of Fame the first year he was eligible.

Yet he was embarrassed that he'd had to play nice, be a good boy, do what needed to be done in order to get in by simmering down his doubters, critics, and all those he'd purposely disrespected along the way. "It's like what the Monkees are going to have to do to get in," he said, putting himself down in a quizzical half-bitter, half-ironic tone that I've never heard come out of any other human mouth in quite the same way. "This is what oldies acts do."

Only a couple of years after he'd said, "I can't buy my way into *Rolling Stone*," there he was, in 2004, sitting for a proper, incisive interview with the incisive, heavyweight critic Anthony DeCurtis.

And though many agreed that Prince's "arrogant slamming of his guitar at the end was tasteless and disrespectful to the other artists on the stage with them," as Alan Leeds told Ronin Ro after the epic guitar solo at the Rock and Roll Hall of Fame induction ceremonies that same year, enough approved of the performance to make it worth Prince lying about to burnish his own image as a genius-provocateur. Even though George Harrison was his favorite Beatle, Prince claimed never to have heard the song before. Despite a lifetime spent focusing on every note Harrison played as if he were splitting an individual atom, Prince contended he had never practiced the solo once.

Prince bore false witness so well that he bragged about it: "I lie so well that *I* believe my own lies, I really do. I think that's why I got so good at it—if I could make myself believe my own lies, I knew they would work," he told me in 2005. "I also knew it would work if the lie was so big, so sick, that no one would think anybody would dare make up such shenanigans."

It was one of the perils of kayfabe, the science of pro-wrestling fakery. Prince had "bought his own gimmick"—believed he was what he pretended to be—but knew it. As oxymoronic as it sounds, he was proud he was such a master of self-deception.

For this he made no apologies. He loved the book *Homicide*, upon which our favorite television show of the 1990s was based. At the time he read it, he was well into his lifelong study of prevarication. He mailed the book back to me, and as he'd done in my Walt Frazier's guide to youngsters about basketball and cool, long sections were underlined.

Among them:

It was the job of the homicide detective to determine, I reread, "who's lying, who's lying more, and who's lying the most. . . . Are they lying? Of course, they're lying. Everyone lies. Are they lying more than they ordinarily would? Probably. Why are they lying? To a homicide detective the earth spins on an axis of denial in an orbit of deceit."

And: "It is a God-given truth: Everyone lies. And this most basic of axioms has three corollaries:

A. Murderers lie because they have to.
B. Witnesses and other participants lie because they think they have to.
C. Everybody else lies for the sheer joy of it."

And: "How does a detective know if he has the right man? Nervousness, fear, confusion, hostility, a story that changes or contradicts itself—all are signs that the man in an interrogation room is lying, particularly in the eyes of someone as naturally suspicious as a detective. Unfortunately, these are also signs of a human being in a state of high stress. . . . [Homicide investigator] Terry McLarney once mused that the best way to unsettle a suspect would be to post in all three interrogation rooms a written list of those behavior patterns that indicate deception:

Uncooperative

Too cooperative

Talks too much

Talks too little

Gets his story perfectly straight

Fucks his story up

Blinks too much, avoids eye contact

Doesn't blink. Stares

And so Prince lied. He was a vegan—except when he felt like tasting the rib tips at Rudolph's Barbecue, a few hundred yards from my apartment. So he was a Jehovah's Witness—except when he threw himself massive birthday celebrations fit for a dozen celebrities or strove for the kind of secular fame non-Witnesses were famous for.

He knew all the fine gradations possible for properly propagating falsehoods, misconceptions, or ridiculous bullshit about himself. When Prince wanted to, he could see situations so clearly that he was automatically aware, it seemed, of when a grandiose whopper was called for to sway a credulous girlfriend, reporter, or musician; when a half-truth would do; and when nothing more was needed to get what he wanted than a slightly alternate version of the truth. He knew how to lie by staying silent, and how to lie by nonverbal playacting, changing the expression on his face from a smart-ass grin to a grimace that would sink a U-boat.

More than a master of the half-truth, he was equally adept at the half-lie, sometimes drawing you in with a faux secret he told you conspiratorially, as if you were the only one to know. He actually had a philosophy about his unwillingness to keep a secret if he could figure out how spilling the beans served to his advantage, even as a put-down he'd use against those who'd confided in him.

There was usually an agenda behind Prince's lying: to placate a girl; to frighten a musician; to goof on a journalist. And yet:

He lied about his mother.

He lied about his family.

He lied about his race, telling reporters early in his career he was half black, half white, when both his parents were African American.

He was ambiguous about his sexual identity, even though he was the straightest male I've ever met.

He lied about his record label.

And he lied about Minneapolis, saying he would never leave, all the while trying to break away, to Toronto, L.A., Spain.

He lied about Amiir, and he lied about me to other reporters.

And yet he never cut me off, and I never stopped taking his calls or meeting up with him. The clock on both our lives was ticking, and both of us were oddly stopped. Sometimes synchronicity isn't such a fun thing.

Prince, unlike Fitzgerald, would successfully traverse the almost impossible rocky terrain of the comeback trail, perceptions hithering and thithering all the way from international icon to cosmic idiot, then finally back on up, all the way to the cosmic pantheon of artists. It would be an astonishing closing third act for the Prince passion play, indeed.

In many ways his comeback provided many of the best moments and self-satisfying redemptions of his career and life. Broken, Prince would still be elected to the Rock and Roll Hall of Fame in 2004, slashing one of the most galvanic guitar solos in history the night he was inducted.

Still to come was his 2007 halftime show at the Super Bowl, still considered the greatest performance at the year's most globally watched event. And then on to almost as a decade in which he was lauded, arguably but persuasively, as the greatest live performer on the planet.

And yet he was cracked, as badly as the later hack Fitzgerald, or the embittered, alcoholic, and survivor of multiple suicide attempts, Dorothy Parker—who, having sold her soul to what she considered the onerous craft of screenwriting, would stand at the bar at the Garden of Allah, the Hollywood smart set's residential complex of choice, and wail: "I used to be a poet."

With the death of Amiir and the tipping point reached by the disintegration of his body, Prince retreated.

And in 1997, I noticed, he no longer was looking to soak up information from outside sources. He either no longer cared most strongly about learning what moved other people, or he still cared deeply—it was just that so much of his energy now had to be poured into living through the pain.

Early on in his still-teenaged career, he'd sucked Chris Moon dry of knowledge on what button did what in Chris Moon's Sound 80 Studio. He'd taken in every morsel of knowledge about Joni Mitchell from Moon, and/or Owen Husney's wife and/or Lisa Coleman. Coleman also introduced Prince to the wide world of classical music: The first notes he heard her play were Mozart's. Everyone who had ever been involved with him in business or closely in life had taught him something critical to his success or iconic to his shtick.

Two of his early handlers claim to have given him the idea and persuaded him to go professionally by only his first name; one of them also claimed he gave Prince the notion of making purple his brand-name color. The director of *Purple Rain* insisted at their first meeting, out of nowhere, that Prince include a scene of his father physically abusing him and his mother.

From André Cymone, Prince got the Iceberg Slim attitude, and when he opened for Rick James in 1980, Prince studied the fabled and fading star of funk music, looking for the weakness. Saxophonist Eric Leeds turned Prince on to jazz and the majesty of Miles Davis's trumpet; Wendy Melvoin and Prince communed on mental and intellectual levels whose essence I wouldn't dare to presume.

But he grew more reserved, and his life got more compartmentalized. In our conversations I recognized fewer of the names in passing. What used to be sentences were now sentence fragments, and I rarely hazarded a confident guess as to what he was thinking. He seemed driven back upon himself, in a search to figure out who he was, if he made babies that only died and his body only hurt.

"Dorothy Parker suffered the constant fear of being rejected by those she granted access to her private self," wrote James R. Gaines in *Wit's End* (1977), his chronicle of the legendary wits who inhabited the main table in the lobby of Manhattan's Algonquin Hotel in the 1920s.

As with Prince, it was "a fear she fashioned into such a multi-faceted personality that even her closest friends still disagree about what she was really like."

I don't think anybody really "knew" Prince again, at least in the way he'd allow through the end of century—1999, to be exact.

20

MINNESOTA MEAN

Ben: (giving his fiancée advice for soon meeting his
divorced, warring parents) Best thing to do is distract
them with innocuous stuff they care about.

Leslie: Great, like what?

Ben: Well they're white people from Minnesota, so
hockey, fishing, skiing, sailing and after a few drinks, put
on a Prince album; don't mention the Green Bay Packers
or the state of Iowa . . .

—*Parks and Recreation*, season 5, episode 6, "Ben's
Parents"

Don't mention it.

Minnesota's license plates read "Land of 10,000 Lakes." A more accurate motto for Minnesota's existential ethos might be "Let's Pretend."

So many, it seems, play "Let's Pretend" in Minneapolis. For those who do it's mostly a matter of little white lies, because, granted, you didn't want to hurt anybody's feelings.

But there is also a deep spring of deception running beneath those 10,000 lakes—of keeping things pleasant at-the-moment, no matter the seriousness of the situation: In Minneapolis it's a tradition that people often simply go into denial rather than face the harsh truths:

—The alcoholic or drug addict on whom friends never dream of pulling an intervention.

—The gay man playing it straight.

—A family not confronting that for four successive generations a Funny Uncle has been taking advantage of each succeeding group of teenage nieces.

—The husband who doesn't show up at family functions on holidays for several years, and nobody dares asks "why?"

—The suicidal depressive who is not encouraged to seek therapy.

Keep it pleasant. Don't rock the boat.

And so we pretend. And worse. In any case, you just don't talk about it.

So pretend Prince is not dead. Hard to do, but think back. I remember the time he turned to me in 1993 while driving through Minneapolis's Uptown neighborhood, and said: "I counted it as an honest day for my father if he only told me half the truths."

"It's more like pretending," I said, trying again.

"I feel you," he said.

"You should," I said. "You pretend better than anyone. You do an excellent impersonation of yourself."

"How's that?" he replied.

"Pretend," I said.

"Too easy," he shot back with a cackle.

In any case, you usually don't talk about stuff here—especially about knowing Prince. For almost a decade after I moved back home from New York I lived in the Belmont, a funky old residential hotel that was perhaps the closest thing Minneapolis had to the Chelsea Hotel.

In time I became hang-out pals with my neighbor Stacia Lang—who I never knew was Prince's lead designer at Paisley Park for years in the 1990s. Stacia was responsible for the "butt pants" with which Prince stole the 1991 MTV Music Awards by performing the sensual "Gett Off" in seemingly see-through pants that revealed his ass. (Years later it was revealed Stacia had sewn flesh colored panels where his cheeks would have shone.)

Year after year we hung out—I knew she was a designer and had done some freelance work, I guessed for Prince, but I wasn't sure. And she never said a word. And I had just quit writing about him for print and was on to other circuses when we met.

Stacia, a born and bred small-town Minnesota girl, and me, a born and bred Minneapolis kid, just didn't talk about Prince. If you knew him, or worked for him, you just didn't mention it, and not just because if you did talk you wouldn't know or work for him for long.

We were from Minnesota, and when in doubt, or distress, or feeling joy, you just don't mention it.

Still alive, Prince didn't yet seem like he ruled as the Zeus of the modern cultural pantheon in Minneapolis, but as soon as he was dead, it seemed like he'd always occupied that position. In fact, he was perceived as a pompous, has-been dick by vast segments of the population. Pop-cultural history is a very fluid thing here, dontcha know.

Is it possible that such a person as Prince could thrive, be huzzahed, made the most favorite son, in a distant, peculiarly different galaxy known as Minneapolis, whose Ten Commandments are a Scandinavian ethos known as *jante* (YON-tuh)?

Jante: the social stricture that one musn't be different, get too big for one's britches; where being labeled a "character" is a bad thing. Is it possible a Prince could pop out of this soil?

Well, in, general, no. Indeed, superficially, Minnesota—and even putatively cosmopolitan Minneapolis—would seem the least likely loam to produce and nurture a globally singular talent like Prince.

With exceptions. There exists here a cadre of several thousand loyal Prince enthusiasts who always supported and followed the man, in good times and in bad. Some were members of what I term the Purple People, who belong to dozens, perhaps, of secret Prince Facebook groups. Almost all are exceedingly nice and gracious, and I'm proud to call myself one.

More were simply fans, who always knew we had a gem in our midst. By the end of his life there was the radio station 89.3 FM, the Current, the hepcat station in town that paid proper deference to the man who for so long should have been the Favorite Son, but wasn't.

And luckily for Prince, an astonishing array of writing talent was in town, or at least passing through long enough to make a mark, and try to make sense of it all: among them Richard Abowitz, Jim DeRogatis, Keith Harris, Will Hermes, Jessica Hopper, Martin Keller, Melissa Maerz, Michaelangelo Matos, Ross Raihala Chris Riemenschneider, Andrea Swensson, and Jim Walsh.

How could it come to be that a being like Prince would be allowed to do even a pale impersonation of his real self, in a land where you're allowed to express yourself however you want—*except* as stated in the following 1933 text that enumerated the tenets of monolithic, irony-free *jante,* the religion of social behavior that preaches:

1. You're not to think you are anything special.
2. You're not to think you are as good as we are.
3. You're not to think you are smarter than we are.
4. You're not to imagine yourself better than we are.
5. You're not to think you know more than we do.
6. You're not to think you are more important than we are.
7. You're not to think you are good at anything.
8. You're not to laugh at us.
9. You're not to think anyone cares about you.
10. You're not to think you can teach us anything.

This numbering and description came in a satirical novel called *A Fugitive Crosses His Tracks,* by Norwegian-Danish writer Aksel Sandemose, who showed how, in the fictional Danish town of Jante, conformity, not rocking the boat, keeping things boring, not calling attention to oneself, and not behaving—well, *differently*—were viewed as positives across Scandinavia.

And, by extension, in outer-world boroughs like Minnesota. In the 1960 census Minnesota clocked in at 99 percent white, the overwhelming majority of those inhabitants descendants of Norwegians, Swedes, and Danes—the preachers, teachers, and practitioners of *jante.*

Before I begin carving the turkey that is Minneapolis, I have to admit something personal on the subject that is kind of heinous. Especially since I must cop to hypocrisy as I lampoon the town for its shameless hypocrisy in its feelings for Prince pre- and postmortem.

To begin to understand how alienating a place Minnesota in general and Minneapolis in specific would be for Prince, you first have to understand the "Good Life in Minnesota"—which is how in 1974 *Time* headlined its cover story on the state, a story seemingly dictated by the area's chamber of commerce, featuring a photo of the beflanneled and aggressively Aryan governor Wendell Anderson holding up a just-nabbed walleye. Unremarked upon was how monolithic the Scandinavian ethos of not calling attention to yourself is here, as well as the human pathos of passive-aggressive pleasantness at all costs.

The state and its metropolitan center have grown a bit more diverse in the last half century—though not by much; Minneapolis still ranks as having the fewest people of color of any of the nation's largest fifteen cities (as of 2018, 7 percent of the state self-identified as black.) Meantime, the disparities in median income gap between white and African Americans is the greatest of any state, as is ownership of a high school diploma.

Jante has leaked into every other culture that for some reason has dared set its toe in Minnesota. Part of the genius that was the Coen brothers' production of *Fargo*—which, per the Coens' usual bent sense of logic is in North Dakota—was how the filmmakers showed even Jewish accountants and Vietnamese alumni of Minnesota high schools so comfortably blending into the ethos. The 1998 film skewering Minnesota manners and mores all the way to the Academy Awards' Best Picture was deemed charming in New York and Los Angeles, with audiences coming out of the theaters trying to do the Midwestern accent of "You betcha" and "Heckuva thing."

In Minnesota—not so much. It was, um, *different* (more on "different" shortly). Then again, the Coens have always been considered *different* at home, a point nodded to in *Fargo* when the brothers named William Macy's character, an achingly Minnesota Nice homicidal sociopath, after the Minneapolis *Star Tribune* movie reviewer who'd been panning their internationally lauded work ever since they'd begun experimenting in something called "irony" in *Blood Simple*.

To get a sense of the alienation a black youth growing up in Minnesota might feel, one need simply look at "Ebb Tide,"the first episode of the second season of *The Wire*. In that show two young soldiers in a drug-slinging organization steal a car, and hear on the radio the Lake Woebegone monologue of Garrison Keillor, the apotheosis of Minnesota, the #metoo-ed douchebag who ranks as perhaps the whitest man in America, as the street kids' eyes bug out listening to his tale of rural Midwestern nothingness—asking in response, "Why would anyone live outside Baltimore?"

Jante is basically the same as the parable of the poppy that dares stick its head above the other flowers and is the one to get its head chopped off. It's about not getting too big for your britches, or at least pretending not to.

This is the town that the Purple One would love, and be loved back by? Doubtful, at least on a large scale that extended beyond the professional cognoscenti, the hard-core fans, and those who just liked to cut loose and dance—that in itself is a borderline offense against *jante*, depending on how you're dancing.

This place would love Prince, who in 1985, within the first half hour of talking to me said, "Look, it all boils down to one question. 'Is Prince finally getting too big for his britches?' What I wish people would understand is that I've always thought I was bad. If I didn't think I was bad, I wouldn't have gotten into the business."

This is not the spirit of *janteloven*, Minneapolis, Minnesota, or the fjords. This is hubris.

It's downright—*different*.

True Prince fans call them twenty-firsters, those who believe Prince, while alive, was always honored as king in his hometown—a belief twenty-firsters take as an article of faith. Even twenty-firsters who became lifelong fans on April 21, 2016, call other twenty-firsters by the slur, truly believing that they were there when it counted, and did not come on board the moment they heard Prince was safely dead.

It's a peculiar phenomenon, this believing that we've always believed, and it strikes sometimes even beyond Minnesota's borders.

After President John F. Kennedy was assassinated, 64 percent of the populace said they had voted in 1960 for the slain chief executive, though in fact he'd only beaten Republican nominee Richard Nixon by less than two-tenths of a percentage point.

We here in Minneapolis certainly believed it the night Prince died. The First Avenue Club was thrown open for an all-night dance party; and in downtown Minneapolis buildings and bridges were set aglow with purple neon. Thousands of strangers, hugging and dancing, sang "Purple Rain" and sobbed in one of the most authentic displays of mourning I've ever seen. In fact it was probably the most authentic expression of communal mourning I've ever seen.

How could this be? Minneapolis's putative always-reverent attitude toward Prince? Yet it was the last even semi–big city in the country to play him on the radio? Why didn't Prince—so competitive, so easy to offend, so fast to feel spurned—mind when "Little Red Corvette," his first single to break, rising up to number six on the national pop charts, couldn't even be heard in the Twin Cities?

"Didn't bother me," he said nonchalantly. "I could hear it anywhere else I went in the country."

True . . . but . . . and how about the Minneapolis press corps, a segment of which would hound him to distraction, ridicule his name change, and mock Prince for his general attitude, which—though it would register as midlevel haughty in New York or Los Angeles—would be seen by Minneapolis standards as the behavior of a downright lunatic? Why would the myth emerge fully blown the day he died, even though in the months before he passed, he was truly imprisoned in his own Paisley Park "Xanadu," because contrary to forever legend he couldn't go to the local mall without being mobbed?

"Last time I tried," he said near the end of his life, "four hundred people were jumping all over me."

Alas, the truth is, that except for a handful of local writers and broadcasters, many astonishingly talented, several now-national names, and a population of several thousand hardcore fans whom I call (and count myself a member of) the Purple People, virtually all of Minnesota and most of Minneapolis completely ignored Prince, thought he was a freak, and/or couldn't name two songs of his post "Purple Rain."

The truth is, Minneapolis was never a haven, let alone heaven, for Prince. "No one had heard of him here," said Emily Goldberg, who came to Minneapolis from the East Coast after Prince had done a couple of albums, and was the producer of *The Minneapolis Sound*, a seminal documentary filmed for public television. "My college housemates and I in rural Ohio heard songs from 'Dirty Mind' on a Cleveland radio station and were obsessed with it; we had that album on tonearm drop replay 24/7. I was so excited to be moving to the Prince epicenter, but when I raved about his music here, all I got were blank stares."

Allen Beaulieu, Prince's brilliant principal photographer from the late seventies and early 1980s chuckles now when he remembers how Prince was laughed at then. "People in Minneapolis were not into his music, period," he says. "It is one of the great cultural myths that people in Minneapolis, outside his loyal base, were into Prince since he was teething."

Indeed, it was jarring to walk into First Avenue with Prince one Saturday night not long after *Purple Rain*. He had parked his white Cadillac convertible on the sidewalk in front of the club: literally rock-star parking. Walking unguarded into the packed club, the seas of people parted like a piece of Busby Berkeley choreography. So this is fame, I thought.

And then out of nowhere, like Ruby coming after Oswald, a mamma jamma dressed for *American Bandstand* approached Prince and told him Purple Rain was a sellout: "You're a black man," the white guy declared, commanding, "Be one!"

"And what are *you* doing?" Prince asked, his standard response to anyone who challenged him in those days. And in those days the only place on planet Earth he was being challenged was Minneapolis.

The town's highest-profile press had always been a pox on Paisley Park.

For dramatic purposes they work the Prince beat as if it were an opéra bouffe. One local reporter is a woman Prince saw as a vengeful, provocative temptress who must have been an ex-girlfriend in a previous lifetime. Another is a hapless yet powerful buffoon who for more than four decades has fancied himself the Twin Cities' Bernard

Berenson of rock criticism, when in fact he most resembles Paul Shaffer as Arnie Fufkin, the douchebag publicist in *This Is Spinal Tap*.

Prince believed the past-life-scorned gal pal, who goes by the moniker C.J., to be a combination of the two types of beings that tortured him the most: African American women, and gossip columnists. When he began calling himself an unpronounceable glyph, she referred to him as "Symbolina" in her column, which drove Prince bonkers.

Prince wrote a plaintive, uncharacteristically whiny song about her, and believed a famous Otis Redding–Carla Thomas duet, "Tramp," was written about their previous lives together. (The song Prince wrote about her is "Billy Jack Bitch," on one version of which he can be heard mumbling "C.J.")

The ass clown, Jon Bream, is more pernicious. At best Prince considered him, well, an annoying douchebag. At worst he hated him: When Bream told him in the nineties that his career was over, Prince responded by setting a picture of the rock reviewer afire onstage during *The Arsenio Hall Show*. Bream also dug dirt on the megastar, but with no élan and little accuracy.

In 1984 he published an unauthorized biography of Prince. In it he repeated the musician's early career bullshit about how he learned the real facts of life by seeing the hard-core pornography his wanton mother left lying around the house while he was a young boy.

Running into his mother, the dignified Mattie Shaw, a public school social worker, Bream proudly handed her a copy of the book telling the story of the Marquis de Sade household she apparently ran for Prince in the Twin Cities of Sodom and Gomorrah.

He is necessary to the Prince opera, however, for comic relief in what is really a sad, sad, story. Corrupt—at least by the most minimal standards of his industry—he had, unimaginably, asked Prince between the fall of 1992 and the first few months of 1993 to write a song about him, too, which the musician didn't. I didn't try to pin Prince down for an exact date when he told me of the-then recent request.

I was too shocked: the mere asking of such a thing, according to industry norms, is an egregious breach of journalistic ethics usually considered a firing offense.

A song has monetary value, especially a Prince song. It would guarantee that Jon Bream would be known far and wide by Prince afficionados, as C.J. was as the inspiration for "Billy Jack Bitch." His name itself would be worth more in the commercial marketplace.

"It is appalling that a music critic would ask an artist that," says a former top editor of *Billboard*, now a highly regarded college professor in Los Angeles, and one of the leading consciences of the industry. (I could name him and probably should: when I stab someone I try and do it from the front, and always with my name on it. Not Bream's way, though, and the few times I've righteously hatcheted bullies in print I've tried to do it their way.)

One odd thing, though, is that compared with most people, I honestly love Jon Bream. And I hate Jon Bream.

The reason I am calling him out is the sheer number of new young bands and musicians he has destroyed, made cry, and whose dreams he crushed. Minnesota simply likes its favorite sons and daughters dead.

August Wilson is arguably the greatest American playwright of the last half century, his plays casting a unique and perplexing eye not just on the African American experience in America, but the American experience in America. He lived in St. Paul for a dozen years, where he wrote such marvels as *Fences, Ma Rainey's Black Bottom*, and *Jitney*, but the Guthrie Theater, renowned since the early 1960s as one of the finest regional repertory companies in the world, seemed to favor annual Eastern European pain-and-misery festivals, while across town, the Black Penumbra Theater, always teetering on the brink of financial collapse, was staging Wilson's plays.

Instead of building Wilson a temple, as civic leaders should have, they let him escape to Seattle, where he died in 2005. Mourned across the country, and then, safely dead, he was proclaimed, like Prince would eventually be, as one of Minnesota's forever beloved.

Nor did you need to be black to be an ignored and reviled native. Sinclair Lewis of Sauk Centre, forty miles outside the Twin Cities, was deemed a public enemy after he published lampoons of his hometown in *Main Street* and *Babbitt*. He was not welcomed home even after he won the Nobel Prize for Literature in 1930. Now, of course, "Main Street Days" is a staple theme of Sauk Centre summer festivals.

F. Scott Fitzgerald, who ran down Summit Avenue in St. Paul shrieking the news that his first novel, *This Side of Paradise*, had just been accepted for publication, similarly ridiculed his hometown, in his fiction and off-the-cuff observations, calling it "a museum of architectural failures."

Before Princeton, Fitzgerald was kicked out of the tony St. Paul Academy for drinking, and I have found no evidence that he stopped in Minnesota even once during the last years of his life. Never fear: In 1994, fifty-four years after his death, the World Theater in downtown St. Paul was renamed the Fitzgerald, and two years later, F. Scott was granted a larger-than-life statue in the city that never accepted him while he was alive.

And you didn't need to be a man. Judy Garland spent her life insisting she was from Grand Rapids, Michigan, not Grand Rapids, Minnesota, even though she hailed from the latter as Frances Gumm. The Minnesota locale, however, was where the Gumms were communally shamed and forced out of town by the scandal of Papa Gumm, the film projectionist at the local movie house, getting caught in—shall we say—different circumstances with assorted other men.

Since she died, of course, Grand Rapids, Minnesota, has built a Judy Garland Museum complete with a Yellow Brick Road, a ridiculously overpriced gift shop, and until a couple of years ago, an annual reunion of real-live Munchkins from the original cast of The Wizard of Oz. (The tradition died when the last of the surviving Munchkins became too infirm to travel.)

And what of Bob Dylan, born in 1941 in Duluth, where he spent the first seven years of his life before his family moved north to Hibbing? There was less debate and haggling over his getting the Nobel Prize than over naming the street that encircles the Duluth Civic Center after him. And despite the conventional wisdom that he fled Minnesota and never looked back in the early 1960s, the truth is that Dylan keeps a family compound here and remains close to his extended family, now largely in the Twin Cities, and his friends from summer camp. When Dylan's mother died a few years ago, he wrote a poem for her that he published not in *Granta* or the *Paris Review*, but the *St. Paul Pioneer Press*.

But until he dies—Bob who?

He, like Prince, Scott, Sinclair, August, and Frances, was different, too. Thought he was special.

So after Prince died, the Minnesota Vikings devoted half-time shows to him. When he was alive, the team had turned down an unsolicited song from Prince to replace the tired high school rouser, "Skoal Vikings," which they'd been using since Eisenhower was president.

The University of Minnesota granted the newly dead Prince an honorary Ph.D., a degree they said they'd been considering when he died. Indeed, the mamma jammas had been considering it for a quarter century—I know, because I was asked to write some of the proposals by various departments and schools within the university that wanted to grant him a Ph.D. while he was still alive.

That was an honor Prince would have liked: If his music career foundered, he early on had a backup plan: He would attend the "U of M," get his degree, and teach high school music. But death was a good career move, even academically; Prince's ghost was quickly given his mortarboard, and the university hastily threw together an exhibit, titled Prince from Minneapolis, in its Frank Gehry–designed museum.

I remember the time he turned to me in the mid-2000s, while driving through Minneapolis's Uptown neighborhood, and said: "Does it ever hit you how every mamma jamma in this town is always lying?"

Prince studied body language and the tells of lying as a way of gauging the truthiness—as Stephen Colbert styles it—of what he was being told in the record business. Nothing shadier, that is, except perhaps, the social intercourse that too often passes for civility in Minnesota.

Truthiness certainly.

And yet—both the very best and the very worst people I've ever met in my life are from the Twin Cities. Friends have saved my life here; others have proved "friends" in the worst possible way; once again turning to the Yiddish: "*Beser a guter soyne eyder a shlekter fraynd*"—"Better a good enemy than a bad friend."

Maybe it's not so much the Twin Cities as the Bipolar Cities.

For Prince's entire lifetime he pretended he was Prince. And it worked. Perhaps it is a measure of his greatness that it worked not just in Minneapolis, but all over the world.

He could be a devout Jehovah's Witness while seeing a Hasidic rabbi for tutelage on the Kabbalah. This is the land where disbelief is never suspended, even when, as Prince occasionally did, buy into, in pro wrestling argot, his own "gimmick" or believe his personae and press releases were real.

Even then, when his soul and music and style became shtick, Minneapolis was always the best place to hide out, even when he tried different spots—Los Angeles for a while, several times; Toronto now and again for a few years with his second wife; and a mansion in Spain that ended up being for vacations and a place to stow his first wife after he'd gotten their marriage annulled; even Las Vegas, where he was in residence at the Rio Hotel while performing there in 2006–7.

But let's be real: "Let's Pretend" was a game Prince may have liked playing even more than basketball. The official blood sport of Minnesota in general, and Minneapolis in specific, our home version of "Let's Pretend" even comes with its own philosophy, an ethos known as "Minnesota Nice."

Its flip side is "Minnesota Mean," a singularly corrosive form of passive-aggression so noxious that I hate living here so much, and have lived here for so fucking *long*, that if I didn't love it here so much, and hadn't lived here for so fucking *long*, I'd move tomorrow.

Contradictions, as Walt Whitman liked to point out.

That's Prince.

And that's Minneapolis. The most genuine, generous, authentic, altruistic, friendly, honest, wise, and broad-minded people I've ever known are from here.

I've also never met more awful, phony, narcissistic, self-serving, egotistical hypocrites anywhere in my life.

Too often, unfortunately, especially at first, and among those who aren't your litmus-tested friends, you can't tell the difference.

That's Minnesota Nice and Minnesota Mean, and it's why Prince loved Minneapolis so much that he could simultaneously despise it, knowing it wasn't a place that breathed life and soul and music, but death and a bitter spiritual return to the scene of the crime that had bent him into a human mutant and also made him a star. Prince was a firm believer in the French philosophy of "Jealousy is a fake parasite that feeds on love."

Minneapolis, the actual city, 2020 population 424,256, Prince historically didn't care for all that much: In his first interview ever, in the Central High School paper, he said he was indeed from Minneapolis, "unfortunately." He quit Champagne, a promising local band, as a teen because he sensed he was the only one with dreams of out-of-town success, and as soon as he was out of high school he moved to New Jersey and into his half sister's home to begin shopping himself to record labels.

But then there was his mythical Minneapolis, his pretend Minneapolis. John F. Kennedy's presidency had "Camelot"; *Finian's Rainbow* had mythical "Glocca Morra"; Thornton Wilder had "Our Town"; Harold Hill had River City; and Prince had "Minneapolis." *So* different from the real thing, you know, reality.

He did not revel in being the big fish in a small pond.

In the huge ponds, New York and Los Angeles, no one would dare toss a cross eye at him. If one worked for his record company, a memo *might* have been sent prior to his visit saying: Don't even look Prince in the eye.

But in Minneapolis, after he was already an active success, not to be fucked with by anyone anywhere—except, seemingly, in his hometown, where strangers continued to give him shit to his face.

He would not ignore them but turn on the death stare. "Yeah," he always said. "What are *you* doing?"

The fact is, it was Minneapolis, and most people weren't doing *anything*. I mean on the other side of the aisle there were Hüsker Dü, the Replacements, and Soul Asylum, but they were freakish times. Minnesota was not meant to be hip, and I'm glad I missed the entire decade—the 1980s—when for the only time in history Minneapolis was hip. It's not the way.

And nothing a New York critic said about his music could bother him—in fact, he'd take delight in bad reviews—but Prince could grow livid when he was made fun of or given lousy reviews by local reporters. But mostly it was okay.

Prince was depressed constantly, though he only rarely used the word; he thought it made him sound weak.

Prince was homesick even when he was home, too (like Sarah Silverman), but it was better. And it scratched the itch, the need to replay a drama endlessly, no matter how traumatic, the Fabulous Prince Rogers versus his son Prince Rogers, on a continuous loop, no need ever to leave; not when you're a genius with many millions and no notion of why you feel so bad and lonely and small all the time—and no desire to find out.

For a guy obsessed with hiding out from himself, this was the place, the land of Make Believe, the Land of Nice.

Pleasantness at all costs. It's human nature, of course, but in Minneapolis the seriousness with which this ethos exists is extreme.

But due to a mistake, an anomaly, a weirdness of geographical coincidence, it is a nowhere unto itself. The nearest big city is Chicago—four hundred miles away, six hours by car, a couple of hours to and from via plane—as good as forever away.

In such a land Prince was a nowhere man, which is just what he wanted. As long as he could hear his music delivered across the world and get his paychecks.

There's no there here.

And whatever *is* here seems white.

One needn't live here that long to experience whiteout conditions, even if only while taking a disorienting walk from the driveway to the front door. Putting it mildly, to be caught for even a minute in a Minnesota blizzard producing whiteout conditions is an unholy mind fuck of where-am-I-upside-down terror.

You can no longer tell where the horizon is: Sky and land are indistinguishable; visual points of reference no longer exist. In the most familiar surroundings, you can become so disoriented that if improperly dressed, you can wander yards from your doorstep for hours and freeze to death, never knowing where you were going.

Up is down, nothing is anywhere, *there is no there here.*

And in such a vacuum, where there is nothing, *everything* is possible. Just close your eyes—and pretend.

First, pretend there is something called "the Minneapolis Sound."

There is no such thing as "the Minneapolis Sound."

In jazz, in the 1930s, when the number of African Americans in Minnesota was under 1 percent, it was the sound of Oscar Pettiford, from the same North Minneapolis streets as Prince, learning the bass, eventually becoming the greatest—with Charles Mingus—ever. Oscar Pettiford, from—Minneapolis? *What?* Or Lester Young, the jive-talking hipster with the porkpie hat, who at the same time developed his revolutionary way of playing the tenor saxophone while living in Minneapolis.

Consider the mere fact that the 1937 worldwide hit version by the town's Andrews Sisters of "Bei Mir Bist Du Schön" ("To me you're beautiful") was sung in Yiddish, the street tongue of Eastern European peasant Jews—by a group from Minneapolis, of all places, a northern town somehow labeled in 1948 by Carey McWilliams, editor of the *New Republic* and the leading sociologist of his day, as "the capital of anti-Semitism in America."

First of all, *what?* Minneapolis? The capital? (It's a long story.) With a hit song sung in Yiddish by the Andrews Sisters?

When there's no *there* here, anything can happen.

The next big hit to come out of Minneapolis was in 1963, with the Trashmen, recording "Surfin' Bird" on the local Soma label. The song hit number two on the pop charts, and is an enduring favorite, enjoying several dozen more lives as Peter Griffin's favorite song on *Family Guy.*

The thing is, the Trashmen not only didn't know how to surf—no big deal, only Dennis Wilson of the Beach Boys could actually do it—but they had never even seen the ocean before their song hit.

They got the lingo from a glossary printed in the local paper in 1963 when the Beach Boys first came to town, which included terms like "ho-dad" (a bad-boy greaser), "heavies" (very big waves), and of course "wipeout."

Next came Dave Dudley, recording in the same Minneapolis studio, and coming out with "Six Days on the Road," arguably the best trucker's song ever.

Then there was the song that hit number one in twenty-one countries in 1980, made by Minneapolis producer Stevie Greenberg, with talent drawn from across the Twin Cities, titled "Funkytown," which is most certainly not about how funky Minneapolis is, but about escaping the stultifying sameness of a town that sounds pretty familiar.

Greenberg could get the song on the radio anywhere in the world, but, he said, he could never find it on Minneapolis radio.

And then came "When Doves Cry," from the 1984 *Purple Rain* soundtrack, which reached number one.

And *that* is the Minneapolis Sound. Mix Oscar Pettiford's bass with Lester Young's tenor sax; throw in a Yiddish tune from a group from a town that hates Jews; add a surfing song by a band that has never even seen an ocean; a great trucking song; a disco hit made by a nice Jewish boy in a mixing booth; and then "When Doves Cry."

Only in Minneapolis.

It is a cliché that Miami, New Orleans, and New York are not really part of the United States. The truth is that Minneapolis is not of this galaxy.

In New York or Washington, wise folks say, at least you get stabbed in the front. And Los Angeles, as per the old saw, is where "you go to die of encouragement." In the Twin Cities, you die a slow and smiling death, your soul crushed by a lifetime of false pleasantness, a rigidly enforced culture of passive-aggressiveness, and an unwillingness to offend or confront others, except during "Family Week" at Hazelden/Betty Ford.

For millennia, religious smarties have warned that the devil, to confuse the pious, may appear in the costume of the Lord.

Since no one can tell who's lying, gossip is usually malignantly wrong. And thou art allowed to bear false witness, saying "That's interesting" or "How different" when what you really mean is "That sucks." At least in Los Angeles you can tell who's doing the Pinocchio tap dance. In Minneapolis, says a childhood friend of mine who is now a Hollywood executive, "Unless you've been specifically told otherwise, you have to assume everybody is lying to you."

In Minnesota it is infinitely harder to tell when someone is lying, because virtually no one looks anybody in the eyes, even during sex. (Joke. I know not.)

Knowing that so many are pretending about something, even with the niceties—be it your cooking or new baby—all too often results in "compliment inflation."

Last fall I had to tell the parents of a newborn four times how beautiful their baby was before they believed I really meant it. She's beautiful. She's beautiful. She's beautiful. She's *beautiful*!

And I wasn't even lying!

"Minnesota Nice" is a dialect of contradictions. When someone says, "Well, my truth is that . . . ," they are lying. When someone says, reassuringly, "It's all good," one can be almost certain that all is most definitely not good. Similarly, if you are told "No worries"—it is time to worry.

Similarly, because everyone knows the importance of pretending, flattery, or not-mentioning the obvious for the sake of pleasantness, few believe a simply uttered compliment, simply uttered once.

"You have a beautiful baby" can be easily reckoned to mean "does your monkey want a banana?"

And so, to be believed, one says, "you have a beautiful baby. Seriously, a beautiful baby. What a beautiful, beautiful, *beautiful* baby."

Ah, the truth is accepted.

So, if this is *such* a land of hypocrisy, passive-aggression, and back-stabbing *why* have I stayed for decades and will, no doubt, will remain here for the rest of my life?

Because I love it here.

I love it here. Seriously, I love it here. What a beautiful, beautiful, beautiful city filled with my most favorite, favorite, favorite people in the world.

4real.

As my grandparents, no fans of Minnesota Nice, would say: the *emes*.

The truth.

21

CODA

The greatest way to live with honor in this world is to be what one pretends to be.

—Socrates, the first great explainer of "kayfabe"

I'd known Prince the last thirty-one years of his life, and not once during that time did I presume to call him my "friend." It always sounded presumptuous.

I'd never taken seriously the notion that I was Prince's actual friend even when he'd actually used that word in our correspondence over the decades.

(This is not a humblebrag, the late great comedy writer Harris Wittels's neologism for a boast barely camouflaged by self-deprecation—for example, tweeting: "I can't believe I'm the same putz who was just nominated for an Academy Award." I'm not. Even after Prince died I still have never called him my friend.)

In all the time I'd known him, I would have felt like an utter phony if I'd presented myself as someone who "knew" Prince, as much as one could know him. Indeed, even though I'd last talked to him, in a melodramatic conversation that still haunts me, only three weeks before he died in 2016, I could no longer even remember what he *sounded* like. The cadences. The rhythms. The way he sounded when he laughed, lampooned somebody else, or yes, even made fun of himself.

As wimpy and unprofessional as it sounds, I simply couldn't listen anymore to the tapes of Prince and me again, go over the transcripts, or even look at the notes of our conversations I'd referred to time after time while writing this book. His voice had become too painful to hear one more time, literally unlistenable to, and I couldn't bear to see the generation's worth of scribbled notes on legal pads and index cards spilling out of shoeboxes and two battered suitcases in my living room.

There were ghosts there dating from our midtwenties into deep middle age, ghosts of both of us I could no longer stand to try to make sense of. The tapes were impossible to listen to, to hear the midtwenties hopefulness in both our voices when we first began talking to each other. We didn't talk in the beginning about being masters of our own universes, but about each being in love forever with the princess in our own fairy tales, with whom we shared adventures and would one day both have families with. His was Susannah Melvoin.

Such bullshit, I thought decades later. People always leave, I now knew, and when they didn't, I had often idiotically left of my own accord. We'd both outsmarted ourselves, and suddenly we were both old and alone.

And that, to be pathetically honest, is how the bulk of our telephone conversations went the last ten years of his life. Thank *gawd* I'd had the good sense, or shame, to leave all that out of this book, because who wants to read quotations of two old fucks feeling sorry for themselves—*ourselves*—because we hadn't known what we hadn't known when we still had the chance?

Prince and I had lost the remnants of our youth and grown past middle middle age, living only a score of miles away from each other. He was an off-the-charts genius—hell, an off-the-easels-that-*held*-the-charts virtuoso and internationally recognized cultural icon—and I . . . well . . . *wasn't*. Yet we did have some interesting things in common. And there was an odd synchronicity to the pattern of our lives, especially revolving around settling down and having a family, or at least a Real Life—whatever that was—that even he noticed. And Prince was never big on noticing other people's lives.

So *fuck* if I was going to listen to *those* tapes or read those transcripts again. I'd occasionally send snippets of him talking about God or death or how he was the baddest man on the planet to friends as bonbons of good karma, but I could no longer listen. And now I could no longer remember his voice, what he sounded like when he was elated or depressed or just talking about the Minnesota Vikings' quarterback situation.

He had a well-documented history of erasing his accumulated pasts— especially people pasts, be they male friends or female lovers—and I was never sure if the conversation we might be having would be our last. You wonder these things when someone calls you in the middle of the night once a week for a month and a half—and then you don't hear from him for a year and a half. For someone so aware of human nature, he could be remarkably, unfathomably unself-aware of the same nature that beat in his own heart.

So when I asked him why Morris Day had bad-mouthed him so viciously after *Purple Rain*, quitting Prince's creation the Time, which had made Day a funk, movie, and comic star, he responded analytically:

"Morris," he said, "always wanted to be a solo act himself, the star, period. But when you're broke and selling shoes someplace, you don't think about asking such a thing." Then Prince had given him an identifiable, monetizable character, and "I think Morris [was] trying to create his own identity."

Prince made the last four words sound like an elongated version of "fool."

He then broke out of his flash of anger. "And one of the ways of [creating your own identity]," he said matter of factly, "is trying to pretend the past didn't exist."

Hmmm. Prince would molt himself a dozen, a score, an inumerable number of times by doing just that—pretending the past didn't exist, as well as most of the people who inhabited that past and often helped Prince along the way. He was aware of the habit in a past-tense way by his midtwenties, discussed it as a pathology of his youth, but never seemed to notice the collateral damage he inflicted when he was himself in the middle of shedding a skin—and virtually all those around him—one more time.

"I was very angry when I was young," he'd reminisce, "and I was very quick to turn my back on anyone, never to be seen again." Then, a month later, he would be very quick to turn his back on anyone, never to be seen again.

And why not me? Maybe he did at times, and I just didn't notice. Maybe because I wasn't on his payroll, never asked for anything, because I didn't want anything. Or maybe I seemed not to care enough at the time, unlike everybody else around him. There is nothing I care more about than friendship—nothing. Friends had saved my life many times, and if someone was mean to a friend, I used to like to think, in less humble times, that I made for a terrible enemy.

But my friends, the people I actually called friends and didn't feel presumptuous calling them that, didn't phone once a week for a month and a half, then disappear for a year and a half. Ever since that he must have wanted me specifically to do *this*, and needed in particular to make sure and do *that*. And of all the things I must do, so many said, I must write the real story—as if I'd ever pretended to comprehend anything near the real story since I met him.

These weren't friends who had, as Prince once put it, "gone Trekkie"—they didn't believe in Ouija boards and psychic vibrations and orgone boxes. (I have plenty of those friends, too, and I don't even want to begin telling you how detailed their instructions are of what Prince wanted me to do, in life and in death.)

Prince wanted me to write his biography or he wouldn't have let me tape him and take notes on our conversations for thirty-one years, insisted trusted friends who lived permanently on planet Earth, as well as trusted friends who didn't.

Alas, not once—*ever*—did I indicate to him I was interested in writing the story of his actual life; since my last interview had run back when, I'd published eight books on topics ranging from vaudeville to bush-league baseball to the Hasidim, and I'd never once typed a word proposing a book on Prince that only *I* could write.

I wasn't interested, and I was sure all along I'd be telling at best a piece of a portion of the truth. There *had* to be others like me, each playing a different set role in Prince's existence. For the last several years of his life, I figured, I'd been his middle-of-the-night guy, that's all—his angst guy—I reminded myself always.

After he died, I realized I'd known him too well in life, and he hadn't been gone nearly long enough to approach him as a legitimate historian. And writing a personal memoir of him, I figured, would be as authentic as a Munchkin member of the Lollipop Guild who'd passed Judy Garland twice at the MGM commissary pulling a memoir out of his ass about his friendship with Dorothy from Kansas.

As Prince would say in imitation of Stanley, the basso profundo African American paper salesman in *The Office*—"Ain't gonna happen."

Nor did he indicate even once that he cared.

Andrew Carnegie, the nineteenth-century American plutocrat and robber baron once said, "There is the good reason that people do things, and then there is the *real* reason."

For Prince, the real reason he did something was no reason at all, much of the time, except for that he *could*. Everyone who actually knew him even slightly beyond the game of pretend he liked to play with almost all of the world almost all of the time knew this—or they didn't know him at all.

Frankly, I think he had other things on his mind than answers that ended with me. And frankly, I had other things on my mind, too.

I decided I wanted to offer and promise the truth, at least as I experienced and witnessed it. People ranging from Prince's greatest enemies to Prince himself had (and have) successfully so muddied the waters with bullshit, falsehood, self-aggrandizement, and deceit, while Prince, often for his own amusement did exactly the same thing.

So who was Prince?

One must cast a gimlet eye even at personal recollections of Prince. Even if face-to-face accounts are well intentioned, one believes and remembers with time what one wants to: as the old Russian proverb goes: "He lies like an eyewitness."

And where does that leave me?

The most important, meaningful thing Prince ever said to me was about why in 1987 he shelved at literally the last possible second the infamous *Black Album*. The record was the devil's handiwork, he'd decided, and a half dozen stories have emerged over the years as to how he came to that conclusion.

"I was very angry a lot of the time back then," he'd told me, "and that was reflected in that album. I suddenly realized that we can die at any moment, and we'd be judged by the last thing we left behind. I didn't want that angry, bitter thing to be the last thing."

At sixty, as I'm writing this, I feel mortality as more than the ethereal concept I perceived it to be when I first talked to Prince when I was twenty-six. I've seen enough people my age die at the proverbial moment, which I guess leaves me open, too. And so I have indeed come to believe we'll be judged by the last thing we leave behind.

A couple of years after Prince died, I went to see the band the Family perform at the Dakota, an intimate music room seating a few hundred, a venue that Prince had favored his final decade as a favorite spot to quietly, invisibly see new, often mellower, national talent from his reserved table.

A generation before, with the dissolution of the Time, the Family had been at the top of Prince's stable of offshoot bands, founded at the height of his personal *Purple Rain* power, a brilliant ensemble conjured from his imagination and brought to life as another facet of his personality and multiple personae.

He'd been selling, as it happened, a lot of albums. More than anybody. No one was going to say no to the Family, Maserati, Mint Condition, et al. So many records, in fact, that the Time, ostensibly the supporting act of *Purple Rain* had fractiously, ruinously broken up when faced with their own palpable success—and the promise of more, more, more. Morris Day, whom Prince genuinely was amazed at for his terrific comic performance in *Purple Rain*, was also an idiot, the boss felt, for in effect breaking up the Time by leaving the band to be on his own, just as they were on the precipice of serious fame and money.

So big deal if Morris Day—freckle-faced errand boy Morris Day!—was suddenly on *The David Letterman Show* dressed in pimp's regalia and cane, boasting about his women. Didn't he know, Prince asked, that *he*, Prince, was responsible for his success and probably for any continued success, and that was just the fact?

Soon enough *Purple Rain* and Morris Day made it so the Time didn't exist. They were quickly replaced by the Family, made up in part of members of the defunct Time—a band Prince was convinced would be a major moneymaker. The Family, goes the accepted Prince lore, was a mostly white version of the mostly black version of the Time. It was a mighty crown to inherit: Under his dictatorial tutelage the Time had become so good that they were the only band Prince sincerely claimed he was "afraid" of.

Meantime, the Family's lead singer was Susannah Melvoin, the winsome identical twin of Wendy Melvoin of Lisa and Wendy of the Revolution fame.

Susannah had a brain, a spine, and a great laugh, and in 1986 had finally walked out on Prince—walked out on *Prince*!—after he refused to stop stepping out with other girls. Despite promises, Prince could not keep a pact of fidelity, and Susannah split from Minneapolis back to the San Fernando Valley and an apartment with her sister and Lisa Coleman.

The stomp-out was not the only thing that doomed the band: The original Family had broken up after one album when Susannah's colead singer "Saint" Paul Peterson quit the group in a dispute with Prince about money, or rather the lack of it in the pockets of the musicians, whom Prince paid a salary of three hundred dollars a week. That album included the first recording of "Nothing Compares 2 U," which Sinéad O'Connor would turn into an international hit in 1990.

The band has reunited and put out several albums in the years since, and has been a touring entity again in the last several years, with almost the whole original lineup: Jellybean Johnson, Peterson, and Eric Leeds, from whom Prince would learn and copy many jazz stylings.

And Susannah.

I had never met Susannah, but she was the reason I'd gotten to talk to Prince in the first place, back in the mideighties. Though I'd been working at *Newsweek* for four years by then, I was still relatively a twenty-six-year old cub reporter, and was too dumb to try and angle an apt moment to ask. Wendy and Lisa, who I was interviewing instead, spoke on his behalf, the deal being Prince could say nothing if he appeared on the *Rolling Stone* cover with them.

I wasn't Jimmy Olsen, the go-get-'em, opportunistic boy reporter on Clark Kent/Superman's *Daily Planet*. But Wendy and Lisa told Susannah I was an okay guy, I guess—and she talked Prince into giving an interview. Or at least into checking me out. Susannah didn't know me from Adam Ant, but she took a chance.

And after Prince died, she sent me a LinkedIn message saying something very special to me, the unsolicited words that made me know—good Christ!—that he knew who I *was* beyond an occasionally useful tool all these years, and I guess that that, or I, or something mattered to him:

> *Neal, I cannot tell you the many times he mentioned you with the deepest respect and love. Only a small few could say they were really loved by him. Without too much of my own grief sprinkled in this, I felt deeply loved by him as well. Stay in touch. Love and Kindness, Susannah*

I didn't meet Susannah on my first reporting adventure with Prince—or ever. But she also figured in my first discussion of the leitmotif of loneliness that would prove such a fruitful topic of conversation for so many years between Prince and me:

> *"Sometimes* [he'd said the first time we talked] *it gets lonely here* [at his infamous purple house.] *To be perfectly honest, I wish more of my friends would come by. A lot of times they think I don't want to be bothered. When I told Susannah you were coming over, she said*

"Is there something I can do? Do you want me to come by to make it seem like you have friends coming by?"

I said no, that would be lying. And she just put her head down, because she knew she doesn't come by to see me as much as she wants to, or as much as she thinks I want her to. See, you did some-thing good, and you didn't even know it!

A *compliment*! From *Prince*! There weren't a lot over the years, but more than you'd expect.

And then, backstage, back in the present, thirty-four years later, after the Family's quite excellent show, I met the cause of it all, Su-sannah Melvoin, as well as the band. I had seen them *practice* once when we were all young, but had never been introduced.

Wow, did I owe her! And then she said what I took to be the greatest compliment.

"You were the only reporter," she said, "who made Prince sound like he really sounded."

I allowed myself to be flattered: It had been no magic trick or spe-cial talent on my part, but simply a matter of being able to transcribe tapes and/or read my own handwriting. For more than thirty years, I'd just been among the reporters Prince had let tape or take notes on the pretend-sly of our conversations, greater and lesser.

"Thank you, Susannah." I didn't know what else to say, and soon it was time to head off into the Minneapolis night.

I replayed her words over and over to myself.

"You were the only reporter who made Prince sound like he re-ally sounded."

Once upon a time. It had been three years and change since he'd been dead.

And so I watched, over and over, the videos for "Raspberry Beret" and his shredding of "While My Guitar Gently Weeps" at the 2004 Rock and Roll Hall of Fame induction ceremonies. Prince? Lonely? With those hordes of the most beautiful women and the strongest men in the world always surrounding him? That so many people found this fact so astounding never failed to astound *me*.

But where was Prince? Who was he? Despite what Susannah

Melvoin said I'd once done, I'd forgotten what he actually sounded like—the tenor of his laugh, the snap of his anger. Who was *I* to write his biography, a veritable memoir, if I couldn't remember what he sounded like—or walked like or, at times, even looked like?

"Really, I'm normal," Prince said around the turn of the century, speaking in all earnestness and honesty, as he occasionally did with the press. "A little high strung, maybe, But normal."

And there, in a couple of sentences, was the truth about Prince's self-conception: He really was a Minneapolis guy. He was, no matter how weird he got—though he still saw himself, according to Minneapolis norms—*normal*.

If instead he sucked, he would be *different*, and one wouldn't say, "He's an asshole," one would say, "He's *different*." And if you were so different from normal that you were described as a *character*?

In Brooklyn or Portland that might be a high-end compliment, but in Minneapolis—egads! S/he is a character. S/he is not normal. S/he is different, which is as bad as a freak, but not as awful as a character.

In Minneapolis it's not a lingo, it's a worldview. It doesn't matter if one is black, Jewish, or (increasingly) Somali, it is what happens when a monolithic Scandinavian ethos of self-abnegation and loathing becomes so bent by modernity that the town is simultaneously proud of boasting the country's largest shopping mall—and the largest ball of twine on earth rolled by one man.

And why does this matter? Because it is the ultimate contradiction that an artistic personality as brilliantly fractured as Prince's could be comfortable in a place like Minneapolis, where, as he said, "I can go out and not get jumped on"—in light of what eventually happened to George Floyd, a tragically ironic thing to say about being an African American male in this city.

Tragically, for Prince, long before *his* end, he also preferred not to go out because he preferred to be alone. He just didn't want, above all, to die that way. Tragedy to the ninth power, he couldn't choreograph his death as he did his life.

And so it goes in a town where he said he could no longer go out and not get jumped on, that he preferred to be alone because "I make everyone else feel small," that one sees in retrospect he was looking at his own imminent death.

Alas, in a town where to be "normal" is—to be normal, Prince wanted above all to be "sick." Sadly, if you're Prince, that meant, ultimately, he'd get neither what he wanted or needed most.

Sick? If you were an artist, in Minneapolis, sick *wasn't* the requisite "normal." It was going where no human had dared to go. Amazingly, he had the genius to somehow pull it off and stay here. Good for him and us, even the local curmudgeons agree—now that he's gone.

He always cared desperately about his legacy, about how far his "sickness" would take him, what he *did* and had done. But he was beyond completely disinterested in anybody knowing who he actually *was*—he seemed determined that nobody would.

And so he lied. Well, not lied but "teased," as he put it, or engaged, as Don King liked to say, in "trickeration."

It was nothing unique to Prince as a transcendent artist who happened to be African American.

"As a black child," wrote James McBride, James Brown's brilliant biographer in *Kill 'Em and Leave*:

> [Brown] was an expert at knowing what white people expected of him, secure in the knowledge that white folks didn't care enough about him, or black history, or black music, to even pay attention to what he said. As long as you could dance and sing and entertain them, they didn't care what you did or did not do. Sell yourself and get paid. They were going to believe whatever they wanted to about you anyway. So tell 'em anything. And he did.

And so, McBride went on, "There's lots of versions of [his] story: a white version, a black version, a record company version. There's even an official version in his [auto] biography. . . . So what's real?"

Being black, or even a musician, was not necessary for this desire or need to obfuscate. In 1984 Philip Roth told the *Paris Review*: "Making fake biography, false history, concocting a half-imaginary existence out of the actual drama of my life is my life." Roth went on, "There has to be some pleasure in this life, and that's it." Some writers, Roth said, "pretend to be more lovable than they are and some pretend to be less." Artistically, he said is "beside the point. Literature isn't a moral beauty contest. Its power arises from the authority and audacity with which the impersonation is pulled off; the belief it inspires is what counts."

What Prince would have liked was that his music survived in its entirety—but only the legend, *a* legend, just about *any* legend, of his life. He admired bluesman Robert Johnson almost as much for how little was actually known about him as he mourned how little of his output survived.

In 2018 the *New York Times* began running a regular feature named "Overlooked," obituaries of the deserving who were denied "them when they died," beginning in 1851, largely because of race, sex, sexual orientation, or disinterest. When they wrote up Robert Johnson on September 25, 2019, some eighty years after he died, I slapped the paper and thought, *That's* the kind of obituary Prince would have wanted.

Wrote Reggie Ugwu in the *Times*:

> Little about the life Robert Leroy Johnson lived in his brief 27 years, from approximately May 1911 until he died mysteriously in 1938, was documented. A birth certificate, if he had one, has never been found.
>
> What is known can be summarized on a postcard: He is thought to have been born out of wedlock in May 1911 in Mississippi and raised there. . . . and yet . . . he became one of the most famous guitarists who had ever lived, hailed as a lost prophet who, the dubious story goes, sold his soul to the devil and epitomized Mississippi Delta blues in the bargain.

That, Prince would have said, was *sick*.

Finding Prince in the murk is difficult despite the sheer tonnage of ink spilled on him during his lifetime. So much depends on the mind and motives of the teller. One is reminded of the parable of the elephant and the group of blind men who discover the beast—and try to decipher what it looks like by each touching only one small part of the elephant's body, be it a tusk or the animal's flank. Based on their limited knowledge, each then tries to conceptualize the unique enormity of the elephant using their compromised senses and grossly conflicting data.

An example might be Prince's relationship to his Revolution bandmates Wendy Melvoin and Lisa Coleman, a friendship that I obviously knew less about the closer I got. When I first interviewed Prince, still in the flush of the *Purple Rain* gold rush, he gushed about the Revolution: "I personally love this band more than any other group I've ever played with," he said. "Everybody knows what they have to do. *I* know what I have to do."

Beyond their exquisite musicianship, Wendy and Lisa were amulets of good karma who added to his own luster: "Wendy makes me seem all right in the eyes of the audience. She keeps a smile on her face. When I sneer she smiles. It's not premeditated, she just does it. It's a good contrast," he said.

Lisa Coleman, meanwhile, he continued, "is like my sister. She'll play what the average person won't. She'll press two notes with one finger, so the chord is a lot larger. She's more abstract."

A year later the musical love affair seemed bonded by Superglue. "The group's latest album, *Parade: Music from the Motion Picture Under the Cherry Moon*, contains two songs—'Sometimes It Snows in April' and 'Mountains'—cowritten by Lisa and Wendy," I wrote in *Rolling Stone*. "They have also begun writing songs for Prince's third movie. They're not sure what it's about, but Prince has let it be known he'll shape his film to suit their songs."

Within months Prince had dissolved the Revolution. And when Wendy and Lisa put out their first album, Prince dismissed it—as well as their feelings of hurt toward him—as if they were mere acquaintances hopelessly out of step with what was going on musically in the world, or psychologically with their once unbreakable-seeming friendship.

In the end I utilized Virginia Woolf's notion of trying to comprehend the incomprehensible via shards of a broken mirror that might reflect certain basic truths undecipherable if faced head-on. I thought Woolf put the idea quite well in describing those who knew English poet Samuel Taylor Coleridge, as collected in Richard Armour's *Coleridge the Talker*.

"Two pious American editors have collected the comments of this various company, and they are of course, various," wrote Woolf:

> Yet it is the only way of getting at the truth—to have it broken into many splinters by many mirrors and so select. The truth about Coleridge the talker seems to have been that he rapt some listeners to the seventh heaven, bored others to extinction; in the same way his eyes were brown to some, grey to others, and again a very bright blue. But there is one point upon which all who listened are agreed; not one of them could remember a single word he said.

In splintered visions of broken mirror glass, I might get a more rounded picture of the entire Prince than even if I could stand listening to his voice or rereading the words he said to me. If I couldn't trust myself to hear as much as possible of *him* in his voice, perhaps I could see him even more clearly in the shards that reflected parts of who he was.

If I looked closer at what he liked, perhaps I could see better what he was like. And so, in my office, I put up not pictures of Prince, but photographs and mementos of who and what he liked, admired, was once influenced by, or reminded me of him: a black-and-white, eleven-by-fourteen-inch photo of "Pistol" Pete Maravich, the tragic leading scorer in college basketball history. Maravich was taking a jump shot in the late 1960s for Louisiana State University, his trademark floppy socks and hippy-boy hair blowing in the wind.

Petar "Press" Maravich, his father as well as basketball coach through college, both made and destroyed his son, the Pistol, "the first white man who played like a nigger," Prince said as he'd taken the highlight reel off the DVD of Pete Maravich's college years, when he'd averaged a still-unsurpassed 44.9 points a game.

Next to that picture I had a color eight-by-ten close-up of Pete Maravich, only his head and his uniform visible as he pensively cradled a basketball, looking sadder than the whole outdoors.

Unlike John Nelson with Prince, Press Maravich hadn't tried to thwart his son's desire to take his talent down the road of his father's never-achieved ambitions. Rather, Press had funneled his own failed bad basketball karma into a quest to make his son both the greatest and the most-fun-to-watch hoops player in history.

Press almost succeeded. But in creating the perfect, twirling monster for the basketball floor, Press had turned his own son into an alien at dealing with human life. Pistol died at forty, literally of a broken heart (he'd had an undiagnosed coronary defect.)

Then came a sixteen-by-twenty-inch poster of Walt Frazier passing off the basketball from his own dribble underneath the legs of a splayed-in-midair, ginormous, seven-foot-tall Wilt Chamberlain. Walt Frazier was the author of Prince's favorite book growing up, *Rockin' Steady: A Guide to Basketball and Cool.*

"Everyone has a certain rhythm that he dribbles to," Frazier had opined, and Prince had not just one or two, but dozens.

He'd underlined sentences in my copy of the book for emphasis, if never any explanation: "*When you're playing good, you can't sleep too long because you can't wait to wake up. You're excited. You can't wait for the next game, the next day. Usually I can't wait to get my act going again.*"

Style—the man with the ultracool alter ego named Clyde lectured young Prince—was all about fitting your mood to your style:

> So it's about four-thirty or five now. I pick what I'm going to wear to the game. What's my mood? If I feel like steppin' out I'll maybe wear a Clyde-type ensemble. Maybe I'll do seals and minks, doing it all when I'm feeling good. But when I haven't been playing good, nothing else interests me. Not dressing up, not chicks—nothing means nothing.

But not Prince. No way had the music *ever* meant nothing. Had nothing about the spectacle he'd create every day and night in the studio or an auditorium or club meant *nothing*?

Oh yes.

> During the *Dirty Mind* period I'd go into fits of depression and get physically ill. A lot had to do with the band's situation, the fact that I couldn't make people in the band understand how great we could all be together if we all played our part. A lot also had to do with being in love with someone and not getting any love back. And there was the fact that I didn't talk much with my father and sister.

And how did he get over feeling, well, *un*-Clyde?

Paisley Park hadn't been built yet, but that didn't stop Prince from trying to use it as a metaphor for . . . something. "Paisley Park is the only way I can say I got over it. Paisley Park is the place one should find in oneself, where one can go when one is alone."

To seek out a place where one can go when one is alone to recapture one's spirit? Those seemed the specifications one wanted for one's own coffin, and next to the picture of Walt Frazier I put an eight-by-ten black-and-white photo of "Xanadu," Charles Foster Kane's grandiose tomb for the living and dying in *Citizen Kane, his* Paisley Park.

Next to that came the professional-wrestling section of the wall: It seemed appropriate that extra space was being devoted to that questionable art, considering that Prince had constructed much of his life out of the pro-wrestling notion of kayfabe, of never letting them see that there was an actual human being behind the curtain, that the Prince you saw acting peculiar on MTV or at the French Open or the Los Angeles Lakers game was actually the Prince who lived in the outside world and inside his head.

Some would say it was also tragically appropriate, considering that what had consumed and almost destroyed Prince was that, in the parlance of professional wrestling, he had "bought his own gimmick." He had come to believe that the "Prince" character he had perfected was, in fact, Prince. For the last fifteen years of his life, luckily, he had—once again in the parlance of pro wrestling—remembered how he had "gotten over" in the first place—and that life would now be a matter of his getting back there.

Which he did. And that is why lives should be lived in three acts, and Prince's story is not a tragedy. He bought his own gimmick—but he also remembered to give "them" what had originally gotten him "over"—himself, Prince, Prince Rogers Nelson, Skipper, whomever, whatever. However, it was one person up there, capable of playing all those instruments.

And so there is an eight-by-ten color photo of a madly scowling Mad Dog Vachon, minus his lower front teeth, and his 290-pound brother Butcher Vachon. And this was the 1960s, back when 290 pounds *meant* something! Mad Dog and Butcher, the baddest French-Canadians Montreal has ever produced, are each in a grappling, growling pose, a golden World Tag Team Wrestling Championship belt atop each one's trunks.

They had been bad, bad guys, who when interviewed on television had voices that sounded like they had swallowed a wasp. And Prince did a frighteningly spot-on imitation of both brothers, his Mad Dog Vachon being of particular righteousness. But what reminded me of Prince most about Mad Dog was not the former's imitation, but the latter's level of "sickness," and how much that impressed Prince: One of Prince's most critical litmus test of how funky, or outrageous, or just plain new something was, as always, by how *sick* it was.

"To be sick is to do something nobody else would do," he'd said in 1985.

They called him Mad Dog, and Prince loved him. "He let them take his fake leg and let another guy beat another guy over the head with it!" Prince had exclaimed when I told him the news. "That is *sick*."

Yes, the "retired" Mad Dog Vachon, for his final act, had agreed to go through with a "bit" where his prosthetic leg would be "forcibly" removed at ringside and used by another wrestler to bludgeon a third? Prince then offered one of his great gut laughs, the kind he was so rarely able or willing to summon in his screen performances: "There is a man willing to sacrifice for his *art*," he said.

Next on the wall beside the Vachon brothers were their always archnemeses, an eight-by-ten shot of the lovably and always morally vague Crusher and his kayfabe "cousin," Dick the Bruiser, aka William Fritz Afflis, who took up pro wrestling after retiring from the Green Bay Packers. In the photograph, taken in the mid-1950s, Crusher and Bruiser are shown frozen in fury, their faces smeared in blood, their rippling arms holding up folding chairs in the middle of the ring, seats which they will no doubt soon be laying upon the head of an unfortunate, anonymous wrestler who already lies on the mat at their mercy. It matters not that whatever they're about to do is patently illegal; it is Bruiser and Crusher, and nobody did a better imitation of Crusher than Prince.

And why did he like Crusher? "They made a hit out of him," he recalled, of the eponymous ode to the wrestler, remembering the lyrics to the Nova's 1962 ditty that charted briefly with lyrics about headlocks and eye-gouges.

But what did Crusher have to do with Don King, the malevolent boxing promoter addicted to polysyllabic pronouncements and graced with gravity-defying hair who'd learned his big words and Shakespeare after he kicked a man to death in the streets of Cleveland?

"He made everything seem new," Prince said, pausing. "Even when it was old."

And last in the rogues' hall of fame of professional wrestlers was a photo of the all-time grappling "heel" Gorgeous George, in a Liberace-worthy mink, his effeminate golden locks pinned back with what were called "Georgie Pins," which he'd toss to the angry crowds booing him as if he'd turned the manliest endeavor that existed into a debutante ball. George had unlocked the secret that would inspire, all three men would admit, Muhammad Ali to be the loudest, most braggadocious big mouth in sports; Little Richard, in rock, to be the most outrageous; and James Brown to be the baddest. Even if the masses couldn't stand or didn't understand you, George understood: They would fill an auditorium to see the heretofore unseen, to be positively *outraged*.

Muhammad Ali was still Cassius Clay when he saw Gorgeous George draw a huge mob of wrestling fans who hated him. It was the passion Clay tapped into when he saw George and his outrage draw fifteen thousand shrieking patrons to an auditorium, as Jonathan Eig reports in his seminal biography, *Ali*. "I said," Eig quotes Ali later, "this is a *goooood* idea."

While George incited wrestling fans of the 1950s by prancing, and Ali recited poetry in the ring, Prince, pretended he was this character, Prince.

It worked. He'd "gotten over" in the biggest sense possible in rock and roll. And to get the attention he needed when he was nobody, he had both the talent and the understanding of the lessons in showmanship of those who influenced him, who had in turn been inspired by Gorgeous George.

And then there was a twenty-by-twenty-seven-inch poster for the 1965 Bob Dylan documentary, *Don't Look Back*. It was one of my favorite movies, the first cinema verité full documentary, by D. A. Pennebaker, as he followed Bob Dylan around his 1966 tour of Britain. "He never crossed over," Prince, said, repeating his line over and over.

I'd made him watch the film, and noted the footage Pennebaker had put in of a *very* young Dylan very early in his career playing "The Lonesome Death of Hattie Carroll," the true story of ass-backward racial injustice, in a Southern field before a small audience of what seem to be sharecroppers and their families.

"What do you call that?" I asked.

"Notice that he knew enough to make sure there was a camera crew in that field?" Prince asked.

He was right. Prince, like Dylan, was hip to the ways of the media when the media still thought they were the one-dimensional kayfabe characters each had created. Like Dylan, Prince had proved how far one could go by going way too far.

And next to that, symbolizing "betrayal" beyond Wendy and Lisa is an eight-and-a-half-by-eleven color photo of the Revolution right at the time of *Purple Rain*. Prince—the only picture of him I have in the room—drummer Bobby Z. Rivkin, keyboardist Matt "Dr." Fink, Lisa Coleman, and Wendy Melvoin on guitar.

And here is Prince on the band that seemed to be for all time, not just a prelude to something called the New Power Generation.

It would never end because the Revolution *communicated*. Said Prince:

> Sometimes everybody in the band comes over, and we have very long talks. They're very few and far between, and I do a lot of the talking. Whenever we're done, one of them will come up to me and say:
>
> "Take care of yourself. You know I really love you."
>
> I think they love me so much, and I love them so much, that if they came over all the time I wouldn't be able to be to them what I am, and they wouldn't be able to do for me what they do. I think we come together with what we've concocted in our heads, it's cool. I can't imagine a better situation, a better band, a better reason to go out in the universe and try something new.

Men, men, men, oh so many men before I land on a woman on my office wall, a lovely shot of Billie Holiday standing at the microphone. Prince had evinced disdain for Holiday's self-dissipation— "She stopped listening for how people were finishing their sentences, and got fried," he said in disdain, the kind of disdain for drug addicts who'd sacrificed their careers and lives that would keep him too ashamed to seek help at the end, when he could have saved himself.

The women who weren't victims, it hit me as I stared up again at the collage of faces he sometimes turned into victims, or scalawags. I had a picture of his mother, Mattie, at around the time she'd gotten married to John Nelson, and began singing for the Prince Rogers Trio. She looked nothing like the libertine wild woman he'd tell tales of for as long as she lived, when he wouldn't make a life move without consulting Mattie Shaw for her opinion and counsel.

Symbolizing the damage he could do with his bullshit, simply concerning his mother, was a picture of his forever hairdresser, Kim Berry. I had always enjoyed Berry's interviews when I stumbled upon them; the interview she gave a hair salon magazine after Prince's death was one of the best pieces. She had been on speaking terms with Prince for almost as long as me, and she was right down there with him, literally in his head, or at least his hair, almost every day.

But he had to bullshit even Kim, just enough so that when her book, *Diamonds and Curlz* (sic) came out in 2019, she painted a false and disturbing picture of Mattie as an out-and-out dope fiend that ruined the book.

Kim's book painted Mattie Shaw as an irreedemable drug addict. It was untrue, of course, as all his tales of his mother were; never mind that on planet Earth she was a long-serving social worker specializing in addiction issues. Berry wrote:

> Prince told me that his mother had been addicted to drugs, and once, when she ran out of cash and couldn't get money from his stepfather, she snuck into Prince's room and took what she could find. He had been saving that money for a new guitar. For the rest of his life, that moment clung to Prince like the smell of grease from a fish fry. It impacted the way he trusted and treated women; it forced him to protect his music—and his money—fiercely.

One lie from Prince and Berry's importance to the historical record was destroyed. "Prince knew his mother used to run from one relationship to the next to feed her drug habit," she went on, "never providing the nurturing love that he needed as a child (and as a man.) As a result, he never displayed any real respect for any of the women who came into his life after that."

The problem is that this wasn't Mattie Shaw. She wasn't a drug addict, she was a social worker with a special expertise in drug addiction. Cindy Stoewer, the student who worked a couple of hours a day in the school office across the hall from Mattie remembers coming to her with questions about what she worried was her own mother's addiction to playing bingo. "I was really worried," Stoewer recalls. "And I remember talking to Mattie about that. I remember saying, 'I think she's addicted. What do I do about my mom being addicted to bingo?'"

She continues:

> And I remember Mattie telling me signs to look for with addiction. [Is] she ignoring things she should be doing? Is she making excuses for things? Is she taking money away from these things that are really important? Can she not pay her bills because she's spending too much money? I remember getting some real specifics. I remember her style. She wasn't bossy, she was wise and smart, but she wouldn't say "You do this, you do that." She *listened*. And there was always a joy to her.

And still Kim Berry went on about the wreckage she believed Mattie had caused Prince based on his one lie that she'd been a degenerate drug addict. She did this and that to feed her monkey, he said, and it ruined him; and all the women, Berry noticed, looked like the mother who supposedly tortured him.

"Prince definitely had a type. He liked his women petite," she wrote, "and after he broke things off with Vanity (his first true love) most of the women he dated, as well as both of the women he married, had a similar look. I liked to say they were 'Vanity-esque.'"

They were, in fact, Mattie Shaw–esque: There was an element of revenge in the way he treated women, but it was from how he was teased and forever bettered and beaten out for the girls of his dreams, it seemed, back in junior high and high school—often by friends or his half-brother Duane. His tastes grew catholic, however, when he began playing in bands and the women came running.

And on and on it went, my walls of Prince mirrors. There was a picture of Minnesota Vikings quarterback Joe Kapp, in 1969, taking the ball in a snap from Vikings center and football Hall of Famer Mick Tingelhoff. That Vikings team had been of my time as well as Prince's.

That hometown team went to the Super Bowl when he was eleven and I was ten, and was heavily favored to beat the Kansas City Chiefs. Though, oddly, I never asked him what the Vikes hideously losing that big game had done to him as a prepubescent, I myself was never the same. I honestly believe that that 23–7 wipeout of my team as a child had given me my tragic sense of life. But who cares?

Prince had never stopped caring about the Vikings—nicknamed back then (with a nod to Sheb Wooley's 1950s novelty hit) "the Purple People Eaters"—and had even gone so far as to write them a new theme song—a submission they rejected. If nothing so symbolized the rejection of his hometown, that was it: Turning down a Prince composition in favor of keeping their half-century-old jingle that sounded like a mediocre high school jingle rouser.

As soon as Prince was dead, of course, the Vikings had the one-hundred-plus musicians of the august Minnesota Orchestra take the field at halftime and played a full orchestral version of "Purple Rain," a version that went viral, while only a few newspapers dug up the fact that the man himself, already long in full fame, had sent them an unsolicited and *free* composition that by mere virtue of its composer would have given the Vikes the funkiest team song through eternity in professional or college sports—and they had turned it down.

Minneapolis.

He could be so self-contradictory that it sometimes verged on self-mockery. When I asked him, for instance, about those who doubted the sincerity of his conversion to the righteous and nonprofane path of Jehovah, he retorted: "Yeah, those are the same people who will tell you I never fucked Kim Basinger."

Facts, as such, didn't matter. He would have been amused that any reporter in the world—including several who were scouring the globe for hints about whether Prince had grown up a Seventh-day Adventist—could have contacted his old friend André Cymone and learned the name and location of the Adventist church the two attended growing up.

There were contradictions even in who had access to the moribund Prince and his Paisley Park temple: Three years before he died, a police report filed about a minor nonspecified incident at Paisley Park noted that "Only Prince had a key and he was the one who would let people in or out."

And yet when medical personnel got to Paisley Park to find Prince in an elevator, dead since well before dawn, half a dozen people were inside in various states of hysteria. And while his death certificate should just as meaningfully have included "shame" as "fentanyl" as a cause of Prince's death, how could embarrassment possibly have been listed as a fatal contributing factor for a man who had absolutely no problem performing live on national television with his butt cheeks apparently proudly exposed for the world to see?

He died partly of the shame of addiction? The same man who unashamedly appeared before one hundred thousand booing Rolling Stones fans in the Los Angeles Coliseum throwing deadly missiles of full bottles of booze at him, a slight, sexually ambiguous figure wearing lingerie, who dared sing the sexually ambiguous "Jack U Off" while the mob waited for the headliners to take the stage and play "Street Fighting Man."

I am convinced he died spiritually, inside his consciousness if not his soul, from the combined effects of the death two decades before of his days-old son Amiir, as well as the fact that he could no longer dance, and sooner rather than later would no longer have the strength in his arms to play guitar or even the piano. Yet still . . .

In reality to die, literally of shame, afraid to admit he needed help. For help with an addiction that stemmed from a lifetime of work-related injuries sustained from jumping off thirty-foot speakers in high heels—from literally giving his fans, for decades, far more than they'd paid for?

This wasn't the shame of a Michael Jackson overdosing on surgical anesthesia he needed in order to take a nap; or Elvis falling off the toilet dead after swallowing a Walgreen's distribution center worth of fourteen different drugs including Demerol, amytal, and codeine.

Hazelden—which had saved the likes of Eric Clapton and Pearl Jam's Mike McCready with no apparent harm to their careers, was so close.

But the boss had to say yes. And the boss said no. It would have been too disgraceful, after a lifetime of lecturing and firing subordinates about and over drugs, after decades of press clippings about clean living, vegan living, and the superhuman strength of the little fellow who seemingly never needed to sleep to create, let alone narcotics to get through the day.

And so shame killed, while Prince's lackeys scrambled like Keystone Kops for help, any kind of help, from any kind of source, be it even a West Coast doctor nobody seemed to have heard of, who in turn sent for triage his premed son on a flight to Minneapolis armed with naloxone to suss out the situation, while Prince literally already lay dead.

It was, like virtually everything else in Prince's life, a seemingly incomprehensible contradiction. Unless one knew of the power of addiction, so much stronger than even one hundred thousand white macho meatballs booing a twenty-three-year-old black man standing before them wearing lingerie and a guitar.

There was really nothing one could do to stop someone from killing themselves if they were too hurt and ashamed to want to continue.

I knew but didn't really internalize that critical fact until a few years after Prince's family rendered him into ash. A different thought occurred to me after I talked to Prince on the phone less than a month before he died.

I'd realized then, as Prince called me "mamma jamma" one last time, what Dallas radio reporter Roy Jenkins understood in November 1963 as he watched President John Kennedy's limousine unexpectedly speed up.

"Something is wrong here," Jenkins had said into his microphone, stricken with the heebie-jeebies, "something is terribly wrong."

I didn't have a microphone, but panicked—I think sideways when panicked—and came up with a cuckoo scheme. Otherwise, I'd never have done what I did, like a handful of his old friends did on their own.

With the only tool I might have, I tried.

And so André Cymone pretended he was homeless, deep on the skids, as he texted Prince with pleas to be allowed to come stay with him at Paisley Park. Alan Leeds, just about as close to Prince as anybody who'd ever worked for him, was given a patronizing "nothing wrong here" when he called Paisley Park after the Moline incident, told not to worry by someone he'd thought was a friend, not a bullshitter willing to play enabler to a superstar about to croak.

There wasn't much I could do that last month he was alive. I don't have a whole lot of markers out there. So my plan—to call out to him through the newspaper in the hopes he'd get in touch—perhaps wasn't as cockamamy as it sounded. Perhaps. I'd come to know a college housemate's brother, the late great Baker Saunders, a well-known bass player in recovery. He'd become an inspirational figure to many in the Hazelden community who'd stuck around the Twin Cities after getting out of rehab in an attempt to avoid old bad friends and habits.

Baker had become friends and jamming buddies with Pearl Jam's Mike McCready, another Hazelden graduate, and had been hired first by Pearl Jam, to accompany them on tour both to serve as a resident wise man—and to clean out the minibar before McCready got to his hotel room. Later he even joined an all-sober band McCready had started as a side project, Mad Season, and recorded a hit album with them.

Meantime, a few years earlier I'd bizarrely intersected with Kurt Cobain while writing a book on the music industry, and had even wangled a night's stay at the house he shared with his wife, Courtney Love, and baby, Frances Bean. He'd seemed clean to me that day, but within a year Cobain had vaulted the wall of a California rehab he'd checked into, and headed to Seattle on the lam for what would prove to be his last days on earth before sticking a shotgun in his mouth.

What, I asked Baker, should people who had any way to contact someone in trouble do in those situations?

"Call them out, do whatever you have to do to have them call you," Baker said.

After he'd escaped the rehab center, half the world seemed to be looking for Cobain, but to no avail. In that situation I'd asked Baker, what should one do? "Whatever you have to get a hold of him and to come in out of the cold. By any means necessary."

Now, in the last weeks of Prince's life, my only means was through people I knew at the newspaper who could print veiled pleas to get Prince to get in touch with me. I knew he acted most aggressively, or acted at all, when he was angry, so I decided to give his archenemy— the gossip columnist C.J. at the *Star Tribune*, the only weapon I had—the first interview I'd given in decades about the little purple guy.

I called him out, revealing to Minneapolis (falsely) what a "nightmare" it would be to work with him again. I told the columnist about his "time capsule" and final testament I'd written for him so long before, and provided such juicy details about him that the national must-read *Adweek* ran two installments of my videotaped interview in their gossip column.

I knew people at Hazelden—I'd done several stories on recovery, and had even been locked up there for a week for their quit-smoking program, which was run on the tenets of the Twelve Steps ("I'm Neal," I'd tell my group, "and I'm a nicotine addict." My group would roar back, "Hi, Neal!").

Now, days before Prince would become another opioid casualty, I called a friend who worked at Hazelden and told him someone famous probably needed a bed. I didn't hear aye or nay, just as I never heard back from Prince. But I literally almost threw up in horror a few years later while reading Jay Corn's locally produced investigative book on Prince's death.

Apparently, the morning Prince died—in fact he was already entering rigor mortis in the elevator—Kirk Johnson, Prince's personal assistant Meron Bekure, and Dr. Howard Kornfeld's dipshit son, Andrew, were enjoying a leisurely breakfast at a hotel restaurant near Paisley Park before going over and checking on the boss, who was already a corpse.

Both Johnson and Meron "nonchalantly shared [that] it wasn't unusual to 'not check on Prince for a while,'" said Andrew later, horrified.

"He's alone?" Andrew asked in disbelief. The unanimated "yes" answers from Kirk and Meron sent a pang stinging through Andrew's gut, and he suggested they try to find Prince.

Wrote Corn: "Two incoming calls, received during breakfast with Kirk and Andrew at 9:20 and 9:21, appeared to be from the intake division of Hazelden. . . . Neither were answered."

Motherfuckers.

I have no idea if I had anything to do with those calls, but I highly doubt it—I had neither Meron nor Kirk's phone numbers to give my sources I'd contacted at Hazelden, and I suspect some third party had reached out.

But still, the motherfuckers.

While André was pretending to be homeless to get hold of Prince and Alan was vainly quizzing people he thought were his friends at Paisley Park about Prince's condition, calls from the world's leading rehab center to the few people who actually had access to Prince were going unanswered while the three amigos enjoyed breakfast. Not that it mattered—Prince had already been dead for hours—but it *does*. I don't know what he deserved, and he deserved better than that.

Or did he? Prince, literally terminally lonely, had become so alone by turning virtually everyone he dealt with into a servant. And as Samuel Johnson wrote:

> "The danger of betraying our weaknesses to our servants, and the impossibility of concealing it from them, may be justly considered as one motive to a regular . . . life. No condition is more hateful or despicable than he who has put himself in the power of his servants."

Maybe, maybe not. But Prince—a man who found it despicable to be even symbolically under the thumb of beloved music industry titans and mensches like Mo Ostin and Lenny Waronker—was most certainly not going to put himself under the power of servants like his personal assistant and property manager Kirk Johnson, or an unknown premed student named Andrew Kornfeld.

For if he was nothing else, Prince, as he liked to remind me, was bad, too bad to put himself under anybody's power. Sans snark, it was too fucking bad.

And then, three plus years postmortem, having seen the reunited Family and Susannah Melvoin, I needed to remember what Prince sounded like again. I couldn't remember. With time the myth had replaced the man.

I opened up my computer and listened to the first question I ever asked Prince. It was 1985, and as per my usual interviewing style, I didn't so much pose a query as begin babbling a run-on something that usually makes the subject interrupt me and say something just to get me to stop not making sense.

"In people's minds it all boils down to 'Is Prince getting too big for his britches?'" he began his first answer. "I wish people would understand that I always thought I was bad. I wouldn't have got into the business if I didn't think I was bad."

I recognized the voice.

It was a friend.

POSTSCRIPT: PRINCELIT

Jack Gladney, the narrator of Don DeLillo's brilliant absurdist 1985 novel *White Noise*, is a professor at College-on-the-Hill, as well as the international founder of an entirely new field of academic discipline officially known as Hitler Studies. One hopeful on staff says to Gladney, "I love what you've done for Hitler. Someday I hope to do the same for Elvis."

Life aped art in 2006, when the *New York Times*'s Richard Sandomir declared the existence of a new literary genre entitled "MickLit" devoted to the never-ending excavating and explicating of every possible happenstance in the life of Mickey Mantle, the New York Yankee home-run hitter and forever aw-shucks All-American Boy of the 1950s and 1960s.

Mantle played baseball like Prince played music—with an artistry, industry, and sense of style so profound they transcended their particular art forms, ascending to that pantheon of cultural icons so preternaturally *good* at what they did that they in effect beat their own games. For that we asked only for them to be who they were, or to at least pretend who we wanted them to be, forever.

By 2010—fifteen years after Mantle's death—an estimated thirty full-scale biographies had been written of the in-truth quite miserable and misery-making Mantle, including a half dozen volumes the slugger and members of his driven-mad family had eagerly cooperated on. Some of the books tried to explain with a nostalgic patina the how and why of what he did on the baseball diamond. Others focused on why Mickey Mantle fared so poorly as a human being.

Finally, in 2010, Jane Leavy came up with *The Last Boy*, a sweeping, incisive, and creatively constructed life story of a tragically heroic forever-masked man—a book that made it possible to say there was a definitive Mickey Mantle biography.

Or was there?

Not that her work had brought an end to MickLit: if anything it accelerated the musings. As Leavy noted in the introduction to the paperback version of her masterpiece, "The packaging and repackaging, construction and deconstruction of [Mantle's] memory continues unabated [as] writers recalibrate his memory and recycle recollections."

And what was the point again, even of Leavy's meritorious work? She'd interviewed 563 people, from the man who designed Mantle's rookie-year baseball card to Eric Kandel, winner of the 2000 Nobel Prize in Physiology or Medicine.

Leavy asked Kandel for an explanation for the superhuman power behind Mantle's scientifically impossible but quite real home run swing. And then she asked about the slugger's inability to explain how he created his own magic.

Kandel answered wittily: "I think your question is not dramatically different than asking, 'What makes Mozart Mozart?'"

Forget comparisons: We won't know for decades if Prince was a new Mozart or Rudy Vallée, an almost entirely forgotten crooner who in the late 1920s and 30s became one of the first pop music superstars. I'm betting heavily Prince's genius is for real. One either believes it or not, but until that question is answered, let's call what is happening and will continue to happen "PrinceLit."

The sheer number of actually quite worthy books and articles about this guy that have been published (or regularly republished post mortem from the back catalog of Prince life stories and artistic dissections) since his 1984 *Purple Rain* breakthrough is astonishing.

There have been reportage and criticism, biographies and memoirs, oral histories and tomes of revenge and fond remembrances; deconstructions of his discography, not to mention comic and coloring books for adults. There have been so-called pathographies positing theories about every one of Prince's warts, faux pas, and social miscues, real or imagined; and hagiographies all but concluding, that, well, Prince is God.

I'm guessing not. Yet he certainly was so contradictory in manner and multiplicity of personalities, that for proper illustration I had to go back to the unlikely, perhaps-hallucinatory-in-comparison figure of Lyndon Johnson, the U.S. commander in chief from Lee Harvey Oswald's third shot, to President-elect Richard Nixon putting his hand on his inaugural Bible, to find a just-so combination of idealism, vision, power, and pure batshit craziness. (Again, one can only go so far. For Prince the Time was a side project from his Revolution, while for LBJ the side project to his Great Society was the Vietnam War.)

In reviewing Johnson aide Joseph Califano's memoirs in 1991, the *Los Angeles Times* lauded the former adviser for making it possible to "see the L.B.J. who was part Machiavelli, part Falstaff, part Fagin, part Robespierre, part Robin Hood, and part American Original. The view is worth the price of admission."

Keyboardist Morris Hayes lasted two decades with the New Power Generation—longer than anyone in the NPG, Prince's post-Revolution, long-lived backing band with a revolving door of local musicians. Hayes survived longer than any other member of NPG because he was able to deduce on any particular day which Prince he'd be dealing with.

"I theorized that there were five of him," he told C.J., the Minneapolis *Star Tribune* gossipeuse and Prince tormentor in 2018:

> I would study the different versions of Prince. There was what I
> call "The Purple Rain Prince" I first saw when I went to the movies
> and I thought that's what Prince was. When I got in the band, there
> was this really tough band leader and I was like, "Oooh, this guy is
> mean. Woooo, he's rough." That's No. 2. No. 3 was the guy [who]
> was the basketball playing [character], talk about each other's mom-
> mas and joke around. And then there was the sad Prince, the one
> [who] was having a bad day—so you're going to have a bad day. The
> other one [5] was the guy [who] would give you the shirt off his back.
> What I started doing was, before I would say anything, I would see
> who showed up today. Then I'd be like, "OK No. 2 is here. If you're
> not on your A-Game, you're going to have a headache today." That
> really helped me . . . I'd just let him talk and everything was like, "I
> know what I'm dealing with today," and I stayed.

How many personalities did he have? I'm convinced it is impossible for any person to know; I doubt whether he had any idea himself.
Less than two weeks after he died, the *New York Times* cracked the
truth of how Prince was able to make sure no one knew his whole
story: "Unlike many stars of his magnitude, who are known to employ
extensive entourages and teams of staffers to handle everyday business, Prince was also surprisingly autonomous, friends and associates
said, often driving himself around and making appointments without
the knowledge of his assistant[s]. Such insistence on maintaining his
independence may have made keeping a secret easier, they said."

And yet, despite the Rubik's Cubes that made up Prince's forever-
clashing personalities—a multiplicity of personalities for whom
"multifaceted" seems a pitiful understatement—another common
denominator of many of such types is to be a complete unknown
as an actual human being. To *be*, most definitely—perhaps known
as the best in the world, certainly. But to be *known*? *Understood*?
That's *not* what becomes a legend most.

Lyndon Johnson, like Prince, was obsessed with secrecy. Later in life he once had four hundred copies of his college yearbook defaced, cut apart to remove what he considered embarrassing parts of his biography. Alone?

And these loners of the masses often accepted their contradictions as natural. Califano described LBJ as "brave and brutal, compassionate and cruel, incredibly intelligent and infuriatingly insensitive. . . . with a shrewd and uncanny instinct for the jugular of his allies and adversaries."

There are just those who don't want to be known for who they "are" but for what they "do."

And yet Prince had just accepted $2.5 million from Random House to tell his autobiography shortly before he died: What could indicate a desire to be known more than that?

Depends.

As McBride discovered while investigating James Brown, the subject had no interest that the truth be related; in fact Brown seemed to take delight in what bullshit there was inside its pages. "'I was laughing because Brown didn't even want to do that book. He just told the [ghostwriter] anything he wanted,'" said Charles Bobbit, his personal manager for forty-one years. 'He had a lot of stuff in his family, his family life, that he didn't want to come out.'"

Similarly, Prince had told me years ago that he would like to do a book of his life—but one that would be so full of half-truths, whole lies, blot-outs of huge sections of his past, that whatever he ended up with would in fact be a novel. Perverse as it seems, by leaving only twenty-nine pages of handwritten narrative behind, Prince almost guaranteed a fantastic memoir might well come out. Indeed, *The Beautiful Ones*, Prince's ostensible memoir, is in fact an illustrative and artfully-written delight, edited by Dan Piepenbring, who was only twenty-nine and without a book credit when Prince picked him to collaborate.

Piepenbring was the perfect choice, adding insight and élan in a monograph-length narrative that he composed after only three months' worth of sporadic phone calls and meetings with Prince. The book is chock-full of fascinating photos, goodies, and handwritten gewgaws from Prince's life and estate, and he managed to pull it off. Yeah, Dan!

And yet, Prince as the Square John seems impossible to imagine. In *End of the Century*, the brilliant 2003 documentary on the Ramones, Joey Ramone's brother posits the not-illogical conclusion that if Joey Ramone hadn't become Joey Ramone, he would have ended up in a mental hospital or assisted-care facility. He was just too . . . Joey.

And Prince . . . not a star? Could he have survived?

Chris Moon has opined on what should have been. (Moon can take credit as being Prince's first producer by virtue of his allowing the green teenager free rein of his Sound 80 studio in Minneapolis in the mid-1970s.) At the end of the combination biopic/documentary *When Doves Cry*, Moon pronounces:

"I'm not sure having help make Prince famous [and] achieve his dreams was ultimately what he needed," Moon said. "What would have been [if all] I had done is introduce him to a nice girl and he had had a couple of children and gone to work at the factory and grown up as an old man sitting on his rocking chair, never famous? I think perhaps . . . I would been proud of that."

I don't know. Baby, he was a star!

Or he'd have been nothing.

As it was, he left plenty to go around for the purveyors of PrinceLit.

I hesitate to name one favorite Prince book for fear of leaving five worthy works off the list. I also fear logrolling the entire rock-crit establishment, almost none of whom I know but who are not generally known as a crowd that enjoys having their asses kissed by an outsider. And so, like Michael Scott on Prince's favorite show, *The Office*, I am distributing the equivalent of "the Dundies," the individual awards Scott would hand out each year at a ceremony for Dunder Mifflin Paper Company employees.

For the best book that reminded me of one of my favorite movies I give the Dundie to Alan Light's *Let's Go Crazy*, his retelling of a generation that came of age during *Purple Rain*—and provided a perfect snapshot of a moment in time, just as Richard Linklater's film *Dazed and Confused* could have been a documentary of my high school years.

Dig If You Will the Picture by Ben Greenman was an Old Testament lamentation for what had been lost by Prince's death; and a New Testament love-thy-neighbor encomium to the joy and just plain *dance* commandment embedded in Prince's music and performance that he brought fresh, seemingly, to each demonstration. Greenman offered to Prince a wish, a dream, a prayer of mourning.

Touré's *I Would Die 4 U* as expected made steam come out of my ears like Popeye's immediately after he ate spinach—but I had to admit at the end, no matter how much I want to disagree with the man, that he's right.

Alex Hahn and Laura Tiebert, co-authors of *The Rise of Prince*, provided the necessary spadework for digging up the truth about Prince while he was on the rise, while Jim Walsh, with *The Gold Experience*, delineated not just the tick-tock behind Prince's nineties decline, but also the critical backbone behind the slide. Ronin Ro and Mick Wall provided a veteran music journalist's ability to get the then-this-happened-then-that-happened exegesis of Prince's life and career leavened with apt commentary.

In many ways, oddly, I feel the finest straight biography of Prince is James McBride's saga of James Brown. The men were different; the pressure was often the same.

There is such great and terrible criticism written on Prince's music that perhaps the one thing we don't need is any more. Questlove, an authentic friend of Prince, was prescient enough to be able to look back and note that Prince hadn't, contrary to conventional wisdom, made a feeble, ultimately moribund attempt at catching up to the future that had become the present. With a sample box, who needed to be able to play twenty-nine instruments better than any twenty-nine instrumentalists he could find?

A bad rap, wrote Questlove, for:

> at heart, [Prince] was more hip-hop than anyone. . . . Prince was an outlaw. When he was giving interviews on the regular to Cynthia Horner in *Right On!* magazine, he was telling tall tales left and right.

That was hip-hop. He built a crew, a posse, around his look and his sense of style. That was hip-hop. He had beef (with Rick James). He had his own vanity label (Paisley Park Records). He had parents up in arms over the content of his songs to the point where they had to invent the Parental Advisory warning. Hip-hop, hip-hop, hip-hop.

And then what else need be said, or should even be uttered, after Robert Christgau's 1980 review of *Dirty Mind*, where he somehow begins a sentence with the words "Brashly lubricious," and by the middle of the same sentence uses the phrase "fuckbook fantasies"? The man has passion.

Wrote Christgau about Prince forty years ago:

> After going gold in 1979 as an utterly uncrossed over falsetto love man, he takes care of the songwriting, transmutes the persona, revs up the guitar, muscles into the vocals, leans down hard on a rock-steady, funk-tinged four-four, and conceptualizes—about sex, mostly. Thus he becomes the first commercially viable artist in a decade to claim the visionary high ground of Lennon and Dylan and Hendrix (and Jim Morrison), whose rebel turf has been ceded to such marginal heroes-by-fiat as Patti Smith and John Rotten-Lydon. Brashly lubricious where the typical love man plays the lead in "He's So Shy," he specializes here in full-fledged fuckbook fantasies—the kid sleeps with his sister and digs it, sleeps with his girlfriend's boyfriend and doesn't, stops a wedding by gamahuching the bride on her way to church.

"Gamahuching"?

Me? On the question of who Prince "is," or "was," or "will be," I defer to the man—and the one time in the thirty-one years I knew him when he didn't swat away like a pesky gnat my infinite queries about who he thought he was, or who he reminded himself of, or who he wanted to be, or be like. He was wholly *sui generis*, he always said— though not in the Latin—"unto himself."

He made a point of announcing "I'm bad," unquestionably unaware that the way he'd grown up had made him feel that way in both diametrically opposite meanings of the term.

But one day—April 19, 1994—he let on with a curious piece of self-awareness regarding who he might be compared to. Just that once. He was picking me up to go to Rudolph's Barbecue joint about four blocks from my apartment in Uptown. I'd brought a copy of the soundtracks of one of my favorite blaxploitation films of the 1970s.

Prince always fancied himself a bit of a "Shaft" kind of character— though he'd never admit it, just as he'd never cop to still forever affecting the memoir title of his favorite basketball player when he was fourteen, Walt "Clyde" Frazier of the New York Knicks. *Rockin' Steady: A Guide to Basketball and Cool* was the book, and Prince could still quote from it like it was Ezekiel.

And he still defined the name of fictional African American private eye John Shaft as meaning "bad motherfucker." But the song Prince opened up to that one time wasn't the original, totemic, magnificent Isaac Hayes version of the theme from *Shaft*.

Rather, it is from the third and last in the series: the little-seen *Shaft's Big Score*. The theme, "Blowin' Your Mind," was played by the comparatively good but unbrilliant O. C. Smith singing about John Shaft.

We sat and listened.

> He's a smooth cat
> And knows where it's at
> A bad spade
> Don't pull your blade
> A super brother
> A gone mother
> A cool dude
> And shovels his food

"You want to know who I am?" Prince asked, about to come out with the first straight answer to the question. "Him. That's me. That guy he's singing about."

I looked over at him. He was, I had to admit, a smooth cat who knew where it was at. Using the nomenclature of the time, with all due respect, he was indeed a bad spade, and only an idiot would even think of pulling a blade. He was a super brother, a truly gone mother. A cool dude, definitely.

And he did shovel his food. Half the time. The other half he'd eat so slowly that you'd think your head would explode waiting for him to finish.

I wish he'd liked more people.

I wish, in pro-wrestling's phony kayfabe ethos, Prince hadn't, over the decades, bought into his own gimmick.

I wish Al Nuness had let him try out for the tenth-grade basketball team at Minneapolis Central High School.

I wish, just once, I'd told him we were friends.

"Show me a hero," wrote Prince's *lontzman* F. Scott Fitzgerald, "and I'll write you a tragedy."

ACKNOWLEDGMENTS

I write sans a grain of hyperbole that neither I, nor this book, would be alive today if not for the beneficence and love of hundreds of people from every stage of my life who stepped in to save me when an aggregate of traumas almost swallowed me alive while working on these pages.

Typing now in the midst of a pandemic, it clanks with hideous narcissism not to heed Humphrey Bogart's words in *Casablanca* that the problems of one woebegone writer don't "amount to a hill of beans in this crazy world." But it will be a cold day in Minneapolis that I forget the help my universe—which I had no idea existed—gave me going on with both life and this book. Led by Emily Goldberg, my soul sister, GoFundMe queen (and maker of the definitive documentary *The Minneapolis Sound*), those hundreds gave me the votes of confidence to keep typing every time I wanted to quit this biography of a hometown hero. Thank you all. 4real.

But enough of the appropriately purple prose—to thank one name who helped means leaving out fifty, so I'll resist my natural tendency to logorrhea and simply thank those who brought this book directly to life (many of whom are also on that other list. I still owe a lot of you thank-yous—and they're coming.)

First, I must thank my lifelong agent, Suzanne Gluck, at William

Morris Endeavor, for shepherding this book to existence, literally leading me by the hand and explaining my stammers to editors across New York. Her volunteer consigliere and my friend in this effort, Sasha Emerson, was also notable in her support. Suzanne's noble assistants Clio Seraphim and Andrea Blatt were never less than . . . noble. Thanks, dudes!

I knew from the first second I met her that St. Martin's Press executive editor Elizabeth Beier "got" both this book and Prince in ways I hadn't even thought of, and it was an honor and privilege to benefit from her hands-on care. Assistant editor Hannah Phillips, meantime, put up with so much, for so long, in such good spirits and with wise counsel that I am forever in her debt. "Hanner" is a true general in the Purple Army.

I also owe muchly to the whole team at St. Martin's: I never use the word "fabulous," but there is no other word to describe copyeditors Jenna Dolan and Susan Llewelyn, production editor Eric C. Meyer, lawyer Laury Frieber, production manager Vincent Stanley, interior designer Kelly Too, jacket designer Rob Grom, marketing director Martin Quinn, and publicist extraordinaire Rebecca Lang. Fabulous! Many thanks to Guy Oldfield, director of Macmillan Audio, director Elishia Chave, and in the Minneapolis studio, engineer Heather Benneson, and many thanks to Sabrina Taitz at WME for making it happen.

In Prince podcast-ville, thanks to magician Kristen Vaurio and the folks at Best Case, Allie Gallo, Kevin Pham, and Adam Pincus.

Meantime, back on Planet Me, I was able to utilize the editing talents and word wisdom of Marya Hornbacher. In Chicago, Allison Mansfield provided more editorial insights. Kris Vruno provided desperately needed help with the intricacies of all things social media, with an assist from Beth Bowman who I owe big time. Hannah Kampf contributed her press wisdom from the left coast while Malka F. Margolies, my first ever and publicist for life, has been a much better friend than I deserve. Richard Mammen and the Reverend James Nelson of Change, Inc. were able to provide much needed insights on Minneapolis's Northside, as did my late father, Markle Karlen, who grew up there. Peggy Orenstein was an unflagging source of friendship, love, and editorial guidance, and Elizabeth Ess was always available as a Prince scholar, interpreter, and friend.

Abbie Kane not only provided my own bedroom in her house to write a book (again!), she gave me her unique insights into the Minneapolis music scene gleaned from a lifetime of being right in the middle of it. Also providing shelter to work were my great friends Henrietta Saunders and Richard Day in Chicago; Chuck and Soraya Strouse in Miami; good vibes were tossed in by our Hope Street comrades Jonathan Levy and Carole Katz, while Art Simon and Barbara Berger gave me room for my suitcases of papers in New York and Grand Rapids, Minnesota; while my sister Bonnie lent me her old bedroom to type in.

Sebastian Joe's coffee shop, where I've written most of nine books, was always there (and open until midnight weekends). Thanks 4everything Pellizzer brothers and Greg Hefferan—space and good karma (you too for granting me immortality there, long ago alumnus Bill Bates.) Gemma Vennewitz, Alfredo Barrera-Martinez, Austin, Chloe, Meredith, Sophia and EVERYBODY. Lynn Casale and all the fine folks at the Loft Literary Center provided swell space and vibes; Philip Edwards of Friends of the Hennepin County Library chipped in with encouraging good karma.

Other writers, editors, and experts on Prince in specific and/or music in general were invariably kind and helpful. Across the country they include (but are not limited to) Richard Abowitz, Laura Billing Coleman, the swell Alex Hahn and the wonderful, wonderful Laura Tiebert, Chris Heath, Steve Hochman, Geoffrey Mayfield, Duane Tudahl; in the Twin Cities, Corey Anderson, Frank Bures, Tim Campbell, Susie Eaton Hopper, Neal Justin, Martin Keller, Josh "Just FINISH" Leventhal, Steve Marsh, Tim Nolan, Robynne Robinson, Josh Rosengren, Jim Walsh, and Brad Zellar were unfailingly helpful and kind. And Dara Moskowitz Grumdahl—I owe you one from last time.

Thanks for keeping me alive, Dr. Badrinath Konety, and to Beth Bowman for running a Pentagon of social media and Mark Jones of Arts District Imageworks for his heroic work making photographs visible. Christy DeSmith is a saint and I can never repay her.

As for photographs, thanks to the fine artists Craig Helgeson,

Tommy Smith, and Virginia Turbett; Edward Hathaway in Special Collections at the Hennepin County Library helped me track down photos of the Prince Rogers Trio in action. Patrick Coleman at the Minnesota Historical Society provided expert advice.

Special kudos to André Cymone and Katherine Anderson for their help in so many areas—from photos to fact checking to expert commentary. Stacia Lang, my beloved former Belmont chum and Prince's designer, was cheated out of far more space due her here; Mi-Ling Stone Poole was totally ripped off of space to tell her story. SORRY!

Big, repentant sorries go out to Bernie, Christy, Michael and Kate; as well to all those I interviewed but words didn't find their way into the text—early versions of which were read by Richard Mammen, my amigo, the mentsh Mike Gelfand, Tom Bartel and Kris Henning, Christy Kujawa, Judy Brunswick and Fawn Bernhardt-Norvell. Joe Voyles—you bastard! And thanks FOJ. And thanks especially to the Baseball Buddies Caravan for all their indulgences.

And finally and most of all, goes a heart as big as the Ritz to my soul mate Michelle Kasimor Streitz, who came along to give me hope, a place to stay and work through the night, innumerable meals, a keen editorial and spiritual eye as a Prince expert who used to work for the man himself, as well as immeasurable help tracking down and when necessary taking photos. Thanks most of all for your unconditional love and support. I owe ya.

And first, and finally, Prince. Thanks.

TIMELINE

JUNE 7, 1958

Prince (Prince Rogers Nelson) is born at Mt. Sinai Hospital in Minneapolis, Minnesota. He's named after his father's jazz combo, the Prince Rogers Trio.

APRIL 7, 1978

Prince's debut album, *For You*, reaches number 163 in the US and contains his first Top 100 entry: "Soft and Wet," which reaches 92.

OCTOBER 19, 1979

Prince's second album, *Prince*, contains the number 1 R&B hit "I Wanna Be Your Lover" and the original version of "I Feel for You," later a hit for Chaka Khan. It's his first certified Platinum album, signifying sales over one million.

OCTOBER 8, 1980

Prince's third album, *Dirty Mind*, hints at the lascivious songs within, including "Head" and "Sister." The record's biggest hit is the modest "Uptown," which goes to number 5 on the R&B chart.

JUNE 2, 1981

Prince plays the Lyceum Ballroom in London. He does not play the UK again for five years.

OCTOBER 11, 1981

Prince fails to charm the crowd when he opens for the Rolling Stones in Los Angeles and gets booed off the stage. He decides never to open for another band.

OCTOBER 27, 1982

Prince releases his fifth album, *1999*, and at this point he and history intersect. It sells more than five million copies worldwide, propelled by both "1999" and "Little Red Corvette."

NOVEMBER 11, 1982

Prince begins his *1999* tour. The opening acts are the Time and Vanity 6.

MAY 21, 1983

"Little Red Corvette" goes to number 6 in the US. This is Prince's first Top 10 hit. The video also breaks through on MTV, one of the first on the network by a black artist.

JULY 7, 1984

"When Doves Cry," from his upcoming movie *Purple Rain*, goes to number 1.

JULY 27, 1984

Prince stars in a mythical version of himself in *Purple Rain*, a cultural watershed.

AUGUST 4, 1984

The *Purple Rain* soundtrack hits number 1 in the United States, where it stays for an astonishing twenty-two weeks.

SEPTEMBER 29, 1984

"Let's Go Crazy" by Prince and the Revolution hits number 1.

NOVEMBER 4, 1984

Prince kicks off his *Purple Rain* tour with a show in Detroit. His opening act is Sheila E., whose song "The Glamorous Life," written by Prince, reaches number 7 in the United States.

MARCH 25, 1985

Prince wins an Oscar for Best Original Score for the film *Purple Rain*.

APRIL 22, 1985

Prince releases his seventh album, *Around the World in a Day*. It's his first issued on his Paisley Park label and primarily recorded at his Paisley Park studios.

JUNE 1, 1985

The Prince album *Around the World in a Day,* featuring "Raspberry Beret" and "Pop Life," goes to number 1 in the United States.

SEPTEMBER 12, 1985

Rolling Stone publishes its interview with Prince, who has not spoken to the press in three years.

APRIL 19, 1986

Prince hits number 1 in the United States with "Kiss." The Bangles, meantime, hit number 2 with "Manic Monday," which he wrote.

JULY 2, 1986

Under the Cherry Moon, Prince's second film, hits theaters. Prince directs.

MARCH 29, 1987

Prince is named Worst Actor and Worst Director for *Under the Cherry Moon* at the 7th Golden Raspberry Awards. The film also earns Razzies for Worst Picture (tied with *Howard the Duck*), and Worst Original Song ("Love or Money").

MARCH 30, 1987

Prince releases to critical acclaim his ninth album, *Sign o' the Times*.

MAY 10, 1988

Prince releases his tenth album, *Lovesexy*. The record becomes his first number one album in the UK.

AUGUST 20, 1990

Prince releases his album *Graffiti Bridge*, containing "Thieves in the Temple."

JULY 28, 1992

Prince trademarks the male/female glyph he has been using on various album covers and promotional materials. He later redesigns the symbol and uses it as his unpronounceable name.

AUGUST 31, 1992

Prince signs an extension with Warner Bros. Records reportedly worth one hundred million dollars. It wasn't.

OCTOBER 13, 1992

Prince releases an album with an unsayable symbol on the cover that later becomes his name. The record becomes known as the "Love Symbol" album.

JUNE 7, 1993

On his thirty-fifth birthday Prince changes his name to an unpronounceable glyph, making him, literally, an icon.

FEBRUARY 22, 1994

Prince is granted the trademark on the symbol he has been using in lieu of his name.

FEBRUARY 14, 1996

Prince, thirty-seven, marries a model and belly dancer, Mayte Garcia, twenty-two. The marriage is annulled three years later, and Garcia takes up with Tommy Lee of Mötley Crüe.

FEBRUARY 25, 1999

Prince sues nine fan websites to prevent unauthorized downloads of his music, a complex legal argument since it still hasn't been decided in court whether he is Prince or not.

MAY 16, 2000

Prince reassumes his own name when his Warner Bros. Records contract terminates.

FEBRUARY 14, 2001

Prince launches the NPG Music Club in order to directly deal with his fans. It runs until 2006, when Prince shuts it down.

MARCH 15, 2004

Prince is inducted to the Rock and Roll Hall of Fame in New York, where he wordlessly blows an all-star ensemble off the stage with one historic guitar solo.

MARCH 27, 2004

Prince kicks off his *Musicology* tour with a show in Nevada. The average ticket costs sixty-one dollars, which includes a copy of the *Musicology* album. These are counted as sales according to *Billboard*, so the album rises to number 3. *Musicology* is 2004's highest-grossing tour.

FEBRUARY 4, 2007

Prince plays the 2007 Super Bowl halftime show in Miami in a downpour, taking astonishing command of a rain-soaked stage and finishing with "Purple Rain." To quote a YouTube comment: "When Prince plays 'Purple Rain' the rain gets wet."

JULY 15, 2007

Prince gives away free copies of *Planet Earth*, with the UK newspaper *Mail on Sunday*. The unconventional distribution rankles record retailers but helps promote his run of twenty-one shows at the O2 Arena in London, which sell out.

APRIL 27, 2008

Prince plays Coachella, covering Radiohead.

MARCH 24, 2009

Prince launches Lotusflow3r.com, which offers online access to all his music and video output for seventy-seven dollars a year—the length of time the service lasts.

MARCH 17, 2016

Mayte Garcia sells a collection of his memorabilia at auction.

APRIL 14, 2016

In Atlanta, Prince ends his last concert ever with "Purple Rain."

APRIL 21, 2016

Prince dies at age fifty-seven of a fentanyl overdose, which is ruled accidental.

MAY 7, 2016

Following his death, Prince's music experiences a sales revival, taking the top two spots on the *Billboard* albums chart and four of the top ten. *The Very Best of Prince* reaches number 1, and *Purple Rain* comes in at number 2. In the days after his passing, Prince's overall sales increase 44,000 percent.

OCTOBER 6, 2016

Prince's Paisley Park Museum opens.

AUGUST 14, 2017

Pantone announces a new color—an original hue of purple named Love Symbol #2, the color of Prince's once unpronounceable name glyph.

NOTES

1. MEMOIRS OF AN AMNESIAC

1 *Eiffel Tower purple: People* special issue, spring 2016, https://people
.com/celebrity/prince-dead-purple-rain-eiffel-tower-new-orleans
-superdome-light-up.

1 The New Yorker*'s purple rain cover: The New Yorker*, May 2, 2016.

1 New York Times *headline story: New York Times*, April 22, 2016,
front page.

1 *Minneapolis skyline purple: People* special issue, spring 2016, p. 25

3 *"Most memoirists enter a complicated relationship with the truth"*:
Ben Ratliff's introduction to Mezz Mezzrow's *Really the Blues* (New
York: New York Review of Books Classics, 2016), pp. x–xi.

4 *Breakup with Kim Basinger:* Alan Leeds in the Prince biopic/documen-
tary *When Doves Cry* (2017, dir. Nyrita Thompson, ITV).

5 *"I never did find too many people to relate to":* Interview with André
Cymone, June 25, 2019, Minneapolis.

9 *"I can make people famous for fifteen minutes":* Phone call with
Prince, Feb. 22, 1988.

9 *"My head feels like a pinball machine":* Phone call with Prince, Dec.
21, 2008.

9 *"I would be advising Prince not to sue [his own fans]":* Minneapolis
City Pages, June 29, 1999.

2. LAST CALL

10 *Phone call from Prince:* March 28, 2016.

12   *Susannah Melvoin as Prince's fiancée:* There is overwhelming evidence from many credible people that Susannah Melvoin wore what was generally regarded as an engagement ring from Prince. Not that her own accounting isn't credible simply on its own. I know her: She is a radical truth teller (and quite a swell person).

12   *The songs Melvoin inspired Prince to write include "Nothing Compares 2 U" and "The Beautiful Ones":* Ronin Ro, *Prince: Inside the Music and the Masks* (New York: St. Martin's Press, 2016), p. 91.

12   *"Forever in My Life:"* ibid., pp. 153–54.

12   *"If I Was Your Girlfriend":* ibid., p. 57.

12   *"Wally":* Hahn and Tiebert, *The Rise of Prince,* Kindle ed., chap. 24.

12   *"Um, how are you?":* Phone call, March 28, 2016.

13   *"He always loved his sitcoms":* Phone interview with André Cymone, Sept. 12, 2018.

13   *"There is a lot about Prince that people don't understand":* Interview with Cymone, June 25, 2018.

13   *Bernadette Anderson takes Prince into her home for high school:* Hahn and Tiebert, *The Rise of Prince,* Kindle ed., chap. 3.

13   *Prince's two favorite television shows were* The Wire *and* The Office: Cymone interview, June 25, 2018.

14   *Prince used line from Dorothy Parker's "Big Blonde":* He quoted: "She wanted to be married. She was nearing thirty now, and she did hot take the years well" at Rudolph's Barbecue, Minneapolis, April 17, 1992.

14   *"'The Office' Is Netflix's Most Popular Show":* Nina Metz, *Chicago Tribune,* July 3, 2019, entertainment section television column, p.1.

15   *Creed Bratton of* The Office *uses "mamma jamma" in conversation:* aired May 19, 2011, season 7, episode 24, "Search Committee," Deedle-Dee Productions, NBC, Internet Movie Data Base.

15   *JFK co-opting Ben Bradlee and others with nicknames:* Garry Wills, *The Kennedy Imprisonment: A Meditation on Power* (Boston: Mariner Books, 2002), p. 113.

15   "It is better to be feared than loved": Niccolò Machiavelli, *The Prince* (New York: Atheneum Classics, 2020).

17   *"real dark night of the soul":* F. Scott Fitzgerald, *The Crack-Up* (New York: New Directions, 1945), p. 332.

17   *Prince recorded thirty-nine studio albums and four soundtracks:* He sold more than one hundred million units, won seven Grammys, one Academy Award, had five number 1 hits and forty Top 100 hits. *Newsweek: Prince Special Commemorative Edition: The Life and Death of a Musical Genius,* June 30, 2016, pp. 74–75.

18   *Stanley (Leslie David Baker) on* The Office *says, "fighting the power and eating what we wanted:* aired September 25, 2008, season 5,

episode 1, "Weight Loss," Deedle-Dee Productions, NBC, Internet Movie Data Base.

18   *Prince's plane makes emergency landing in Moline, Illinois:* "Clues to the Mystery of Prince's Final Days," John Eligon and Serge F. Kovaleski, *New York Times,* April 22, 2016, Section A, p. 3.

18   *André Cymone trying to text Prince after Moline:* Interview with Cymone, June 25, 2018.

19   *Trying to get truth about Prince's condition after Moline:* Alan Leeds, biopic/documentary *When Doves Cry.*

20   *"Big Sleep" used by Raymond Chandler as euphemism for death:* Robert McCrum, "The Best Novels No. 62—The Big Sleep," *The Guardian,* Nov. 24, 2014., Culture section, home page.

20   *Kirk Johnson tells EMS Prince is fine after he's treated with naloxone after the Moline overdose:* Ibid.

20   *Phaedra Ellis-Lamkins connects Prince's people with Dr. Howard Kornfeld, California drug rehabilitation center owner/director:* Hahn and Tiebert, *The Rise of Prince,* Kindle ed., prologue, part 4.

21   *Transcript of call to 911 alerting authorities to Prince's death:* Sewell Chan, "Sheriff Releases Transcript of 911 Call From Prince's Home,"*New York Times,* April 22, 2016.

3. THE POWER OF THE JUST-DEAD

23   *Auden poem, "In Memory of W. B. Yeats":* 1939, poets.org https://poets.org/poem/memory-w-b-yeats.

23   *"Live conformists" quote: The Neurotic's Notebook,* Mignon McLaughlin (Indianapolis: Howard W. Sams publishers, 1960).

25   *Poem about suicide sent to Prince:* Dorothy Parker, "Résumé," *The Portable Dorothy Parker* (New York: Penguin Classics, 206), pp. 39–40.

25   *Prince album sales up 44,000 percent in three days after his death:* Ben Sisario, "Prince Rockets to No. 1 as Fans Buy (Yes, Buy) His Albums," *New York Times,* April 25, 2016, Section C, p. 3.

26   *Prince conquers the charts after death:* Keith Caulfield, "Prince Sets Record with Five Albums in Top 10," *Billboard,* May 3, 2016, https://www.billboard.com/articles/columns/chart-beat/7356812/prince-sets-record-five-albums-top-10-billboard-200.

26   *Prince captures top spots on charts:* "Prince Rules at No. 1 & 2 on Billboard Chart with 'The Very Best of' and 'Purple Rain,'" *Billboard,* April 24, 2016, https://www.billboard.com/articles/columns/chart-beat/7341816/prince-number-1-and-2-on-billboard-200-albums-chart-very-best-of-purple-rain-albums

26   *Obama tweets upon Prince's death: Billboard,* April 21, 2016, https://www.billboard.com/articles/news/7341563/prince-death-president-obama-statement.

27   *Trump tweets upon Prince's death:* Jessie Katz, "Donald Trump Mourns Prince on Twitter: 'I Met Prince on Numerous Occasions,'" *Billboard,* April 22, 2016, https://www.billboard.com/articles/news /7341660/prince-donald-trump-twitter.

27   *Prince died of fentanyl overdose:* Joe Coscarelli and Sheila M. Eldred, "Prince's Overdose Death Results in No Criminal Charges," *New York Times,* April 19, 2018, Section A, p. 17.

28   *Bobby Shriver at Paisley Park:* Chris Heath, "Prince's Closest Friends Share Their Best Prince Stories," *GQ,* Dec. 2016, https://www.gq.com /story/prince-stories.

29   *Prince spent more playing and practicing the guitar than anyone in history of recorded music:* Hahn and Tiebert, *The Rise of Prince,* Kindle ed., forward.

30   *Kevin in* The Office *says to take any ten-thousand-to-one bet:* aired 4/12/2007 Season 3 episode 20, "Product Recall," Deedle-Dee Productions, NBC, Internet Movie Data Base.

30   *"Chopsticks" first piece Prince learned on the piano, and played it at Paisley Park April 17, 2016:* Hahn and Tiebert, *The Rise of Prince,* Kindle, prologue, part 4.

30   *Prince at Paisley Park performance, Jan. 21, 2016, talks about father:* This was the last time he'd play in Minnesota; he started with theme from TV show *Batman,* first piece he played at age seven, telling crowd: "I thought I would never be able to play like he did and he never missed a opportunity to remind me of." Hahn and Tiebert, ibid., prologue, part 3.

32   *John Nelson first black employee at Honeywell:* Ropeadope Records, posthumous release of *The John L. Nelson Project* album, March 2, 2018, press release with record.

32   *John and Mattie separated in 1968:* Mick Wall, *Prince: Purple Reign* (London: Orion Books, 2016), Kindle ed., chap. 2.

32   *Comeback:* "Baby I'm a Star, Again: How a Seeming Has-Been Spent Months Preparing to Reclaim the Center Stage," *Wall Street Journal,* March 31, 2004. https://www.wsj.com/articles/SB1080694182 91869750.

32   *Musicology sold 1.4 million copies and earned Prince $9.1 million:* Ro, *Prince,* p. 338.

4. KILL 'EM AND LEAVE 2.0

36   *Echoes of Prince in James Brown:* James McBride, *Kill 'Em and Leave: Searching for James Brown and the American Soul* (New York: Spiegel and Grau, 2016), pp. 50–7.

37   *"I was always an expert at turning my back":* Prince, July 2, 1985.

37   *"A long time ago we knew each other for a short period of time"*: The
        Big Chill, directed by Lawrence Kasdan, Columbia Pictures, 1983.

38   *"Everything has been said [so] that nobody will ever know what really
        was"*: Prince, Dec. 11, 2004.

38   *"You did not get to know James Brown"*: McBride, *Kill 'Em and
        Leave*, quoting Brown's lawyer, Buddy Dallas, pp. 10–11.

39   *188 acres of Paisley Park sold off to develop 169 homes*: "Prince's es-
        tate to assume management of Paisley Park," Minneapolis *Star Tri-
        bune*, Aug. 26, 2019.

39   *hundreds of acres of Paisley Park*: Paisley Park studio (7801 Audubon
        Road., Chanhassen, owned by PRN Music Corp.), nine acres valued
        at $7.01 million, according to Carver County property tax records;
        7021 Galpin Blvd., Chanhassen, 187 acres with an estimated value of
        $16.43 million, according to Carver County property tax records.

39   *A will is a major plot point of* Graffiti Bridge: Ro, *Prince*, p. 192.

39   *Prince as "dynamic funk enigma"*: *Los Angeles Times*, March 16, 2004,
        https://www.latimes.com/archives/la-xpm-2004-mar-16-na-rock16
        -story.html

40   *"Mick Jagger should fold up his penis and go home"*: "The Rock Critic
        Robert Christgau's Big-Hearted Theory of Pop," *The New Yorker*,
        May 22, 2019. https://www.newyorker.com/books/under-review/the
        -rock-critic-robert-christgaus-big-hearted-theory-of-pop.

41   *"Anybody can do it"* Neal Karlen, *Babes in Toyland: The Making and
        Selling of a Rock and Roll Band* (New York: Random House, 1994),
        epigraph.

42   For You, *recorded when he was nineteen*: Ro, *Prince*, p. 27.

43   *"The proper way to read the book"*: John Leland, *Hip: The History*
        (New York: HarperCollins, 2004), Kindle ed., preface.

44   *"Hip comes of the haphazard"*: ibid.

45   *Eric Clapton, "You either hate him or love him"*: Prince: Musical Por-
        trait, directed by Albert Magnoli, British Film Institute, 1989.

46   *"Tell all the truth but tell it slant—"*: Emily Dickinson (poem 1263],
        The Poems of Emily Dickinson (Cambridge, MA; Harvard College).

46   *"The Riddle we can guess/We speedily despise"*: ibid.

46   *"Brown was always foggy about his past"*: McBride, *Kill 'Em and
        Leave*, p. 33.

47   *"Lyndon Johnson was 13 of the most interesting people"*: Bill Moyers,
        https://billmoyers.com/2014/05/08/an-interview-with-bill-moyers
        /5/18/14.

49   *meaning of Norman Mailer coinage "factoid"*: https://merriam-webster
        .com/dictionary/factoid.

50   *"It is hard to write about genius"*: letter from Alison Mansfield, June
        29, 2018.

51   *"created a new place"*: Jack Newfield, *Sugar Ray Robinson: The Bright Lights and Dark Shadows of a Chamption,* Ross Greenburg, executive producer, HBO documentary, 1998.

52   *Bunk has code with Omar: The Wire,* season 1, episode 7, "One Arrest," written by David Simon & Ed Burns, HBO Productions, 2002.

52   *Pete Hamill discussing Miles Davis telling Sugar Ray Robinson to retire: Sugar Ray Robinson: The Bright Lights and Dark Shadows of a Chamption,* Ross Greenburg, executive producer, HBO documentary, 1998.

52   *"But Prince ain't no nigger"*: John Turturro as Pino, *Do the Right Thing,* Spike Lee, director, 40 Acres & a Mule Filmworks, 1989.

5. DADDY DEAREST I: THE BAD SON

54   *Singing "The Crusher":* June 30, 1985.

55   *Don King kicked a man to death:* Newfield, *The Life and Crimes of Don King,* pp. 4–6.

55   *"He's a wretched, slimy, reptilian motherfucker":* Mike Tyson on Don King, quoted in Gage Skidmore. "Happy 86th Birthday, Don King," *Huffington Post,* Aug. 20, 2016.

57   *"My father's a little sick, just like I am":* Prince interview, June 29, 1985.

58   *"That [bad] stuff about my past and my father hitting everybody":* Prince interview, June 8, 1986.

60   *Badmouths mother to Kim Berry:* Kim Berry and Andrea Williams, *Diamonds and Curlz,* (Los Angeles: Kim B On Set Publishing, 2019) Kindle ed., chap. 5.

61   *children abused by the father blame the mother:* Phyllis Chesler, "Why Honor Killing Is Not Just a Muslim Problem," *Tablet,* April 15, 2018.

62   *Prince drove like a proper Minnesotan:* Interview, July 14, 1988.

63   *Kinji Shibuya wrestling background:* Prowrestling, fandom.com.

63   *Calvin Griffith as racist:* John Kerr, *Calvin: Baseball's Last Dinosaur* (Dubuque, IA: Wisdom Publishers, 2016), p. 134.

65   *Falling asleep in Prince's car:* June 30, 1985.

67   *Critique of Arthur Miller documentary:* Amanda Petrusch, *The New Yorker,* 2018, https://www.newyorker.com/culture/culture -desk/a-dau ghters-view-of-arthur-miller.

69   *John Nelson on A Current Affair:* https://www.youtube.com/watch?v =Byr-TaMi0gA.

70   *Honeywell in Vietnam:* Ronnie Dugger, "The Company As Target," *New York Times,* Sept. 20, 1987, Section six, p. 30.

6. DADDY DEAREST II: THE GOOD SON

No notes for this chapter.

7. "THE PROBLEM FOR SUPERHEROES IS WHAT TO DO BETWEEN PHONE BOOTHS"

88   *"Me? We!":* George Plimpton on Ali composing short poem, *When We Were Kings* documentary on Muhammad Ali, 1996.

90   *Ali song, "Black Superman":* Jonny Wakeline & the Kinshasa Band, songfacts.com

91   *how Bruce Banner become Incredible Hulk:* Marvel Comics biography, https://www.marvel.com/characters/hulk-bruce-banner/in-comics/profile.

93   *André Cymone:* Interview, June 25, 2018.

93   *André Cymone:* ibid.

96   *"I didn't fight fair":* Prince, Aug. 19, 1988.

96   *takes credit for André:* Prince interview, July 1, 1985.

97   *"I've got six kids":* André Cymone interview, Aug. 12, 2019.

98   *Half-sister Sharon thought Prince's favorite color was orange:* https://www.thecurrent.org/feature/2018/03/05/sharon-nelson-on-her-fathers-music-impact-on-prince.

98   *Lack of proof that Prince grew up a Seventh-day Adventist:* "Was the Rock Star Prince an Adventist?", *Adventist Today,* April 24, 2016.

99   *Nick Cave's "Who knows? My life could be quite interesting if you ask the right fucking questions":* Rolling Stone, 1987.

99   *Official name of Adventist magazine, Adventist Today.*

99   *Only Prince had the key for admittance to Paisley Park:* Hahn and Tiebert, *The Rise of Prince,* Kindle ed., prologue.

99   *Prince's ashes displayed in the ceiling of Paisley Park:* "Paisley Park, Prince's Lonely Palace," by Amanda Petrusich, *The New Yorker,* June 25, 2018, https://www.newyorker.com/magazine/2018/06/25/paisley-park-princes-lonely-palace.

8. BALLER

102   *Dylan living in the Sigma Alpha Mu house:* "Minnesober," by Neal Karlen, *The New York Times Sunday Magazine,* May 28, 1995, https://www.nytimes.com/1995/05/28/magazine/greetings-from-minnesober.html.

106   *Meaning of doing something "sick":* Prince, July 4, 1985.

107   *Al Nuness, member of University of Minnesota Hall of Fame:* "M Club announcement, HOF class of 2016," https://gophersports.com/sports/2018/5/21/sports-m-club-spec-rel-hof-nuness-html.aspx.

107   *Prince hates old coach every day:* Interview, Nov. 12, 1998.

108   *One-on-one:* Dec. 3, 1991.

108   *Prince playing basketball in heels:* "Samuel L. Jackson says he has proof Charlie Murphy's Prince story is true," *USA Today,* May 19, 2016, https://ftw.usatoday.com/2016/05/prince-charlie-murphy-basketball -samuel-l-jackson-story.

109   *Richard Robinson his ninth-grade coach:* https://www.scout.com /Article/5-2-Prince-Used-to-be-a-High-School-Basketball-Player -74995035/Scout.com 4/21/2016.

109   *Jimmy Jam on Prince's basketball skill:* Rob Tannenbaum, "Producer Jimmy Jam Pays Tribute to 'Ultra Sharp, Ultra Witty' Prince: 'His Talent Was Singular, Second to Nobody,'" Rob Tannenbaum, *Billboard,* April 26, 2016, https://www.billboard.com/articles/columns/pop /7348342/jimmy-jam-remembers-prince.

112   *Einstein's "If I were not a":* https://www.goodreads.com/quotes/7603 -if-i-were-not-a-physicist-i-would-probably-be

113   *David "DVS" Schwartz on playing Prince in basketball:* Quoted in Chris Payne, "Playing Basketball: Collaborator Breaks Down His Trash-Talkin' Game," *Billboard,* June 7, 2016, https://www .billboard.com/articles/columns/pop/7393692/prince-basketball-video -interview-david-schwartz-daisy-chain.

114   *"Nuness played himself by not playing me":* Interview, July 22, 2010.

9. HIGH SCHOOL

116   *"I play with Grand Central Corporation":* Lisa Crawford's interview with Prince for the Central High newspaper, his first interview ever, Feb. 16, 1976.

117   *Prince's high school music teacher:* Interview with Katherine Doepke, May 17, 2018.

119   *"Now, they could rewrite history":* Oral history with André Cymone, June 25, 2018.

123   *"I just knew him as Mattie Baker's son":* Oral history with Cindy Stoewer, July 26, 2018.

10. THE TEENAGE AUTEUR

125   *Mo Ostin kicked in a million dollars personally for* Purple Rain: Wall, "Prince: Purple Reign," Kindle ed., chap. 5.

126   *Sinatra, Mafia, Mo Ostin:* Kitty Kelley, *His Way: The Unauthorized Biography of Frank Sinatra* (New York: Bantam, 2010), p. 330.

128   *"I understand what he's trying to do":* Lenny Waronker to Owen Husney, Ro, *Prince,* p. 26

129   *Michael Jackson, James Brown, Prince, together August 20, 1983:*
        https://www.youtube.com/watch?v=lHaFj7gOWh4.

130   *Michael Jackson table tennis:* Ro, *Prince*, pp. 142–43.

131   *Miles Davis disrespecting Duke Ellington, Charles Mingus:* "You see
        the way they can fuck up music," *Downbeat*, 1958; reprinted in *Open
        Culture*, "Miles Davis Dishes Dirt on His Fellow Jazz Musicians: 'The
        Trombone Player Should Be Shot'; That Ornette is 'F-ing Up the Trum-
        pet.'"

131   *"Miles Davis and James Brown, who [had] similar reputations for
        being cantankerous and outrageous":* McBride, *Kill 'Em and Leave*,
        p. 10.

131   *"'the cool' was at work":* ibid., p. 8.

131   *"the people who walk that land":* ibid., pp. 8–9.

133   *"Sometimes it is a very wise thing to simulate madness":* Machiavelli,
        Discourses on Livy, book 3, chap. 2 (1517).

133   *Acting insane as a diplomatic strategy: Herman Kahn, Thinking About
        the Unthinkable,* quoted in Jonathan Stevenson, *New York Times*, Oct.
        26, 2017, https://www.nytimes.com/2017/10/26/opinion/the-madness
        -behind-trumps-madman-strategy.html.

133   *Kayfabe and Gorgeous George and his effect on Dylan, James Brown,
        Little Richard, and Muhammd Ali:* John Capouya, *Gorgeous George:
        The Outrageous Bad-Boy Wrestler Who Created American Pop Cul-
        ture* (New York: HarperCollins, 2008), epigraph.

134   *Kayfabe and marine drill instructor:* Mike Edison, *You Are a Complete
        Disappointment*, (New York: Sterling, 2018) Kindle ed., chap. 1.

134   *Kayfabe examples:* Mike Edison, *Dirty! Dirty! Dirty!* (Berkeley, CA:
        Soft Skull Press) Kindle ed, chap. 2.

136   *Bob Merlis, Warner's not going to push interviews:* "In the Beginning,"
        Prince / An Oral History, Minneapolis *Star Tribune*, April 21, 2016,
        https://www.startribune.com/prince-an-oral-history-in-the-beginning
        /51508747.

136   *Dez Dickerson about* American Bandstand *and Dick Clark:* Wall,
        Prince: Purple Reign, Kindle ed., chap. 3.

11. *PURPLE RAIN:* "DANCIN' IN THE DARK"

139   *"Dancin' in the Dark":* Light, *Let's Go Crazy*, p. 170.

141   *Grauman's opening:* Lisa Coleman, "Oral History: Prince's Life, as
        Told by the People Who Knew Him Best," Minneapolis *Star Tribune*,
        June 7, 2019, https://www.startribune.com/the-life-of-prince-as-told
        -by-the-people-who-knew-him/376586581.

141   *Ali, "I don't have to be what you want me to be. I know where I'm
        going and I know the truth":* "Clay Discusses His Future, Liston

and Black Muslims," by Robert Lipsyte, *New York Times*, Feb. 27, 1964.

142   *Jim Carrey:* Chris Smith, *Jim and Andy: The Great Beyond,* with Jim Carrey and Danny DeVito, directed and produced by Chris Smith.

144   *Prince tracking mud over Santana's floor:* Owen Husney, Minneapolis *Star Tribune* June 7, 2019, https://www.startribune.com/the-life-of -prince-as-told-by-the-people-who-knew-him/376586.

144   *Prince mocking Bruce Springsteen:* "Oral History: Prince's Life, as Told by the People Who Knew Him Best," Minneapolis *Star Tribune,* April 29, 2016, https://www.startribune.com/prince-an-oral-history -in-the-beginning/51508747.

146   *"They weren't fighting for the championship of the world":* "Muhammed Ali: What They Said,"American sportswriter Jerry Izenberg on Ali-Frazier III, the "Thrilla in Manila," BBC.com, June 6, 2016, https://www.bbc.com/sport/boxing/16289663.

151   *Razzies for Prince for* Under the Cherry Moon: IMDb.

12. IN THIS LIFE YOU'RE ON YOUR OWN

No notes for this chapter.

13. THE CRACK-UP, ACT 1

159   *Prince married to Mayte, Feb. 14:* Ro, *Prince,* p. 272.
159   *Prince was fifteen years older:* ibid.
160   *Wedding details:* ibid.
163   *"walking around . . . muttering 'fucking Janet Jackson!'":* "Planet Janet, Sept. 27, 2016. http://planetjanet.invisionzone.com/topic/14565 -welp-we-can-dead-that-assumption-of-prince-not-liking-janet-now.
163   *Jim Walsh on* Chaos and Disorder: *The Gold Experience* (St. Paul: Minnesota Historical Society Press, 2017).
163   *"tossed-off works":* ibid, p. 56.
164   *the album was "dark and unhappy":* Ro, *Prince,* p. 276.
164   *Mayte was "barefoot and pregnant" and happy:* ibid., p. 273.
164   *"Of course all life is a matter of breaking down":* F. Scott Fitzgerald, "The Crack-Up," *Esquire,* Feb. 1936.
165   *Jay Leno, "the artist who formerly sold records":* "Royal Prerogative: The Hidden Side of Prince," *Q magazine,* April 22, 2016.
165   *Amiir dies:* "Prince's Closest Friends Share Their Best Prince Stories," by Chris Heath, "Prince's Closest Friends Share Their Best Prince Stories," *GQ,* Dec. 2016, https://www.gq.com/story/prince-stories.
170   *Prince comatose on Oprah:* Ro, *Prince,* p. 286.

14. THE CRACK-UP, ACT 2

175   Feb. 18 , 2004, *Chappelle's Show,* how. IMDb.

176   *Prince and his posse beating Eddie Murphy's crew at basketball:* https:// www.youtube.com/watch?v=ff8LEx9Mw54.

176   *Jackson confirms Prince was playing basketball "church shoes":* Charles Curtis, "Samuel L. Jackson Says He Has Proof Charlie Murphy's Prince Story Is Real," *USA Today,* May 19, 2016.

177   *"Daisy Chain" video:* https://www.youtube.com/watch?v=w1tW8ja 3QG4.

178   *"another sort of blow that comes from within":* Fizgerald, "The Crack-Up," *Esquire,* March 7, 2017, https://www.esquire.com/lifestyle /a4310/the-crack-up.

178   *"You don't feel [the inner blows]":* ibid

15. THE CRACK-UP, ACT 3: A HAS-BEEN IS BORN, 1998

192   *Rockin' Steady: A Guide to Basketball and Cool:* Walt Frazier and Ira Berkow (Chicago: Triumph Books, 1974).

192   *"Cool is having an attitude, too, of how you carry yourself":* ibid., p. 24.

192   *"Cool is my style":* ibid., p. 17.

192   *"CATCHING A FLY WHEN THE FLY IS IN A SEATED POSITION":* ibid., p. 131.

193   *Frazier book taught at Yale:* ibid., p. 7.

193   *"I happened to meet President Obama":* ibid., p. 7.

193   *Ro, Warner Records, "reacted to growing fan and media nostalgia":* Ro, *Prince,* p. 295.

193   *"Never has the simple servicing":* Bob Merlis, ibid.

194   *Clive Davis paid for kid's bar mitzvah:* Ben Fong-Torres, "Clive Davis Ousted; Payola Coverup Charged," *Rolling Stone,* July 5, 1973, https://www.rollingstone.com/music/music-news/clive-davis-ousted -payola-coverup-charged-37191.

195   *"I thought you'd":* Ro, *Prince,* p. 303.

195   *"Sugar daddy once":* ibid., p. 300.

195   *"he runs like a thief":* ibid.

195   *"He wasn't broke":* ibid., p. 30.

196   *"threaded up":* Frazier, *Rockin' Steady,* p. 16.

196   *"fine vines":* Iceberg Slim, *Pimp: The Story of My Life* (Los Angeles: Cash Money Content, 1987), p. 302.

197   *"A Current Affair":* https://www.youtube.com/watch?v=Byr-TaMi0g A&t=21s.

197   *Dylan's house for sale on eBay:* David Browne, "Forget Guitars. Buy a Rocker's Childhood Home," *Rolling Stone*, Aug. 22, 2018, https://www.rollingstone.com/music/music-features/bob-dylan-kurt-cobain-tom-petty-childhood-homes-870593.

16. THE NEW MILLENNIUM: YOU GOTTA SERVE SOMEBODY—JEHOVAH AND BOB DYLAN'S RABBI

204   "Performed at the Mayo Clinic by a hip replacement specialist," surgery at the Mayo Cinic with orthopedic surgeon named 'Dr. Trousdale,'" Corn, *Death of Prince,* Kindle ed., chap. 62.

204   "*I don't think our boy is going to make it*'": Ricky Peterson on George Benson, Minneapolis *Star Tribune*, April 29, 2016, https://www.startribune.com/prince-an-oral-history-in-the-beginning/51508747.

17. "WHILE MY GUITAR GENTLY WEEPS"

213   *My grandfather giving homemade wine to the neighborhood Gentiles:* Neal Karlen, "Wine That Burns in the Lamp of Memory," *New York Times*, June 30, 1996, https://www.nytimes.com/1998/12/24/garden/close-to-home-wine-that-burns-in-the-lamp-of-memory.html.

213   "*Murderapolis*": Dirk Johnson, "Nice City's Nasty Distinction: Murders Soar in Minneapolis," *New York Times,* June 30, 1996, https://www.nytimes.com/1996/06/30/us/nice-city-s-nasty-distinction-murders-soar-in-minneapolis.html.

18. SONNY LISTON'S GRAVE

222   "*would mow Ali's grass*": BBC News, "When Muhammad Ali Met Prince," June 5, 2016, https://www.bbc.com/news/world-us-canada-36455642.

224   *Holmes sobbing over Ali:* Jonathan Eig, *Ali: A Life* (Boston: Houghton Mifflin Harcourt, 2017), p. 489.

225   *Creamer's regrets:* Douglas Martin, "Robert W. Creamer, Biographer of Babe Ruth, Dies at 90," *New York Times*, July 19, 2012. https://www.nytimes.com/2019/09/25.

19. LAUGHS, LIES, AND LEARNING FROM OTHERS

227   *Prince making joke about Bobby Z. Rivkin's shirt too loud,* Minneapolis *Star Tribune*, June 7, 2019, https://www.startribune.com/the-life-of-prince-as-told-by-the-people-who-knew-him/376586581.

228   *not being able to take notes:* Chris Heath, "Prince's Closest Friends Share Their Best Prince Stories," *GQ*, Dec. 2016 https://www.gq.com/story/prince-stories.

228   *him making me take notes in 1990:* ibid.

230   *Prince keeping a notebook of jokes:* Interview with André Cymone, June 25, 2019.

230   *Fooling Chaka Khan:* Chris Heath, "Prince's Closest Friends Share Their Best Prince Stories," *GQ*, Dec. 2016, https://www.gq.com/prince-stories.

233   *jive in Airplane!:* https://www.urbandictionary.com/define.php?term =jive&utm_source=search-action.

233   *Abbott and Costello "the password is what?":* https://www.youtube .com/watch?v=xect030DfSQ.

234   *Prince doing Stanley, "don't go sniffin' around my daughter":* "Take Your Daughter to Work Day," season 2, episode 18.

235   *Prince's Rock and Roll Hall of Fame performance:* Ro, *Prince*, Kindle ed., chap. 4.

236   *"Everyone lies":* David Simon, *Homicide*, (New York: Holt, 2007), p. 35.

236   *"How does a detective know?":* ibid., p. 215.

238   *Super Bowl performance:* https://www.youtube.com/watch?v=7N N3gsSf-Ys.

239   *"I used to be a poet":* "Baby Moguls: From Pablum to Porsche," Neal Karlen, *New York Times*, Mar. 21, 1993, https://www.nytimes.com /1993/03/21/movies/film-baby-moguls-from-pablum-to-porsche .html.

240   *"Dorothy Parker suffered the constant fear":* James R. Gaines, *Wit's End* (New York: Harcourt Brace Jovanovich, 1977), p. 78.

20. MINNESOTA MEAN

250   *August Wilson:* "August Wilson: The Man Behind the Legacy," centertheatregroup.org, https://www.centertheatregroup.org/programs /students-and-educators/august-wilson-monologue-competition /august-wilson-biography.

250   *Sinclair Lewis:* "If the Shoe (Snowshoe?) Fits, Well," *New York Times*, May 5, 1996.

251   *Judy Garland, Gerald Clarke: Get Happy: The Life of Judy Garland* (New York: Random House, 2000) Kindle ed., chap. 1.

257   *saxophonist Lester Young, from Minneapolis, started trend of playing by his side:* Douglas Henry Daniels, "Lester 'Pres' Young: The Forma- tive Years," Fall 2004, http://collections.mnhs.org/MNHistoryMagazine /articles/59/v59i03p096-109.pdf.

21. CODA

270   *"so much has been written about me . . . let them stay confused:* Chris Heath, "Prince's Closest Friends."

270   *"[Brown] was an expert at knowing what white people expected"*: McBride, *Kill 'Em and Leave*, p. 22.

270   ibid, p. 33.

271   *Philip Roth on playing with character: The Paris Review*, Fall 1984, "Philip Roth, The Art of Fiction, No. 84."

271   *Robert Johnson in* New York Times: Reggie Ugwu, "Overlooked: Robert Johnson, Bluesman Whose Life Was a Riddle," Sept. 25, 2019, https://www.nytimes.com/2019/09/25/obituaries/robert-john-son-overlooked.html.

273   *"two pious American editors"*: Virginia and Leonard Woolf, *Death of the Moth* (Surrey, England: Hogarth Press, 1942), p. 72.

275   *"During the* Dirty Mind *period I'd go into fits of depression"*: p. 33, 2016 "Inside the Pleasure Palace.

277   *Ali, Gorgeous George:* Eig, *Ali*, Kindle ed., p. 83.

280   *"Prince told me that his mother had been addicted to drugs"*: Berry, *Diamonds and Curlz*, Kindle ed.

280   *"Prince knew his mother used to run. . . . any real respect for any of the women"*: ibid., p. 41.

281   *Prince had a type of woman:* ibid.

286   *Hazelden contacted:* Corn, *The Death of Prince Rogers Nelson*, Kindle ed., chap. 33.

287   *How Hazelden reached out:* ibid.

POSTSCRIPT—PRINCELIT

292   *five Prince personalities:* Morris Hayes, quoted in Jay Corn, *The Death of Prince Rogers Nelson: An Investigation.* Kindle ed., chapter 62.

293   *LBJ's shrewd and uncanny instinct for the jugular of his allies and adversaries:* Joseph Califano, *The Triumph and Tragedy of Lyndon Johnson* (New York: Atria Press, 2014) p. 10.

BIBLIOGRAPHY

Azhar, Mobeen. *Prince: Stories from the Purple Underground*. London: Carlton Press, 2016.

Beaulieu, Allen, Jim Walsh, et al. *Prince: Before the Rain*. St. Paul: Minnesota Historical Society Press, 2018.

Berry, Kim, with Andrea Williams. *Diamonds and Curlz: 29 Years Rolling with Rock Royalty PRINCE*. Los Angeles: Kim B On Set Publishing, 2019.

Bream, John. *Prince: Inside the Purple Reign*. New York: Macmillan Publishing Co., 1984.

Bures, Frank, ed. *Under Purple Skies*. Minneapolis: Belt Publishing, 2019.

Capouya, John. *Gorgeous George*. New York: HarperCollins, 2008.

Caro, Robert. *Working*. New York: Alfred A. Knopf, 2019.

Cohen, John, ed. *The Essential Lenny Bruce*. New York: Bell Publishing Company, 1967.

Corn, Jay. *The Death of Prince Rogers Nelson: An Investigation*. Hopkins, MN: JLK Enterprises, 2019.

Dannen, Frederick. *Hit Men: Power Brokers and Fast Money Inside the Music Business*. New York: Anchor, 1990.

Day, Morris, with David Ritz. *On Time: A Princely Life in Funk*. Boston: Da Capo Press, 2019.

Dickerson, Dez. *My Time with Prince*. London: Pavilion Books, 2003.

Earley, Jess, and Chris Stone. *What They Said About Prince Rogers Nelson*. BJH Publications, 2016.

Edison, Mike. *I Have Fun Wherever I Go: Savage Tales of Pot, Porn, Punk Rock, Pro Wrestling, Talking Apes, Evil Bosses, Dirty Blues, American Heroes, and the Most Notorious Magazines in the World*. New York: Farrar, Straus & Giroux, 2008.

————. *You Are a Complete Disappointment: A Triumphant Memoir of Failed Expectations*. New York: Sterling Publishers, 2016.

Frazier, Walt, and Ira Berkow. *Rockin' Steady: A Guide to Basketball and Cool*. Triumph Books, 1974.

Garcia, Mayte. *The Most Beautiful: My Life with Prince*. New York: Hachette Books, 2017.

Goetting, Jay. *Joined at the Hip: A History of Jazz in the Twin Cities*. St. Paul: Minnesota Historical Society Press, 2011.

Greenman, Ben. *Dig If You Will the Picture: Funk, Sex, God and Genius in the Music of Prince*. New York: Henry Holt, 2017.

Guralnick, Peter. *Sweet Soul Music*. Boston: Little, Brown and Company, 2012.

Hahn, Alex, and Laura Tiebert. *The Rise of Prince 1958–1988*. Mat Cat Press, 2017.

Hauser, Thomas. *Muhammad Ali: His Life and Times*. New York: Simon & Schuster, 1991.

Hill, Dave. *Prince: A Pop Life*. New York: Harmony Books, 1989.

Hirshey, Gerri. *Nowhere to Run: The Story of Soul Music*. New York: Times Books, 1984.

Hopper, Jessica. *The First Collection of Criticism by a Living Female Rock Critic*. Chicago: Featherproof Books, 2015.

Iceberg Slim. *Pimp*. Los Angeles: Cash Money Content, 1987.

Ivory, Steven. *Prince*. New York: Putnam Publishing Group, 1984.

Kamp, David, and Steven Daly. *The Rock Snob's Dictionary*. New York: Broadway Books, 2005.

Karlen, Neal. *Augie's Secrets: The Minneapolis Mob and the King of the Hennepin Strip*. St. Paul: Minnesota Historical Society Press, 2013.

Keller, Martin, Greg Helgeson, et al. *Hijinks and Hearsay: Scenester Stories from Minneapolis's Pop Life*. St. Paul: Minnesota Historical Society Press, 2019.

Krull, Kathleen, and Kathryn Hewitt. *Lives of the Musicians*. Boston: Houghton Mifflin, 1993.

Lait, Jack, and Mortimer Lee. *U.S.A. Confidential*, New York: Crown Publishers, 1952.

Lawrence, Sharon. *Jimi Hendrix*. New York: HarperCollins, 2005.

Leland, John. *Hip: The History*. New York: HarperCollins, 2004.

Light, Alan. *Let's Go Crazy: Prince and the Making of* Purple Rain. New York: Atria Books, 2014.

McCann, I. Lisa, Ph.D., and Laurie Anne Pearlman, Ph.D. *Psychologoical Trauma and the Adult Survivor: Theory, Therapy, and Transformation*. Brunner/Mazel Publishers, 1990.

McBride, James. *Kill 'Em and Leave: Searching for James Brown and the American Soul*. New York: Spiegel & Grau, 2016.

Newfield, Jack. *Only in America: The Life and Crimes of Don King*. New York: Spiegel & Grau, 2016.

Mezzrow, Mezz, and Bernard Wolfe. *Really the Blues*. New York: New York Review Books Classics, 2016.

Nilsen, Per. *Dance Music Sex Romance: Prince: The First Decade*. London: SAF Publishing, 2003.

Parker, Dorothy, edited by Marion Meade. *The Portable Dorothy Parker*, rev. ed. New York: Penguin Books, 2006.

Powers, Ann. *Good Booty: Love and Sex, Black and White, Body and Soul in American Music*. New York: HarperCollins, 2017.

Prince. *The Beautiful Ones*, edited by Dan Piepenbring. New York: Random House, 2019.

Remnick, David. *King of the World*. New York: Random House, 1998.

Richards, Keith. *Life*. Boston: Back Bay Books 2010.

Riemenschneider, Chris. *First Avenue: Minnesota's Mainroom*. St. Paul: Minnesota Historical Society Press, 2017.

Ro, Ronin. *Prince: Inside the Music and the Masks*. New York: St. Martin's Press, 2016.

Sefchick, Rick. *Everybody Heard About the Bird: The True Story of 1960s Rock and Roll in Minnesota*. Minneapolis: University of Minnesota Press, 2015.

Sheila E. and Wendy Holden. *The Beat of My Own Drum: A Memoir*. New York: Atria Books, 2014.

Spangler, Earl. *The Negro in Minnesota*. T. S. Dennison Publishers, 1961.

Stein, Seymour, with Gareth Murphy. *Siren Song: My Life in Music*. New York: St. Martin's Press, 2018.

Swensson, Andrea. *Got to Be Something Here: The Rise of the Minneapolis Sound*. Minneapolis: University of Minnesota Press, 2017.

Touré. *I Would Die 4 U: Why Prince Became an Icon*. New York: Atria Books, 1998.

Tudahl, Duane. *Prince and the Purple Rain Era Studio Sessions: 1983 and 1984*. Lanham, MD: Rowman and Littlefield Publishers, 2017.

Valentin, Erich. *Mozart and His World*. New York: Viking Press, 1959.

Walsh, Jim. *Gold Experience: Following Prince in the 90s*. Minneapolis: University of Minnesota Press, 2017.

Whitburn, Joel. *The Billboard Book of Top 40 Albums*. New York: Billboard Books, 1994.

Whittemore, Reed. *Whole Lives: Shapers of Modern Biography*. Baltimore, MD: Johns Hopkins University Press, 1989.

Wide, Steve, with illustrations by Alice Oehr. *Prince A to Z: The Life of an Icon*. Melbourne, Australia: Smith Street Books, 2017.

INDEX

PHOTO CREDITS

[Page 1] Prince's handwriting samples: Photos © Neal Karlen

[Page 2] *Rolling Stone* covers, 1985, 1986: Photos © PMC, courtesy of *Rolling Stone*

[Page 3] *Rolling Stone* cover: Photo © PMC, courtesy of *Rolling Stone*.
Prince Roger's Trio: Photo © The children of John F. Glanton, Sr., Undated

[Page 4] Mattie Shaw: Courtesy of Hennepin County Library
Prince, age twelve: Courtesy of Minneapolis School System
Prince, age thirteen: Courtesy of Minneapolis School System
Prince, ninth grade: Courtesy of Minneapolis School System
Bryant's ninth-grade basketball team: Courtesy of Minneapolis School System

[Page 5] Bernadette Anderson's House: Photo © Michelle Kasimor Streitz, 2020
"Grand Central": Courtesy of André Cymone.
Prince, tenth grade: Courtesy of Hennepin County Library.

[Page 6] Prince in front of Warner Record Executives: Photo © Greg Helgeson, 1979
Dr. Funkenstein's monster: Photo © Greg Helgeson, 1980

[Page 7] "Don't make me black.": Photo © Photofest 1980
"I Wanna Be Your Lover": Photo © Photofest 1979

[Page 8] "All the Critics Love You in New York": Photo © Greg Helgeson, 1980
Prince dancing in front of speakers and drums: Photo © Greg Helgeson, 1980

[Page 9] "You talking to me?": Photo © Virginia Turbett
"I was expert at turning my back on people...": Photo © Photofest 1980

[Page 10] Prince shirtless, onstage: Photo © Tommy Smith III

[Page 11] Apollonia and Prince, *Purple Rain*: Photo © Warner Bros./Photofest
Prince jumping, with guitar in hand: Photo © Warner Bros./Photofest

[Page 12] Wendy Melvoin and Lisa Coleman: Photo © Tommy Smith III
Morris Day of the Time Photo © Tommy Smith III